GRACE & GLORY

Louie Giglio

365 Devotions for a Life
Transformed by Jesus

GRACE & GLORY

passionpublishing

THOMAS NELSON
Since 1798

Grace & Glory

© 2024 Louie Giglio

Published in Nashville, Tennessee, by Thomas Nelson. Thomas Nelson is a registered trademark of HarperCollins Christian Publishing, Inc.

Thomas Nelson titles may be purchased in bulk for educational, business, fund-raising, or sales promotional use. For information, please email SpecialMarkets@ThomasNelson.com.

Unless otherwise noted, Scripture quotations are taken from the Holy Bible, New International Version®, NIV®. Copyright © 1973, 1978, 1984, 2011 by Biblica, Inc.® Used by permission of Zondervan. All rights reserved worldwide. www.zondervan.com. The "NIV" and "New International Version" are trademarks registered in the United States Patent and Trademark Office by Biblica, Inc.®

Scripture quotations marked KJV are taken from the King James Version. Public Domain.

Scripture quotations marked MSG are taken from The Message. Copyright © 1993, 2002, 2018 by Eugene H. Peterson. Used by permission of NavPress. All rights reserved. Represented by Tyndale House Publishers, a Division of Tyndale House Ministries.

Scripture quotations marked NCV are taken from the New Century Version®. Copyright © 2005 by Thomas Nelson. Used by permission. All rights reserved.

Scripture quotations marked NKJV are taken from the New King James Version®. Copyright © 1982 by Thomas Nelson. Used by permission. All rights reserved.

ISBN 978-1-4002-4724-0 (HC)
ISBN 978-1-4002-4728-8 (audio)
ISBN 978-1-4002-4727-1 (ebook)

Printed in Vietnam

24 25 26 27 28 SEV 10 9 8 7 6 5 4 3 2 1

For the LORD *God is a sun and shield:*
the LORD *will give grace and glory:*
no good thing will he withhold
from them that walk uprightly.

PSALM 84:11

CONTENTS

INTRODUCTION

PSALM 84 HAS been a banner text over my life, Shelley's life, and our ministry. It's where we got the term *Doorkeeper* or *Door Holder* to describe the kind of people we wanted to build the Passion Movement with. It's where I've returned time and time again for encouragement of God's blessing, strengthening, and provision for all those who dwell near to Him; even the lowly sparrow has a home near His altar.

It's only fitting, as I set out to put together this journey you're embarking on, that the inspiration would come from Psalm 84. In the King James Version (some of you just gave a little inner shout of praise for the KJV), we read these words in verse 11:

> For the LORD God is a sun and shield: the LORD will give **grace** and **glory**: no good thing will he withhold from them that walk uprightly. (emphasis added)

The Lord will give grace and glory. No good thing will He withhold. It's a stunning promise, one that I believe can change everything for you if you are willing to take Him at

His word and receive this astounding gift of unthinkable generosity.

If God came to most of us and said, "I'll give you any two things you can ask for, just say the words and they're yours," I'm not sure how high on the list of answers we'd find grace and glory. Even now, your mind may have jumped to a dozen other responses: good health, that job you've had your eye on, that relationship you've been pursuing. Or maybe you would have gone more spiritual with something like peace, or in the tradition of Solomon, wisdom. But grace? Glory? Probably not.

And yet, as God always does, He works in exactly the ways that He knows we most need. And the longer I've followed Him, the more I'm convinced that *grace* and *glory* aren't only what most satisfy my heart, but they are the anchors that keep me connected to the throne room, to the cross, and to the awesome and wondrous reality that awaits all of us who are in Jesus Christ.

You don't have to look long or dig deep to realize that *grace* and *glory* are found all throughout Scripture. By *grace* we have been saved (Ephesians 2:8). Beholding His *glory* we are transformed into the likeness of Christ (2 Corinthians 3:18). Through Jesus, we have gained access by faith into *grace*, and we rejoice in the hope of the *glory* of God (Romans 5:1–2).

His grace sustains us as His glory stuns us. His grace drives us to our knees, while His glory evokes our adoration and awe. *Grace and glory* is His nature on display; He is totally set apart and yet intimate and personal. A God who would create the whole cosmos and a hundred billion stars with a single breath and yet still choose to come and die so that we may become His sons and daughters. Grace and glory.

As you journey through these pages, it's my prayer that you find these two threads woven throughout each of these devotions. Some days will draw your eyes more inward, prompting you to reflect on how God is specifically shepherding your heart as His grace abounds in your life. Some days will draw your eyes more upward, as it's good for us to be reminded of how majestic and worthy our great and glorious God is.

But taken together, these days and these devotions will help you find hope, peace, and confidence in the person of Jesus and the work of His resurrection. That's the by-product when grace and glory combine. It's why Peter was able to write in 1 Peter 5:10,

> And the God of all **grace**, who called you to his eternal
> **glory** in Christ, after you have suffered a little while,
> will himself restore you and make you strong, firm and
> steadfast. (emphasis added)

I don't know what you're going through or where you're coming from. But I'm pretty sure that all of us could benefit from being restored, strengthened, and made firm and steady. It doesn't happen overnight but rather day by day, step-by-step. The psalmist said, "No good thing will he withhold from them that walk uprightly."

So start walking on your journey. Our God, the King of Glory, wants to be known by you, and He's already given you every ounce of grace you'll need to follow Him. Press in, and I believe you'll see the Lord work mightily as He draws you to Himself.

By His Grace. For His Glory,

JANUARY

NEW YEAR, NEW PRIORITIES

Commit to the LORD whatever you do,
and he will establish your plans.
PROVERBS 16:3

PRAYER

Lord, in the
macro and
the micro, I
choose to put
You first. Keep
me close to
You this year.

AT THE START of a new year, many of us engage in self-reflection and set fresh goals for the days and months ahead. Which habits will you adopt, and which ones do you want to kick?

As you're dreaming about your future, the God over all creation offers you this choice: if you choose to prioritize His kingdom and His righteousness, everything else you need this year will be added to you.

God is always working on a cosmic scale, holding the universe together—but He is also intentionally focusing on how to give *you* specifically what *you* need. There are things you don't even know you need yet, but He does, and He is working to provide for your life.

When you put God first in your plans, everything else falls into place. You gain perspective of what really matters—making disciples, living for His glory, and using your talents to honor His kingdom. You learn to let go of fleeting whims and desires. As you start this year, start with God. Prayerfully consider His ways and decide today that no matter what else comes, you're going to depend on Him.

LIVING IN THE FULLNESS
OF CONTENTMENT

*"I am the good shepherd. The good shepherd
lays down his life for the sheep."*
JOHN 10:11

NOTHING ON THIS earth will ultimately satisfy the thirst in the human soul. Yet in a world that constantly compares everything, we oftentimes feel like we're missing out or falling short. For you, is this a job? A relationship? Money?

In John's gospel, however, we read that the Enemy comes to steal, kill, and destroy (10:10). He wants to steal your contentment by always highlighting what you're lacking. But that's not the end of the story. Jesus, the Good Shepherd, also comes. And when He does, He brings with Him new life. And not just life, but life to the full! For those of us who have been brought to spiritual life, that means we have everything we need. We can experience a godly fullness that counteracts every feeling of want and lack from the Enemy.

Today, you, too, can declare what David boldly said in Psalm 23. "The LORD is my shepherd; I shall not want" (v. 1 NKJV). You can live a lifestyle characterized by contentment and fullness.

PRAYER

Lord, thank You that You are the Good Shepherd. I gratefully embrace Your fullness of life, and I find contentment in You today.

THERE IS ALWAYS A WAY OUT

*No temptation has overtaken you except
what is common to mankind.*
1 CORINTHIANS 10:13

SLOW DOWN FOR a moment to say these words out loud to God:

"Because of Your victory, I can go forward. I'm opening myself up today for You to create lasting change in my heart. By the same power that raised Jesus from the dead, I trust that You will work in me and guide me through every situation I face today."

This is resurrection power at work, and this is how God invites us to victory. Through Jesus' righteousness, we can reject sin and walk free with Him because He has given us a permanent "way out." This is what it means in 1 Corinthians 10:13 when Paul said, "But when you are tempted, he will also provide a way out so that you can endure it."

Let that sink in.

God. Will. Provide. A. Way. Out.

It's a bedrock truth you can build on. A promise to you from God Almighty. Because of this promise, you can live with assurance of victory. You can stand strong against sin and be holy as God is holy.

GETTING UP OFF
THE STRETCHER

As he approached the town gate, a dead
person was being carried out—the only son
of his mother, and she was a widow.

LUKE 7:12

HAVE YOU EVER felt so sick that you didn't think you'd be able to get out of bed? The kind of weighty malaise that chills your bones and zaps your energy?

Sin is like that, except the consequences are infinitely more dangerous. Before you put your faith in Jesus, your sin puts you on a stretcher heading toward the grave.

But the gospel is actually a gospel of resurrection power. Jesus stops death, lifts you off the stretcher, and brings about new life.

When Jesus walked this earth, He was clear on His purpose and mission—to glorify the Father by conquering death. He often showed up at the right time and at the right place to cross paths with a person's funeral procession.

That's how He is working in your story too. Interrupting death to bring about new life. If He has raised you from the dead, don't spend today living under the power of sin. Rejoice! Jump for joy. You are alive and forever free.

PRAYER

Jesus, Your timing is perfect and Your power unrivaled. I was dead in my sins, but You called me up to new life! Thank You, Jesus, for interrupting my funeral.

THE DIRECTION
OF YOUR LIFE

*For this very reason, make every effort to add to
your faith goodness; and to goodness, knowledge.*
2 PETER 1:5

PRAYER

Lord, I will
persist in my
pursuit of You
and make
every effort to
stay close to
You, because
only by Your
side do I find
life and peace.

YOU HAVE ACCESS to God's best. He loves you, sent
His Son for you, and gives you His Spirit to go with
you day by day. He can't pursue you any more than
He's already pursued you. He is perfect in His faithfulness to you.

So the ball is in your court. Knowing the King
more won't happen out of neutrality; it happens out
of determination. We must prioritize. Press. Persist.
Pursue goodness, knowledge, and self-control. Your
perseverance will produce godliness, and in turn, you
will experience more of His love. Growing in these
qualities requires persistence. Prioritize Him the way
He prioritizes you. Move toward God with affection
and allegiance.

Following His commandments won't earn your
salvation—that's already set by your Father. But
He does give you the choice of which direction you
want your life to go. The way of the world? Or the
way of your heavenly Father? Choosing to grow in
Christlikeness can be hard, but the glory on the other
side of maturation is immeasurably good.

A GOSPEL HEART

*I tell you, now is the time of God's
favor, now is the day of salvation.*
2 CORINTHIANS 6:2

THERE ARE COUNTLESS podcasts and books that promise they can upgrade your life. Bestselling authors share their tried-and-true secrets for how to change your bad habits. Thought leaders travel the globe with advice for how to discover more health and happiness.

There are scores of good teachers out there. But Jesus was different. He wasn't just a good teacher. He didn't come simply to make bad people good people or give a set of tips and tricks for how to live well. He came to make dead people alive—to invite us to be born again by His Spirit, that we may be saved.

The gospel is about our hearts starting to beat again. As followers of Jesus, we are resurrected people. Jesus has done for us what we could never do ourselves. By faith, we trust in the death, burial, and resurrection of Jesus Christ to raise us again and give us new life. The same power that raised us from the dead is the same power that is transforming us to become more like Christ. Ask God to remind you of His resurrection power—you are forever changed by His saving grace.

PRAYER

God, You are saving me today, and through Your power, I experience new life.

7

WORTHY OF ALL GLORY

You are worthy, our Lord and God, to receive glory and honor and power, for you created all things.
REVELATION 4:11

PRAYER

God, I humbly admit my full and entire dependency on You today. All credit, all glory is Yours.

WE'VE ALL EXPERIENCED someone taking the credit for something we've done. Maybe it was a group project back in school. Or an idea in a brainstorming meeting at work. The temptation to make ourselves look good is so strong that it can sometimes filter into our relationship with God.

God does all the work in salvation. He restores us. Cleanses us. Purifies us. Makes us new. But as we live out this gift of new life, we can start to fixate on our own efforts. Our own merit. Our own worthiness. We subtly start to give ourselves the glory. We convince ourselves God is merely a supporter of the things we need Him to do in our lives.

Your life will change dramatically when you truly understand that God is God, and we are only in the story by His wonderful grace. Our lives are meant to amplify how great and how good He is, not how great and how good we think we are. Keep Him first today, and step into the mission He has for you.

THE CALL IS TO SURRENDER COMPLETELY

That person is like a tree planted by streams of water, which yields its fruit in season and whose leaf does not wither—whatever they do prospers.

PSALM 1:3

JESUS LIVES IN you, and when Jesus lives in you, your slate is clean. You are set free from condemnation, and you are given a new life and placed into a new family. This is not a negotiation. This is a call to surrender completely to Jesus. When you do so, you will be like a tree that is planted by streams of living water.

Your sapling of faith will thrive best when you set your mind and heart on Christ daily. God has made a way for you to bear much fruit, but you'll have to do it in His season and in His timing. God's way is not a restriction. It's an overwhelming freedom because you not only prosper but also have protection. Your leaf will not wither.

This kind of life that's dependent fully on the power of the Holy Spirit can be yours, and it's activated by you stepping forward in faith.

PRAYER

Lord, plant me near Your streams of life. Draw forth fruit that is pleasing to You and satisfying to me. Protect me in all that I do, and sustain me as I live fully surrendered.

A SONG THAT RISES TO HEAVEN

Sing to the LORD a new song;
sing to the LORD, all the earth.
PSALM 96:1

WHEN YOU THINK you've finally reached rock bottom, it feels like there's nowhere else to go. You question if God could ever lift you from the depths of the pit you dug for yourself. You may be tempted to think, *I'm shattered. Scared. Desperate. If only you knew my story, what I've done, how far I've fallen.*

When you're at the end of yourself, don't count God out—He's been saving people ever since the garden of Eden. Your sin isn't an anomaly. It's not something He hasn't seen before. There is nothing He cannot redeem, no life He cannot uplift.

From the bottom of the pit, look up and celebrate and worship a God who is bringing you back to life again. You may be in a low moment, but even in your darkest night, God still provides breath in your lungs and a balm for your heart. So with the confidence of the cross rising in your soul, praise Him. Praise the One who has given you the gift of grace and forgiveness today—who has given you new life. Sing a new song of victory, of redemption. Rise up in Him.

EXPLORING THE INEXHAUSTIBLE GOD

"But the Advocate, the Holy Spirit, whom the Father will send in my name, will teach you all things and will remind you of everything I have said to you."
JOHN 14:26

HOW DO YOU get to know—really know—God?

You come to Him through the Word of God and the person of Jesus Christ, who said, "Anyone who has seen me has seen the Father" (John 14:9). You come to know God by discovering His attributes. As theologian A. W. Tozer said in his book *The Knowledge of the Holy*, "An attribute of God is whatever God has in any way revealed as being true of Himself."

You've heard that God is love. God is not some nebulous force of energy in the cosmos. He's a God of personhood, and that includes full will and full emotion. And the thing that drives His will and guides the emotion of God is love. When you look into the love of God, you begin to truly know God. Not just intellectually but personally. And when you know Him personally, you begin to change to be more like Him.

PRAYER

God, thank You for revealing attributes of Your character to me. Help me learn and go deeper into who You are, that I would know You.

11

GRACE-FILLED STRENGTH FOR TODAY

Therefore, if anyone is in Christ, the new creation has come: The old has gone, the new is here!
2 CORINTHIANS 5:17

AS A RECIPIENT of God's grace, you can live confidently knowing all your sin was wiped away when Christ paid your debt. You have a clean slate, but that doesn't give you a free pass to do whatever you want.

You are called to the saving work God set in motion. God can convict you of your sin, but He doesn't force you to confront it. You have to say, "My sin has to go. Not ten or twenty years in the future. Today."

God wants you to live free. Sin no longer has power over you. He has made you a new creation. He wants you to live without the chains that bind you, unfettered from beliefs that limit you. And you can!

Lean toward Jesus in faith and action. It's not a mild action you're taking. It's grace-filled, strong, and even severe. If there's a voice in your head saying, *Life will never change for the better*, that voice isn't the voice of Jesus. That voice of shame and discouragement can—and will—be silenced!

COMPLETELY ALIVE IN THE POWER OF JESUS

Then [Jesus] went up and touched the bier they were carrying him on, and the bearers stood still. He said, "Young man, I say to you, get up!"

LUKE 7:14

PRAYER

Jesus, You called me to get up, so I will no longer live under the rule of sin, but I will honor and glorify Your name alone!

THINK BACK TO a time in your life when you wanted something to change, but had to wait for it. We're not used to shifts happening instantaneously, but when Jesus spoke to the dead man outside of Nain (Luke 7), resurrection was immediate. Scripture describes how the dead man sat up and began to talk, and Jesus gave him back to his mother.

I love that there's an exclamation point in this translation of verse 14. "Get up!" Jesus was reaching with His power and authority into death and commanding that which was dead to come alive again. Jesus wasn't merely hoping something good would happen. He was giving death an order, in effect: *Death, you don't have the power here. I have the power. You will obey!*

That's the same command Jesus is saying to you now: "Get up!" Jesus can intersect your life with intentionality and power, so don't let sin rule over you for one more second today. Claim your new life and go from here with joyful peace.

WORRYING BRINGS NO VALUE TO TODAY

"Do not worry about your life. . . . Look at the birds of the air. . . . Are you not much more valuable than they?"
MATTHEW 6:25–26

THERE'S NOT A single one of us who is immune to worry. We have real, tangible needs. To provide for our families. To put food on the table. To connect with our purpose. To know love. When our needs feel unmet, we swiftly turn to worry.

The reality is that worrying has never once helped meet a tangible need. Planning might. Prayer has. But worry hasn't. Worry just robs you of today.

If you need inspiration to trust in God, just go outside and look around you. The trees, the grass, the animals—God takes care of, protects, and sustains it all. If He can do it for all of creation, He can certainly do it for you.

When you remind yourself of His deep love for you—much greater for you than for any bird of the air—how could you not trust Him? He is faithful to provide all that you need, so don't let worry sit in your mind and heart today.

BURIED AND RAISED
WITH HIM

We were therefore buried with him through baptism
into death in order that . . . we too may live a new life.
ROMANS 6:4

DID YOU KNOW that the Bible calls you a saint? It's
true. This is how you are referred to in Scripture. The
word *saint* simply means that you are a "holy one."
In Christ, you're forgiven of all sin—past, present,
and future. You have a new standing before God,
no longer condemned by sin. You are clothed by the
righteousness of Jesus Christ.

The life you now live is by faith, and you live
because Christ lives in you (Galatians 2:20). When
you became a believer, you were baptized into Christ
Jesus—which means you identified with His death,
burial, and resurrection. Just as Christ was raised from
the dead by the glory of the Father, you, too, are spiritually resurrected into new life.

This changes everything! It changes your affections, your attention, your hopes, and your worship.
It shifts your speech, your actions, your relationships,
your work. You are no longer ruled by sin, but you are
fully alive in Jesus! That's who you are today.

PRAYER

God, because
I have been
crucified with
Christ, I no
longer am
bound to my
old patterns.
By Your mercy,
I am set free!

HE IS ABLE

Now to him who is able to do immeasurably
more than all we ask or imagine.
EPHESIANS 3:20

WHATEVER YOU'RE HOPING for, you can take confidence in this truth: God is able. But just because God is able doesn't mean that your hopes will come to fruition overnight. We tend to expect God to work immediately on our terms, but an almighty God is not confined to earthly rules. What He does in your life may not be exactly as you dreamed or expected, but it is exactly what's best for you and for His glory.

Now, just because God is able doesn't mean you should sit or shrink back. You have a role to play in the miracle story that God is writing in your life. He invites you to join Him as His Spirit works in and through you, spreading the good news of the gospel to those He has divinely put into your path.

As He faithfully leads you, you'll get a glimpse into the stunning truth that God is the God of the impossible, and He wants you to participate in this great story He's writing. Surrender your control of how you think life should be, and pray for opportunities to participate in His wondrous plan and see His majesty in action.

PRAYER

God,
expand my
expectations
so that I would
trust that
You can do
immeasurably
more.

LONGING FOR MORE

Come near to God and he will come near to you.
JAMES 4:8

EACH OF US has felt the tug like we were made for more than just this everyday life on planet Earth. We've all sensed a deeper, inner longing for something or someone more.

Many people throughout history have felt this way, but not all have come to the truthful conclusion that only God, the Creator, made known through Jesus Christ, can fill your deepest inner longing.

How incredible would it be if you experienced God's desire to be known by you? Suddenly, in one glorious revelation, you could find what you've been searching for all along and discover the God who longs to be found by you.

As great as that sounds, there's something more specific God wants to reveal to you about who He is. God wants you to come to know Him as a perfect Father. A Father who gave you life, made you uniquely you, adores you, and wants to be a part of your life. Let that truth wash over you today.

PRAYER

God, because You are a good Father, I'm trusting today that when I come near, You will meet me with love and compassion.

GROWING UP IN CHRIST

Instead, speaking the truth in love, we will
grow to become in every respect the mature body
of him who is the head, that is, Christ.
EPHESIANS 4:15

PRAYER

Jesus, You are the head of all my spiritual growth and maturity. I stay tethered to You today so that the fruit of Your Spirit would grow in me.

IF YOU'VE SPENT any time around babies or young children, you know they are highly prone to imitate what the adults around them say and do.

The same is true in your walk with God. When you first put your faith in Jesus, you are a spiritual infant, and your goal is to imitate God. You do this by first understanding that when you are saved, your identity is changed. You learn to receive the love of Christ into your life, and you grow in learning how to reflect Him to others around you.

Since you are a child born of God, loved and saved by Him, you have God's life inside you. You imitate Him by becoming the eyes of God, the ears of God, the hands of God, the feet of God, and the heart of God to those who are desperate to know Him.

Aim to live like Jesus in all you do. That's how you mature and grow up in Christ, who is the head of all things.

NEW NAME, NEW DESTINY

Paul, an apostle of Christ Jesus by the will of God, to God's holy people in Ephesus, the faithful in Christ Jesus.

EPHESIANS 1:1

IT CAN BE difficult to imagine, but God has the power to change your path, your future, and your destiny. He could even go as far as to change your name, the very thing that identifies who you are!

You can't get too far into Ephesians without stopping at the first word—Paul. That single name is a picture of the gospel. He's saying, "This is who I am. I'm an apostle, an ambassador of Jesus Christ. I'm on a mission for Jesus, and I'm writing to you and letting you know who's writing—*Paul.*"

Saul's name was changed to Paul. Saul was a self-righteous, murderous zealot, and he became a proclaimer of the peace and grace found in Jesus. A dreadful past was changed to an amazing, hope-filled future. God can do this for you today. He can change your name and your destiny. That means you're not what you were.

It doesn't matter what you've done or where you've been. Jesus can turn your life around if you reach out and invite Him in.

PRAYER

God, You demonstrate time and time again Your immense power to rewrite stories. Thank You for calling me by name and into a new relationship with You.

ATTRIBUTES REVEALED

Great is our Lord and mighty in power;
his understanding has no limit.
PSALM 147:5

YOU WERE CREATED to have a relationship with the almighty God. Life and eternal life is knowing God. But how do you actually come to know Him, personally and intimately?

You come through the Word of God and the person of Jesus Christ, who said, "If you've seen me, you've seen the Father." You come with the aid of the Holy Spirit, listening to His promptings and relying on His help to translate the ways of God into your heart.

You also come to know God by looking at His creation. When you witness a great rainstorm, you can see His kindness and mercy poured out. When you see a bolt of lightning and hear the resounding clap of thunder, you observe His power and mightiness on display. When you watch a parent with their child, you can see a mirror of God's tender love and gentle affection.

If you look for Him, you can see His divine attributes all around. He is inviting you in to commit your life to knowing Him more.

SEATED FAR ABOVE IT ALL

*And his incomparably great power for us who believe.
That power is the same as the mighty strength he
exerted when he raised Christ from the dead and
seated him at his right hand in the heavenly realms.*

EPHESIANS 1:19–20

WHEN MARY MAGDALENE went to the tomb where
Jesus' body lay, she found that the heavy stone blocking the entrance had been moved. An angel sent by
the perfect Father rolled the stone away. Turns out,
moving the stone was the easy part. God had already
done the more miraculous work when He called forth
His Son from the depths of Hades. The powers of
darkness trembled as sin and hell were defeated. Jesus
was alive forever, a victorious champion over sin and
death.

We serve a powerful God! When our eyes are
opened with the new "revelation" sight that Paul talks
about in Ephesians 1:17–18, we come to see this: God's
power is limitless and His arm is mighty to save. This
is why Christ is seated "far above all rule and authority" (v. 21).

What is blocking you from accessing the power
of God today? What stone is keeping you from trusting in Jesus' resurrection power? Pray that you might
experience "revelation" sight today.

PRAYER

God, Your
power rose
Jesus from
the dead, and
You've given
that same
power to me
through Your
Spirit. May I
use it to glorify
You today.

21

REMEMBERING GOD'S FAITHFULNESS

"I am the LORD your God, who brought you out of Egypt, out of the land of slavery."
EXODUS 20:2

PRAYER

Lord, help me
to remember
how You've
been faithful
to me.
Restore my
remembering.

IT'S EASY TO look at the ancient Israelites and wonder why they became discouraged with God. We think, *How could they just turn their backs and give up on Him? God had a rich history with these people. He'd chosen them as His own. He'd given them His presence. What happened?*

They forgot.

In the face of the unknown, the Israelites forgot the Lord's faithfulness. All they had to do was remember. God had miraculously removed them from slavery in Egypt. He'd guided them through the wilderness and made water appear. He empowered them to conquer the city of Jericho. Time and time again, God was faithful to His people.

But aren't we just like them? We get caught up and forget that God is with us. We wonder where He is, if He's left us alone. We can't see Him or how He's working.

When we forget that He is faithful, remember that He abounds in steadfast love and faithfulness (Exodus 34:6).

THE STUNNING REDEEMER

*"This is what the Lord says—your Redeemer,
who formed you in the womb: I am the Lord,
the Maker of all things, who stretches out the
heavens, who spreads out the earth by myself."*

ISAIAH 44:24

CATCHING A GLIMPSE of a solar burst some thirteen billion light-years away is stunning. Yet it's far more miraculous to think that the One who fashioned the stars and the galaxies, and everything seen and unseen throughout the universe, stepped onto planet Earth on a rescue mission for lost and sinful people.

When our foolish rebellion separated us from the God who formed us to both know and love Him forever, Jesus spoke up for you and me. And in the end, in human skin, the sinless and perfect Son of God exchanged His life for every twisted thing that we have done. In that single act, the star breather became the sin bearer. The universe Maker became humanity's Savior. It truly is a stupendous and astronomical act of grace.

God didn't leave us unclear on how to measure His love. He displayed the gravity of His affection for us on the cross. Dwell on that reality today, and wonder at the depth of His love for you.

PRAYER

God, how spectacular is Your Word that formed the world and changed my heart. You are my Redeemer!

ANSWERING GOD'S CALL

"Come," he said. Then Peter got down out of the boat, walked on the water and came toward Jesus.
MATTHEW 14:29

IMAGINE THE CONFUSION and terror of the disciples when Jesus called Peter to walk on water. This was a wild request. To step into choppy, windy waves? And walk on them? That's not possible.

But God loves to do the impossible.

Do you ever feel like Jesus is calling you out onto the waves? He knows your limits, your strengths, and your weaknesses. And yet He calls you out onto the water anyway, because every step you take on the choppy waves is an opportunity to strengthen your faith. God supersedes the flawed and failing climate and actually uses it to do the impossible.

If you're being called out of the boat of comfort today, know that saying *yes* to Jesus will never lead you toward less. When you say *yes* and step out in faith, you are exercising your belief in the God of miracles. You're choosing to believe God is capable of grandeur. You're choosing a life of awe and wonder, trusting He can do the impossible in your life.

If Jesus says *come*, then step out onto the water today. He won't let you sink.

CONCENTRATING ON
THE GOOD SHEPHERD

You prepare a table before me in
the presence of my enemies.
PSALM 23:5

IF YOU ARE walking through a season of darkness, if anxiety or lies of the Enemy are weighing you down, take heart. God is not oblivious or unaware of what you are up against. He isn't leading you into fear or paranoia. He isn't putting thoughts of despair in your mind.

Imagine sitting at a table with the Good Shepherd across from you. He has led you through dark valleys to reach this table. Your place at the table doesn't mean that all the difficult circumstances are removed from the equation. In fact, the table was set right in the middle of the hardship and the enemies.

When you realize whose table you are sitting at and how you came to be there, your task simply becomes to dine with and focus on the Good Shepherd, the One who owns the table.

Your invitation, in the midst of chaos, is to put your trust in the One who prompted you to lie down in green pastures, the One who leads you beside quiet waters and restores your soul.

PRAYER

God, thank You for saving me a seat at Your table. Today, I choose to sit down with You, even in the presence of my enemies.

CORRECTIVE LENSES FOR THE SOUL

When anxiety was great within me,
your consolation brought me joy.
PSALM 94:19

Father, I move my heart toward worship because I know that when I look up, I see You and I align myself with Your heart. When I'm in step with You, I can face any challenge.

IF YOU'VE EVER tried seeking peace and joy through your own strength, you know it doesn't work.

When anxiety rises, the most radical decision you can make is to stop fixating on your troubles and instead look to the One who holds your troubles in His hands. Don't withhold your worship from God in the face of fear. Worship is the antidote to all of our worry.

Worship isn't *only* church songs and music. Worship is a way of life. It's a shift of attention that allows you to see God better. Worship is like corrective lenses for your soul, bringing God more clearly into view.

Worship puts God in focus. When the Almighty is in view, the fears in your life begin to flicker and fade. Worship helps you remember that Jesus is fighting for you—and that He has won. Jesus is the all-sufficient source for all you need, available every step of the journey. He is inviting you to come and see what He has done.

SOMETHING IS GOING TO LEAD YOU

"People are slaves to whatever has mastered them."
2 PETER 2:19

THE KEY TO living a godly and holy life is allowing Jesus to shepherd your heart. All of us are shepherded—whether we realize it or not—because we're all led by something. What you let into your heart, whether it's social media trends or the anthem of the world, will end up steering your life and becoming your leader.

Some of you are your own shepherd. You're leading yourself. You're depending on yourself to guide you to still waters and green pastures. If you are living outside of the path Jesus is leading you on, it's likely you are in want.

When you allow Jesus to be your Shepherd, He steps into this stressed-out culture and becomes your replenishing guide. He leads you, watches over you, and gives you rest. When you put your trust in Him and commit to following Him, all the pressure weighing you down is lifted. He is inviting you into a burden-free life today, a life that is godly and holy.

PRAYER

Jesus, You are my Shepherd. Protect me, provide for me, steer me toward goodness and grace. I will follow You alone because You are good and You care for me.

DWELLING IN THE
WORD OF GOD

*In the beginning was the Word, and the Word
was with God, and the Word was God.*
JOHN 1:1

SOMETHING BEAUTIFUL AND transformational
happens when we linger and sit in the Word of God.
Through Christ and the inspired words of the Spirit,
we have access to the very depths of God. We don't
have to settle for a surface-level relationship with our
Savior. Scripture is the revelation of the One who
spoke the cosmos into existence, and it now rests in
your hands.

Something powerful shifts when you realize that
Jesus, the eternal Creator of the universe, is with you
in these pages. So many times we come to read the
Word and fail to acknowledge that Jesus is with us.
When you allow this reality to sink into your heart,
it will change the way you read your Bible. It's not a
chore—it's communion. A kinship. A conversation.

Let your Bible be well-worn as you come to Him
every day with humble curiosity and honest prayers.
Seek and search for His character in the pages as the
Holy Spirit empowers you to uncover His mystery.

REDEMPTION IS HIS CALLING CARD

"I will repay you for the years the locusts have eaten."
JOEL 2:25

CHRIST DIED, AND in three days He rose again from the dead—conquering evil forevermore. The Son of God is an overcomer, and He offers you that same resurrection power in your life today. God can restore and bring about something beautiful from the chaos, and He can rewrite the legacy of devastation in your past. He can and will bring the change that displays His power and love as He leads you forward into life and fullness of joy. This is not some fairy-tale promise or some wishful mumbo jumbo. It's bedrock truth anchored in history at the cross of Jesus.

The prophet Joel proclaimed this. Even if people have hurt you, or circumstances have stolen good and fruitful things from you, even if loss has left your heart like a devastated mountainside, clear-cut of everything beautiful and fruitful and promising—it's not the end of your story. Even if a firestorm of destruction has left your life bare, God is in the business of giving beauty for ashes—of repaying what the locusts have eaten—and that's what He wants to do for you.

PRAYER

God, You are the Great Restorer. Take my chaos and bring about a beautiful display of Your holy renewal in my life.

A RESURRECTION PROMISE

*If there is no resurrection of the dead, then
not even Christ has been raised.*
1 CORINTHIANS 15:13

PRAYER

God, I find
great comfort
in the truth
that Jesus has
been raised
from the dead.
It gives me
confidence that
no matter my
circumstances,
You can bring
dead things
back to life.

WHEN A DIFFICULT season descends on you, sometimes you're there for a short time. Other times, it seems you find yourself in that season for what feels like forever—with the end nowhere in sight.

The good news is that the life Jesus calls us all to enter is a life of resurrection and redemption, where He redeems even the worst of circumstances for His glory and our best. We can trust that our resurrection is possible because Jesus Himself has been resurrected.

Maybe the problems you're wrestling with won't be solved immediately. Yet God offers you His presence in the middle of your problems. In His presence you find a deeper sort of solution, one that holds forth fulfillment, peace, and the hope that He has a wider purpose for your life than you could ever live out on your own.

Resurrection power can be linked to any situation. No occasion is too small for the mighty power of resurrection. If you are in the middle of a hard circumstance, call out to God today. He is near, and He wants to lavish you with gracious confidence.

HIS LIGHT SHINING
THROUGH US

*When Jesus spoke again . . . he said, "I am the
light of the world. Whoever follows me will never
walk in darkness, but will have the light of life."*
JOHN 8:12

God, I choose
to remain in
You today.
Help me see
opportunities
to reflect Your
light to those
around me.

HUMANS ARE BOTH luminous and illuminating,
spiritually speaking. Without God, we were dead in
our sins. But in Christ, we become both carriers of
His divine light and beautiful reflectors of His glory.

Just as the moon reflects the sun's light, God
shines in the darkness and our hearts reflect His light.
When we are in full view of Jesus, His love, grace,
goodness, and power directly impact us. In that place,
in the brightness of His presence, His light will reflect
off us so others can see, no matter how dark the night.

It's amazing to think that, simply by our proximity to Jesus, we can bring hope and life to people
and places trapped in discouragement and despair by
displaying the light that He shines through us.

This knowledge means there's no striving on our
part. No straining to light the world around us. Only
positioning; staying close to the source of all light—
Jesus Christ—and letting that love shine in and
through us to the world around us that's desperately
looking for hope.

JAN 31

LIVING SACRIFICES OF PRAYER

LIVING SACRIFICES OF PRAISE

Therefore, I urge you, brothers and sisters, in view of God's mercy, to offer your bodies as a living sacrifice, holy and pleasing to God— this is your true and proper worship.
ROMANS 12:1

PRAYER

Lord, reveal the areas in my life where I have not put myself on Your altar so I can offer my whole self to You today.

IF YOU'RE NOT careful and intentional, everything in life can quickly become you-centric. It's *your* job. *Your* house. *Your* friends and even *your* dreams and aspirations for the future. But God is gently and steadily inviting you to turn down the dial on *you* and to turn up the dial on *Him*.

God knows that a you-centric universe isn't sturdy enough to withstand the barrage of darkness that comes from living on a broken planet. He knows that if you truly want peace, hope, and security, then you must put your trust in His ways and His guidance. In order to worship Him the way He deserves, you have to depend on Him and sacrifice your self-reliance.

You might be hesitant to put aside your own self-interest. After all, it sounds so countercultural. But it's the only path toward fulfillment and life. When you make your life God-centric, suddenly you find freedom to leverage everything He's given you to worship Him.

FEBRUARY

YOU ACT ON WHAT YOU THINK ABOUT

It is good to praise the Lord and make music to your name, O Most High, proclaiming your love in the morning and your faithfulness at night.
PSALM 92:1–2

PRAYER

God, I do not want to forget Your faithfulness. Rather, help me think about what is right, true, and lovely. Lead my mind toward peace.

THE BIBLE URGES us to stay on the offense with our thought life. Harmful thoughts effortlessly slide past our defenses when we let our mental guard down, tempting us to return to our former ways. The past always looks better in hindsight than it was when you were living through it.

After the children of Israel were released from Egypt, they dreamt of returning to the place of their bondage. Numbers 11:5–6 records how they complained about manna, the miraculous food that God had provided for them in the wilderness. Instead of rejoicing, they remembered with fondness the "leeks, onions, and garlic" of Egypt. How crazy is that?!

If you want to remember God's miraculous works, it helps to build a mental framework that nourishes holy contentment. You'll need a compass that guides you toward peace and beliefs that point you back to Jesus. You'll have to have your heart and mind guarded by the peace of God that comes when your mind is set on the right things.

LET NO SIN REMAIN

*So I find this law at work: Although I want
to do good, evil is right there with me.*

ROMANS 7:21

HAVE YOU FOUND yourself caught in the cycle of trying to change your life but not being able to? No matter how hard you try, the Enemy seems to continue to win in your life?

Satan was defeated on the cross. Thanks to the death, burial, and resurrection of Jesus, Satan is rendered powerless. But Satan can still wriggle and squirm and tempt us to come his way. Just like a dead snake, if we step on Satan's "fangs," he can still poison us and cause serious harm. We're not in heaven yet, and the Enemy is still prowling around on planet Earth.

Even though the Enemy is conquered, his poison will diminish our dreams and weaken the abundant reality of what our lives can be in Christ.

There are two truths to keep in mind. One: Satan was overcome on the cross. Jesus has won the victory. Two: the snake still wriggles. The snake still has venom. Ours is a now-and-not-yet reality. So stay vigilant. Stay ready. And depend on Jesus to sustain you today.

PRAYER

Jesus, help me to remain watchful, and lead me in Your overcoming grace.

TRULY LIVING THROUGH THE CROSS

May I never boast except in the cross of our Lord Jesus Christ, through which the world has been crucified to me, and I to the world.
GALATIANS 6:14

PRAYER

Jesus, when You brought me to life, I was crucified to the world. Its trappings and desires no longer have a hold on me. Thank You for this new resurrection power!

WHEN SOMEONE ASKS you what the gospel is, or to tell the story of Jesus, what do you say?

This is the gospel: Jesus raises the dead. That's how the story of God's salvation plays out. When Jesus was crucified, He covered all of your sin and wrongdoings. The cross was where grace was on display, justice was done, and mankind's case was pleaded before God. Jesus died in your place. Three days later, Jesus was raised from the dead by the power of God. He triumphed over death, hell, sin, and the grave in resurrection. That same resurrection power changes our hearts from the inside out. Resurrection power allows us to stand in the power and provision of a mighty God and truly live.

When you believe this, you realize all striving and boasting is finished. The only thing worth celebrating is the work of Jesus on the cross. Praise God for the gospel!

THE STEADFAST STRENGTH OF GOD

*"When the earth and all its people quake,
it is I who hold its pillars firm."*

PSALM 75:3

HAVE YOU EVER felt like things are tipping closer and closer to being out of control? Like the ground beneath your feet is shaky, and you're not sure where to find solid ground? When life feels like it's falling apart, it can be easy to doubt that God is strong enough to pull things back together.

And yet that is exactly what the Bible says He does. God isn't thrown off-balance or knocked off-kilter by the chaos of the world. He rules above it. Over it. He is perfectly and powerfully working through all things, and that means He is able to calm shaky ground and steady your soul when it feels like you're spiraling.

He is not only able but delights to do it. He's woven His goodness into the fabric of everything around you. He's sustaining you. Protecting you. Covering you. Empowering you.

The more you look to His Word, the more you realize that you never have to doubt His steadfast love or His strength. He's unchanging and unshakable. And He's got you!

PRAYER

God, thank You for showing me Your strength and for holding all things together, including me.

37

GOD ALMIGHTY IS WITH YOU

May the LORD our God be with us as he was with our ancestors; may he never leave us nor forsake us.
1 KINGS 8:57

IF YOU'VE FELT the sting of loss—of resources, of relationships, or especially of death—you know how easy it is to slide from grief into fear. When fear becomes your new operating system, you can easily forget God is right by your side.

Loss is a part of our story as humans. We all walk through devastation, disappointment, and discouragement. There's a valley of the shadow of death, and we all go through it in one way or another.

But how can you come to a place where you can honestly declare that you're not afraid? Of course you won't avoid all the problems around you, but you have a Good Shepherd who is with you as He was with your spiritual fathers. He won't forsake you.

Don't rush by that truth.

God Almighty is with you.

No matter the troubles you're walking through right now, the good news isn't just that God will help you—it's that God is with you.

DAILY DRAWING
CLOSE TO JESUS

FEB 6

The LORD is near to all who call on him,
to all who call on him in truth.
PSALM 145:18

IN ALL SEASONS, you are called to walk with the Good Shepherd. Whether you're saddled with strife or abounding with joy, Jesus wants you to continually rely on His sufficiency, not your own.

We never graduate from being led by our Good Shepherd. We often cling to Jesus when we're being led through the valley of the shadow of death, only to run our own way once we've made it through and are back in the light.

The secret to living truly free is to stay close to Jesus in all things. Stay close when you wake up. When you're working. When you're with your friends, family, or neighbors. Stay close when you're tired and when you're energized. When you're celebrating and when you're sorrowful.

Stay close to Jesus and you will experience not just life, but life to the full. Jesus is close to all those who call on His name, and He is willing and wanting to fulfill the desires of those who daily draw near to Him.

PRAYER

Jesus, I have not grown out of my need for Your shepherding and love. I will follow Your voice as You steer me toward truth and eternal life.

ALIGNED IN CHRIST'S SUFFICIENCY

*Not that we are competent in ourselves
to claim anything for ourselves, but our
competence comes from God.*
2 CORINTHIANS 3:5

PRAYER

Jesus, I
believe that
You are more
than enough
for everything
I need today.
Help me to
trust more
deeply in
Your truth.

TRYING TO PLAY defense to every challenge to our faith can feel overwhelming. But thanks be to God, our ultimate defense isn't all up to us. In fact, the best defense we have is to lean into the all-sufficiency of Jesus. When we start from this source, we suddenly have access to the highest level of protection and provision.

Sufficiency means that Jesus is enough. He is all we need to fulfill God's greatest purposes for our lives. Jesus is not deficient in anything. He is not lacking or inadequate or meager or poor. He's fully competent, fully abounding. Thanks to Jesus, we sit at a banquet table every day—our cups are constantly overflowing.

Jesus is the One who fights the battles for us. Yes, we have some responsibility. We *submit* to Jesus' plan. We *resist* the devil by using His Spirit's power within us. We *align* ourselves with the person and work of Jesus Christ. Yet it's always Jesus who ultimately works on our behalf. Not us. That's why we can trust and depend on Him today.

THE STORY OF ETERNAL LIFE

Jesus said to her, "I am the resurrection and the life."
JOHN 11:25

YOU KNOW THE feeling when you're nearing the last page of a book or waiting for a season finale to drop, and you're anxious to learn how the story ends? It makes for good fiction, but when it comes to real life, we feel restless if we don't know how the story ends. Thankfully, for Christians, the ending is already complete. And the best part is, it's a victorious ending.

This is why Jesus came to earth, taught about the kingdom of heaven, and healed the sick. This is why He carried our sin, was crucified on a cross, and was buried in a borrowed tomb. He came to secure the ending of your story, and He was the only one capable of rewriting that script.

Victory from defeat. Beauty from ashes. Redeemed to be with Him forever.

When the stone was rolled away and Jesus was raised from the dead, He conquered sin, hell, and the grave. He claimed ultimate victory and guaranteed the future victory of all who would follow Him. This is the story of eternal life. It's your story. Jesus is the resurrection and the life forevermore.

PRAYER

God, You went to unbelievable lengths to secure my life for all eternity. May I remember and reflect on Your sacrifice today.

41

MOVING FORWARD AS WE MODEL CHRIST

But grow in the grace and knowledge of our Lord and Savior Jesus Christ.
2 PETER 3:18

HAVE YOU EVER noticed that you start becoming like the people you spend the most time around?

In growing in spiritual maturity, we're called to adopt the behavior and character of God. This means we pattern after Him, copy Him, emulate Him, shadow Him, echo Him, mirror Him. By the close relationship we have with God through Christ, we constantly study how God works and moves. The change in our character doesn't happen all at once.

This work of sanctification actually takes pressure off us, knowing our lives are transformed bit by bit. In our spiritual walks, the key word is *grow*. And growth is gradual. Likewise, Paul told us to "be diligent in these matters; give [ourselves] wholly to them, so that everyone may see [our] progress" (1 Timothy 4:15). The key word there is *progress*.

As you diligently become an imitator of God, you give yourself wholeheartedly to the possibilities of your new genetic makeup. You genuinely develop in your spiritual maturity. Then you move forward in the grace and knowledge of God.

EVEN WHEN YOU CAN'T SEE HIM

Those who led the way rebuked him and told him to be quiet, but he shouted all the more, "Son of David, have mercy on me!"

LUKE 18:39

PRAYER

God, I believe You are working on my behalf. I cry out to You today, and I trust that You hear me.

IN HIS GOSPEL, Luke wrote about a blind man who was begging by the roadside in the city of Jericho. Hearing a commotion, the man learned that Jesus of Nazareth was passing by. Without being able to see Jesus, the man cried out, "Son of David, have mercy on me!" Those in the crowd told him to be quiet, but he yelled even louder. Amazingly, Jesus heard his cries above the chaos, stopped, and healed him (Luke 18:35–43).

You may feel as if God is a billion miles away. You may believe your voice will quiet at the ceiling of the room you are currently in. But there is power that comes through the name of Jesus, and He invites us to call on Him in our times of need.

It doesn't have to be formal. He isn't looking for a rehearsed prayer. He wants your heart—what's really going on. You may not know how He's going to show up in your life, but in faith tell Him you know He can.

WE HAVE BEEN GIVEN ALL WE NEED

*His divine power has given us everything we need
for a godly life through our knowledge of him
who called us by his own glory and goodness.*
2 PETER 1:3

PRAYER

Lord, I do not
want to move
without You.
Each hour,
every moment,
keep me in
step with You.

IT CAN BE easy to say with our lips that "our salvation is by grace alone through faith alone." We can tell others how we believe that Jesus sanctifies us and transforms our lives by His power. But so often, we make the mistake of trying to function as if it all depends on us. We say, "God, thanks for saving me. Thanks for sanctifying me. But I'm good. I've got it from here. Thanks anyway, God. I can do this on my own."

If we truly want to change to become more like Jesus, then we need to understand our constant dependency on the all-sufficiency of Jesus Christ. The change we undergo is more about trusting and less about trying. We've got to make this paradigm shift in our minds. Christ is the real force for us to change.

This is why we can go to Him for all joy. All value. All purpose. All hope. All comfort. All power to resist temptation. All power to change. He, and He alone, can supply all that we need.

DEEPER INTO LOVE

The LORD is compassionate and gracious,
slow to anger, abounding in love.
PSALM 103:8

HOW MAGNIFICENT IT is to serve a God who has revealed Himself to us! He could have chosen to be far off and cast down judgment without ever drawing near to us. But instead, the Creator of the universe decided to come close and reveal Himself to you and to the rest of the world.

How can you know the majesty of God? Look first to His creation. Look to the stars that shine in praise, the trees that grow with grace, and the oceans that roar worship at His great love and power. Look to the life of Jesus, radically generous and a defender of the downcast. He is the holy Prince of Peace, who sacrificially redeemed us for all eternity. And finally, look to His Spirit, who lives within you and accompanies you in His power.

It is impossible to fully understand and know God with our human minds and hearts. That's why He's God! But He has revealed Himself in the perfect capacity for us to know Him. Let Him know through your prayers that you are grateful for His intentional revelation and, by His Spirit, are ready to experience the depths of His love.

PRAYER

God, thank You for revealing Yourself to me. I am only beginning to comprehend the wonders of Your love.

45

THROWING OFF THE OLD DEADNESS

But because of his great love for us, God, who is rich in mercy, made us alive with Christ even when we were dead in transgressions—it is by grace you have been saved.
EPHESIANS 2:4–5

WE CAN READ how the apostle Paul viewed resurrection in Ephesians 2. He wrote that "God, being rich in mercy . . . made us alive together with Christ." That type of resurrection power is displayed when we're saved, and it is also at work through the rest of your life.

The gospel is so much more than a self-help message. Without Christ, we aren't just "bad." We aren't merely unchurched. We don't simply need a little help. Without Christ, we're *dead*. And even after we're made alive, sometimes we struggle with our old state of deadness (Ephesians 4:22–24). The Bible tells us to throw off our old self and take on new attitudes. Just as we put on a jacket and a pair of jeans, we're to put on our new alive self, the self that's created to be like God in true righteousness and holiness.

Just as we put on clothing, we're to put on our new alive self each day. The self that's created to be like God in true righteousness and holiness—set apart and made for a life of abundance of joy.

YOU WERE CREATED ON PURPOSE WITH PURPOSE

But you are a chosen people, a royal priesthood,
a holy nation, God's special possession, that you
may declare the praises of him who called you
out of darkness into his wonderful light.

1 PETER 2:9

PRAYER

God, by Your
Spirit, may
I embrace
my designed
purpose today
and praise
Your name for
all to hear.

AT SOME POINT or another, we've all felt like we don't belong. Maybe you've thought to yourself, *I have no idea what I'm doing here. I don't fit in, and no one would miss me or even notice if I left.*

But when you belong to the family of God, you no longer have to wrestle with not fitting in. You are chosen. You are in a royal priesthood. You are holy. You belong to God. You are created by Him and for Him. You'll never be abandoned.

Created things have purpose. There is just one you. You have a unique calling, a reason for being. It's the second part of this verse.

Your purpose, as one highly valued by God, is to declare the praises of Him who called you out of darkness and into marvelous light. Don't buy into the lie that you are expendable. You're not. Your praise matters because it brings Him glory and echoes out to the people in your life that He is positioning you to serve.

THE BEAUTY IN DYING TO CHRIST

"For whoever wants to save their life will lose it, but whoever loses their life for me and for the gospel will save it."
MARK 8:35

PRAYER

God, show me the joy that comes through the death of my own small-mindedness. Expand my vision to see Your glorious resurrection more clearly.

THERE'S AN OLD blues line that says, "Everybody wants to go to heaven, but nobody wants to die." If we're not careful, we'll cherish the here and now more than the promise of eternity as we push ourselves to the center of our own little galaxies.

Yet in the stars, we see beauty in dying. Even as stars collapse, they often emit fantastic beams of light. Consider their Maker, Jesus Christ, who willingly surrendered to the most glorious death of all. Beyond this, He chose to take our blows, to carry our shame, to bear sin's weight, and to suffer in death. And as gruesome as His last hours were, Jesus' death is still the most beautiful story of redemption this world has ever seen.

So let us model after Jesus. Why should we be afraid to die to ourselves daily while we are still alive here on earth? This "death by choice" frees us from our own small and fading stories, allowing our days to count for something much larger and more enduring than our earthly lives alone could ever be.

A STEADFAST SONG
OF PRAISE

*My heart, O God, is steadfast, my heart is
steadfast; I will sing and make music.*
PSALM 57:7

WHEN DAVID WROTE this psalm of praise, he was
within inches of losing his life. There he was, hiding
in a cave "in the midst of lions" (v. 4), terrified and
crying out to God for help. But then, as we see so
often from David, he shifted his panic into a moment
of praise.

In the midst of the lions in your life, how can you
stir yourself to sing? How can you find the steadfast-
ness to rejoice, to build the confidence that God will
come through no matter what?

Go back to the Word. Embed yourself in
Scripture and witness God's faithfulness for yourself.
Your God doesn't change. His provision and protection are unending. Your future is secure. No matter
what comes in your life, you can praise Him.

As David did, lift your voice and sing a song of
praise. Whether in the middle of scarcity or abundance, choose worship. Watch as God honors that
choice. He delights in the praise of His people, and
He always listens when they surrender and sing.

PRAYER

Father, I
look above
my present
circumstances
with a steadfast
heart and
declare that
I will worship
You for Your
glorious grace!

THE WEIGHTY JOY OF GOD'S INFINITUDE

I can do all this through him who gives me strength.
PHILIPPIANS 4:13

FLICKERS OF GOD'S glory are all around you. The unsearchable riches of Christ are like a huge cavern filled with gold that can never be fully explored. It's an incredibly complex math algorithm that solves all the problems of mankind. It can be tapped into, but it can never be fully understood or written in one sentence on a chalkboard.

This is our God. This is why Paul could write to the Philippians and say that he is empowered through the strength of Jesus to do all things. It's the all-sufficiency of Christ in practice. Paul was showing the church a picture of what it means to explore this unsearchable universe of Christ's grace and glory. What it means to swim in the boundless ocean of Christ's love.

Today, what would it look like for you to explore God's goodness? To step into that cavern of unmeasurable gold, trusting that as you dig deeper and look closer, He will fulfill you in beautiful and holy ways?

YOUR OLD PATTERNS
HAVE BEEN DISRUPTED

God made him who had no sin to be sin for us, so that
in him we might become the righteousness of God.
2 CORINTHIANS 5:21

IF YOU GREW up with a parent who modeled per-petual worrying, or you have an anxious boss, or a nervous friend, you might feel like you could easily tip toward a life marked by fear. Maybe you find your-self looking for the worst in every situation, operating from a place of suspicion, unease, and insecurity.

No matter where you came from or who you're currently surrounded by, you can take confidence that you have a new spiritual reality. In Christ, you are born again. You do not have to sit by and serve an old master like worry or fear. You are not bound to the worrying ways of the world.

If you have put your faith in Christ and are fol-lowing Him, those previous patterns were disrupted the instant you went from death to life. You have a new Father in heaven. He has never worried for one second in His eternal existence, and His security can be your stability as you go about today.

PRAYER

God, would You remind me that Your throne has never been shaken? That because Jesus carried my sin, He can carry my worry?

51

HIS LOVE LEADS US TO COURAGE

"I will not leave you as orphans; I will come to you."
JOHN 14:18

YOUR HEAVENLY FATHER knows everything you're going through. He's been there every step of the way. He's not going to abandon you or walk away from the good work He's doing in your heart.

He's going to continue to heal what's been wronged on this earth and open your eyes to see how astonishingly beautiful He is—and how loved you are by Him. Be assured, "He who began a good work in you will carry it on to completion until the day of Christ Jesus" (Philippians 1:6).

Because you are loved by a perfect Father, you can rely on His truths rooted in the unchanging Word of God and the finished work of Christ on the cross. So today, dig into His Word and keep your eyes fixed on the person of Jesus.

Take courage. You are on God's radar. Receive this truth and breathe it in. He is coming back for you. Live with confidence and reflect it to the world. You are His light, shining like a city on a hill, bringing Him glory as you grow up in holiness to be like Him.

DARKNESS ACCOUNTED FOR

He will not be afraid of evil tidings; his
heart is steadfast, trusting in the LORD.
PSALM 112:7 NKJV

SOMETIMES WE FIND ourselves in the tension of singing anthems our hearts are struggling to believe. Lyrics of praise or psalms about God's goodness can be difficult to recite when you're staring at your life scattered in pieces across the floor.

But in seasons of suffering, you can choose to worship God because your praise is not contingent on the present. Your worship is in response to what God has already done, an echo of the sacrifice God has already made for you. Worship does not deny that life can be dark; rather, it's a declaration that the darkness is ultimately accounted for by Jesus' work on the cross.

If worshiping feels difficult today, remember that you've seen proof of God and experienced His unconditional love through Jesus' sacrifice on the cross. In response to that sacrifice, your life begins to line up with your singing. As you remember this truth, let your heart turn to praise and echo out His glory— not denying your hardship but instead proclaiming the eternal security you have in a God who has overcome it.

PRAYER

God, bring my words and actions into alignment under the banner of Your pleasing and good love.

53

COVERED BY GRACE

*[Christ] was delivered over to death for our sins
and was raised to life for our justification.*
ROMANS 4:25

PRAYER

Jesus, You took on my guilt so I could take on Your freedom and life. You absorbed my trespasses and, through Your death, provided justification for my eternity.

HOW DO WE really know that the work of Christ on the cross was enough? How can we have total confidence that the job was really finished? The answer is Christ's resurrection.

Jesus died physically on the cross, but He also died spiritually when the fellowship and relationship between the Father and the Son was broken. When Jesus was dying, He cried out, asking God why He was forsaken. Have you ever stopped to consider how devastating that moment was? But He didn't end the story there. Shortly after, He also cried out that it was finished.

The great work of redemption was finished, the sin of the entire world was paid for—past, present, and future.

The resurrection of Jesus Christ is the great display of the Father's power. The resurrection shows us that the death of Jesus was enough and we can stand in total confidence that leads us to an unshakable faith. When you go before God today, remember that you are made righteous because of the blood of Jesus. Find peace in the fact that you're covered by grace.

THE CROSSROADS
OF DOUBT

*To those who believed in his name, he gave
the right to become children of God.*
JOHN 1:12

IF YOU HAVEN'T experienced this already, there might be a day where you come to the crossroads of doubt, asking yourself questions such as, *Is God real? Is God powerful? Will God come through for me?* When this happens, there are two options.

The first option is that you listen to the Enemy, who answers these questions with a resounding "No!" The Enemy delights to shut down your questions and pull you away from the Lord.

The second option is to embrace your curiosity and seek answers. Like any father of a young child, God is used to long lists of questions, and He delights to watch you grow in your spiritual confidence. Although we'll never fully comprehend His mystery, God has given all we need to believe in Him. In His Word, by His Spirit, and in all of creation, He reveals Himself.

Even in your questioning, you remain His child; He is not shaken by your doubt. He stands with open arms and invites you to come closer, question by question.

PRAYER

Father, I'm grateful that in the midst of my questions, You are omniscient— all knowing. Help me today to bring all my questions to You as Your child.

THE PERFECTION OF GOD'S LOVE

I pray that the eyes of your heart may be enlightened.
EPHESIANS 1:18

GOD HAS NEVER loved you more because of your good deeds, nor has He ever loved you less because of the sinful acts you have committed. He is love. His love is unchanging. It is the same yesterday, today, and tomorrow. It's unending and eternal. Permanent. His love will fill heaven and be the everlasting source of joy, pleasure, and praise when there is no more measurement of hours, days, or years—when time ceases to exist and all we have is all of Him.

His love is undefeatable and unfailing. It has never lost an inch of ground, never taken a step back in shock or surprise. It has never turned away from you, never given up on you, never stopped pursuing you.

His love is perfect.

And when you get that perfect love in your vision, locked into the center of the eyes of your heart, as Paul said in Ephesians 1:18, you see His power and you embrace His truth. In His love you have the only weapon you'll ever need to extinguish and eradicate sin from your life.

PRAYER

God, may the eyes of my heart be opened to behold Your glorious love today and the great inheritance that awaits me.

RISE AGAIN

For though the righteous fall seven
times, they rise again.
PROVERBS 24:16

WE ALL KNOW what it feels like to keep doing what we don't want to do—to be in the middle of a predicament we feel like we can't get out of, longing for something different, something better, something more.

Many of us try to deny how far we've drifted from God's righteousness, but when we find ourselves in a spiral of bad habits, it can start to change the makeup of our character. You might tell yourself, *I've got everything under control. I can manage this. I'm still okay.* But as these negative patterns seep in over time, you start to become someone you hardly even recognize—resulting in shame, disappointment, and even loneliness as you stay far from the God of love.

If you feel shame while trying to take control of your story, come to the one person who will never shame you. There is a slow-to-anger God inviting you into redemption. When you can't stand on your own, He promises to help you rise. He is not surprised by anything you've done, and He will not let your past define your future. Lay down your life and watch how He helps you rise back up in the days ahead.

PRAYER

God, I repent of how I've strayed from You, and I hold on to Your strong arms as You pull me up in grace.

COUNTERING LIES THROUGH LOVE

When he lies, he speaks his native language, for he is a liar and the father of lies.
JOHN 8:44

PRAYER

Jesus, I speak
Your name into
every shadow
and struggle
today. It is the
highest, most
holy name, and
at Your name,
everything
bows.

THE BIBLE SAYS that Satan, or the Enemy, is the "father of lies." When you start hearing things like "you're worthless" or "you're too far gone," you can know that those lies didn't come from God.

But how do you go one step further and counter those deceptions? You need to replace them with the voice of Jesus, because in Jesus' name, it is possible to shift from being defined by Satan's lies to being defined by Jesus' love.

Change isn't the result of a formula. Transformation might not be immediate for you. Your struggles might not disappear in an instant. But you have the name, power, and authority of the blood of the risen Lord Jesus Christ. You have the power of the cross, the power of Jesus' resurrection. Whatever you're facing may be big, but it is not bigger than the name of Jesus.

When you believe this truth, something is going to shift in you. The victory is already here. Today is the day to ask the Spirit of God to infuse you with the voice of Jesus' love.

THE GREATEST SONG

Praise him, sun and moon; praise him, all you shining stars. Praise him, you highest heavens and you waters above the skies.
PSALM 148:3–4

WE ALL KNOW that stars shine, but as it turns out, they also sing. Every night (and all during the day!) the stars are screaming at the top of their lungs, joining creation as they sing to the One who hung them in their places. And they should praise God! Everything that God made is meant to bear witness to His majesty, sovereignty, and magnificence. Given that the stars have their origin in God, they, too, sing their songs for Him.

But it's not just a cosmic thing; the whole earth is in the mix. The writer of Psalm 148 left no stone unturned in describing a great symphony of epic proportions, one composed of colossal pulsars and mammoth whales, crashing waves and laughing children, tiny birds that flap and flutter, and everything else that comes from the hand of God.

Are you joining in that great symphony? When your life proclaims the worth and holiness of God with fervor and joy, that is the greatest song ever sung.

PRAYER

God, tune my heart to the song of the stars that ceaselessly shout Your wonder and praise!

STAYING CLOSE TO THE SAVIOR

*Trust in the LORD with all your heart and
lean not on your own understanding.*
PROVERBS 3:5

PRAYER

Father, I want
You. Help
me let go of
my need for
control so
that I can
follow You.

IT'S A COMMON desire to want to know what God
is doing with your life and what's coming next. After
all, having access to His blueprint would be nice. But
Scripture tells us that our contentment and joy are
not contingent on knowing all the details of God's
plan. A better understanding of the specifics doesn't
always move us to trust Him more. In fact, it's often
the opposite.

Not knowing what your tomorrow holds makes
you more reliant on Him. He is leading. You are following. When you get that order straightened out, you
begin to experience a deep and active relationship with
God. Instead of a plan, He gives you His promises. He
says to you, *I'm enough. You can trust Me. I poured out
My life for you. I've been faithful from the beginning to
the end. Just follow, and I will lead.*

Loosen your grip from desperately trying to hold
on to a false sense of control. Listen to Him. Go where
He calls. Stay close under His wing. He'll take you
exactly where you need to be.

STAGGERING GRACE

With it he touched my mouth and said,
"See, this has touched your lips; your guilt is
taken away and your sin atoned for."
ISAIAH 6:7

WHEN WAS THE last time you stood in front of something that took your breath away? Maybe you've been to the Sistine Chapel or witnessed the cascading waters of Niagara Falls. When you stand before something majestic, it humbles you.

This is similar to what happened to Isaiah when he had a vision of standing in the throne room of God. Upon seeing the Lord, Isaiah fell on his face, exclaiming, "Woe to me! . . . I am ruined!" (Isaiah 6:5). That's what the presence of God does to a human being. God's glory is more stunning than we could ever imagine, and His holiness illuminates just how unholy we really are. Being in the presence of utter brilliance brings us to our knees.

But Isaiah's story didn't end there, laid flat on the floor trembling in his humanity. No, the perfect God of the universe looked at Isaiah in love and took away his guilt and sin. And today, God offers the same radical grace for you. Let awe fill your spirit and wonder fill your speech as you reflect on the holiness of the throne of God.

PRAYER

Lord, I tremble before You in awe and wonder. Help me see Your holiness with clarity.

UNFATHOMABLE AND UNSEARCHABLE

That I should preach among the Gentiles the unsearchable riches of Christ.
EPHESIANS 3:8 NKJV

PRAYER

God, no one can comprehend You. Yet You invite us to continuously explore the glorious riches of Your grace and goodness. Guide us toward You today.

IN THE FIRST three chapters of Ephesians, Paul noted the challenges of describing and grasping the wonder of Jesus. It isn't easy. Paul simply called the riches of Christ "unsearchable." I love that word. *Unsearchable.* His grace is readily available to us, yet, in its entirety, it's so amazing that it's unfathomable.

Understanding the fullness of God's character is like a child following a trickling brook. With each new step, the child discovers more and more as the brook flows downstream. Soon, the brook he knew well widens into a fast-moving creek with deepening pools and eventually flows into a mighty river. As he continues to walk the bank, he grows to know the river well. Until one day he looks up and the river has flowed into an unmeasurable ocean.

Like our pursuit of the unsearchable riches of Christ, the more you know, the more you learn there's so much more to know. This is a joyous invitation for those who believe in and love God.

MARCH

LIKE A CHILD

And he said: "Truly I tell you, unless you change and become like little children, you will never enter the kingdom of heaven."
MATTHEW 18:3

PRAYER

Jesus, I don't have to have it all figured out to know that You are all that I need. Take my simple and unrefined faith and make it glorious in Your sight.

LET'S BE HONEST. No adult wants to act like a child. To be childlike feels more like something to avoid rather than something to aspire to. So why would Jesus tell us to become like little children to enter the kingdom of heaven? Wouldn't it make more sense to come as our most mature selves? To bring our eloquent prayers and memorized Bible verses before Him?

Hear me when I say that knowing God's Word is a wonderful sword for our souls, and praying with specificity and intentionality has the power to move heaven and earth. But I would argue that what's essential for all of us—whether we've followed Christ for decades or just one day—is that we retain the faith of a child.

All Jesus asks of you is to keep running back to Him like a dawdling little one: eyes wide with wonder at His majesty, full of curiosity and dependent on Him. There, in His arms, you will find paradise.

A TURNAROUND THAT CHANGES THINGS

*Therefore this is what the LORD says: "If you repent,
I will restore you that you may serve me."*
JEREMIAH 15:19

DO YOU EVER find yourself wishing you could have a redo? From some unplanned circumstance? Some mistake or failure? A dashed dream? Some jarring pain?

The good news is that God's in the business of giving fresh starts to people. He gives hope to the hopeless, direction to the directionless, help for those who need help. God is always good, and God's plans will always prevail, even when our plans don't. Or when they need to be changed.

If you're longing for some sort of turnaround or fresh start or new direction, then run to God. Despite feeling scarred or jaded or hopeless, you're never too far. He is able to offer hope and help, encouragement and perspective. He's able to draw near to you if you're frustrated or confused, if you're in sorrow or in pain, if you're disappointed or feel like life doesn't make sense. He is with you when you're surrounded by the rubble, discouraged, troubled, or concerned about your life.

You might be on the brink of giving up, but help is at hand. You might not get the "redo" you wanted, but you'll get an even better promise—God Himself.

PRAYER

God, I ask for a fresh perspective today of Your faithful restoration. Take my difficult circumstances and rework them for Your glory and my good.

AN UNDEFEATABLE JOY

Rejoice in the Lord always. I will say it again: Rejoice!
PHILIPPIANS 4:4

AS A BELIEVER in Christ, you can find an endless source of joy through God's grace. This type of joy isn't dampened by a rainy day or obscured by a dark night. This joy is an anchor, even when the waves of life are stormy. It holds steady, even if water seems to be filling your boat from every side, because it is given by a God who never changes and never fails to show up in your life. It doesn't negate hardship or even sorrow.

But it does eternally permeate your soul.

So how do you get this joy? You spend time in His Word and learn to focus on the things that are immovable—things that are pure, noble, lovely, excellent—and that cannot be devalued or depreciated by darkness.

You begin to focus on heavenly truths, namely, the victory of the cross and the assurance of the future resurrection. Both are set in stone and are catalysts for life-shaping joy. Because of these truths, and the Spirit living within you, joy can be yours every day and in any situation.

SATISFYING THE NEED FOR VALIDATION

And a voice from heaven said, "This is my Son, whom I love; with him I am well pleased."
MATTHEW 3:17

YOU HAVE THE opportunity to walk in an intimate relationship with the God of creation. How stunning is that? You can know God as *a Father*. Not some distant, far-off force who set the world in motion. A Father who loves you. When you see Him clearly for who He is, you can come to know who you truly are in Him.

It's tempting to look elsewhere for validation and affirmation of who you are. There are dozens of distractions trying to define your identity—your job, your talents, even your earthly family. At the core of our desire for validation is the need for the blessing of a father. We want to hear our dad say, "I love you. I'm proud of you. I'm here for you."

This is precisely why God is revealing Himself as a perfect Father. He wants you to live knowing you are His child. When you live from this place of validation, your identity is secure, and you are set free to be a vessel of peace as He leads you.

PRAYER

Father, would Your love for me be the defining mark of my life? May I draw comfort today from Your fatherhood as I stand secure in You.

FIXING YOUR EYES ON JESUS

Consequently, faith comes from hearing the message, and the message is heard through the word about Christ.
ROMANS 10:17

PRAYER

Jesus, I have heard Your truth, so I have faith that You will equip me for every good work. May I keep my eyes on You.

WHAT TAKES UP most of your focus and concentration? What is the topic of conversation when you sit around the dinner table with friends? Are you quick to bring attention to the hardships you're facing, or to the Savior who walks with you?

When you ruminate on your struggles, anxiety is likely to blossom as your faith begins to dwindle. But shifting your attention to Jesus builds up your faith, and faith is the antidote to fear. Faith is saying, "I have confidence in God that He is bigger than whatever I am facing."

This is what Paul meant in Romans 10:17. When you see and hear God in His Word, the Word allows you to hear that Jesus is enough and to see that God is bigger. That builds up your faith, and your faith becomes the weapon you use to take down your struggles. When you hear and see Jesus, things change in your life.

Keep Him in your view today. Fix your eyes on Jesus and follow where He leads.

TAKING A STEP
TOWARD JESUS

*But Jesus immediately said to them: "Take
courage! It is I. Don't be afraid."*
MATTHEW 14:27

SIMILAR TO A storm suddenly wrecking through the
sea, life can change in the blink of an eye. For the
disciples, it was an actual raging storm while they were
crossing the Sea of Galilee. They found themselves in
one of those storms where they weren't certain if they
were going to make it to safety again. That's when
Jesus decided to walk out to His disciples on the water.
The disciples cried out in fear, but Jesus assured them
not to be afraid.

Peter, all big and bold, said, "Lord, if it's you . . .
tell me to come to you on the water" (Matthew 14:28).

Jesus said, "Come" (v. 29).

Can you imagine that?

The visibility wasn't great. The waves and water
and darkness were raging all around. But Peter looked
toward the voice and stepped out onto the water. He
started walking toward Jesus.

Just like He likely said to Peter, Jesus says to us,
*It's okay. I've got you—even in the midst of this storm.
You have nothing to fear.*

PRAYER

Jesus,
because You
have invited
me to walk
out onto the
water toward
Your voice, I
will step out in
faith and move
toward You.

STARTING WITH RIGHTEOUS PRAISE

"But seek first his kingdom and his righteousness, and all these things will be given to you as well."
MATTHEW 6:33

PRAYER

God, would You prick my heart consistently throughout this day so that I would remember to turn to You first before all else? Anoint me. Appoint me. Protect me. Thank You for today. I want to put You first today.

AT THE START of each day, before you look at the weather, scan the news, or check your email, consider orienting yourself first in the truth that matters most: God is great and worthy of all praise.

It's important to aim to start your day with this because there will inevitably be other priorities trying to grab the headline for your day—busy schedules, unexpected stressors, and important conversations. Before you know it, you may find yourself rushing, forgetting to rely on God's power. You start to seek a lesser kingdom of man-made righteousness.

If you really want to see your faith life change, seek Him first. You can't equally seek Him and the things of this world. One always comes before the other. So choose to start with God. Start with praise. Don't wait until the day is over to check in with Him. We are prone to put a thousand things before God. If you prioritize seeking the kingdom of God, everything else will be added to you.

RELINQUISH CONTROL TO GOD

Submit yourselves, then, to God. Resist the devil, and he will flee from you.

JAMES 4:7

WHEN LIFE FEELS like it's spinning out of control, remind yourself that you can't manage the actions of people, events, or nations. You can't dictate or fully know other people's motives, nor can you make people tell the truth, stop lies, defuse threats, or right all wrongs. You cannot personally protect and insulate every person you love from pain.

Thankfully, there is something you *can* do. You can put your confidence in a God who is near and trust that He is working (even through corrupted human decisions) to bring about His overarching plans for our good and His glory.

It all comes down to these two questions: Do you trust Him? And if so, will you relinquish control to Him?

Admitting you're not in charge doesn't imply that you shirk your responsibility for what God gives you to steward or that you fail to pray in faith. Rather, admitting your need for help allows you to realign yourself with the reality that He is actually in control of this world.

PRAYER

Father, I open my hands and release my hold on the things that You were always meant to carry. I put them back in Your hands, knowing You are able to do all things.

YOU'RE IN GOOD HANDS

By the word of the LORD the heavens were made,
their starry host by the breath of his mouth.
PSALM 33:6

PRAYER

God, Your power is unfathomable, and yet You gently and lovingly hold me in Your hands because You are holy and good.

HAVE YOU EVER considered how incomprehensibly big a star actually is? The sun, which is the nearest star to us, is so big that it could fit 1.3 million earths inside it! And the sun isn't a massive star compared to other stars in the cosmos.

So what does it say about God when Scripture tells us that He *breathed* out the stars? First, we instantly know that God isn't our size. He's a beautiful, radiant, limitless, and holy Creator who demands and deserves our awe and devotion.

Second, we're invited to reframe our view of God in light of His holiness. The more clearly we see Him, the more we can rest in the strength and shadow of the One who exhales luminous balls of uncontrollable combustion as if they were merely fireflies on a warm summer night.

If the power of the stars is hard to fathom, how much more so is the power of the One who holds them in place beyond our understanding? If His are the arms that are holding you now, rest and trust. You are in good hands.

ENOUGH! TO OLD WAYS OF LIVING

And God is able to bless you abundantly, so that in all things at all times, having all that you need, you will abound in every good work.
2 CORINTHIANS 9:8

AS DEARLY LOVED children of God, it's up to us to shout, "Enough!" to the old ways of living.

By faith, we can claim the light of Christ to guide our pathways. We must not settle for second-rate living a second longer. We want to truly live, in Jesus' name. So we "throw off everything that hinders and the sin that so easily entangles. And [we] run with perseverance the race marked out for us, fixing our eyes on Jesus" (Hebrews 12:1–2).

In time, we learn to do nothing apart from Christ (John 15:5). We abide in Him. We dwell in Him. We stay close to Him because we learn that He is able to make all grace abound to us in every way. We learn that God has given us unlimited resources, everything we need for life and godliness. In Him, we are enriched in every way, so our job is to simply accept the abundance and rely on Him.

PRAYER

God, no matter my season or circumstance, You are able to make all grace abound to me so that I can cast off my old ways for Your new power today.

THE JUST AND THE JUSTIFIER

He did it to demonstrate his righteousness at the present time, so as to be just and the one who justifies those who have faith in Jesus.
ROMANS 3:26

PRAYER

How powerful is Your salvation over death and the grave! How glorious! Move my heart to depend fully on You today.

WHEN JESUS DIED on the cross, He not only accomplished your eternal salvation, He also put to shame all the counterfeits, false gods, and false security systems in the world who say, "I can be your god. Come to me, and I'll make you feel better. Come to me, and let me run the show."

Today Jesus says to you, *No, we're going to finish off that thinking once and for all. I am the one true Messiah, and My Father is the one true God. He is just, and the Justifier. He's the One who can save, the only One who can bring your heart to life again. My Father is the only Deliverer, the only One who can bring salvation to His people. He's the only One who can break the chains. He's the only One who can open the doors. He is God, and there is no other.*

Hallelujah that God stands alone and above all the things of earth. Lean in to that promise today.

SETTING JESUS ALWAYS BEFORE YOU

I have set the LORD always before me; because He is at my right hand I shall not be moved.

PSALM 16:8 (NKJV)

YOU MAY BE staring down a stressful situation right now. Or you might find yourself unsure about your future and scared about what could happen next. If that is you, take heart, because the Lord is always with you.

Yes, God gives you strength, wisdom, grace, protection, and so many other blessings. But the best and most potent thing you have access to is God Himself. He is at your right hand. Nothing can shake you as long as you are connected to Him.

The term *right hand* in the Old Testament indicated a valued, honored, and even intimate position. If you sat at the right hand of someone, then that was the best seat in the house.

In the New Testament, the equivalent for believers is that Jesus lives in us. Galatians 2:20 tells us that we are crucified with Christ, and we no longer live, but Christ lives in us. When you embrace this reality, and keep Jesus as your focus, you can relax and face any circumstance that arises, because in Christ, you know your future is secure.

PRAYER

Lord, I steady my focus on You alone today. Because You are at my right hand, I will not be shaken.

LIFTED HANDS IN WORSHIP

"The God who made the world and everything in it is the Lord of heaven and earth."
ACTS 17:24

HANDS LIFTED IN praise to God acknowledge that someone exists who's greater than you. That He is reaching down with an outstretched hand, and you're responding to Him in faith.

Hands lifted to heaven, people crying out. It's the way humans respond when they don't know where else to turn. They think, *Someone help me.* You might not know how the help is going to come, but you can know *who* it's coming from—your God, your Maker, the Lord of heaven and earth.

We see hands lifted in praise both in times of jubilant celebration and in times of desperation. We see it all over humanity, and especially in the middle of devastation and ruin. If you've walked through heartbreak or know someone who has, you know the natural posture of the weary and downtrodden—hands lifted in praise.

What would it look like, despite what your surroundings are, if today you opened your hands to God and praised Him for the blessings He's put in your life?

SPIRITUAL AMBITION

Since we have these promises, dear friends, let us purify ourselves from everything that contaminates body and spirit, perfecting holiness out of reverence for God.

2 CORINTHIANS 7:1

WHEN GOD PLACES something on your heart, don't pull away, even if it feels impossible. When God works, He doesn't hold back, and as His followers, we shouldn't either.

God wants you to embrace spiritual ambition. He has a specific purpose for your life, and He wants you to step into it with eagerness and joy. He doesn't want you to be timid or average in the fruit of the Spirit and the gifts that He's given you. He wants you to be the kind of person who has the ambition and maturity to influence heaven and earth.

Are you honoring His calling? Do you embrace impossibility, trusting He will make a way? As you step boldly into His plan, you will continue to grow in your maturity, spiritually fortifying you for the next thing He calls you to. Each time you faithfully answer His call, you prepare yourself for more and more. Be ambitious about what God is ambitious about, and watch the ways He uses your life to make Himself known to those around you.

PRAYER

God, because of Your great promises, I aim for holiness as I revere Your holy name.

A LIFE-SHAPING REVELATION

I want to know Christ—yes, to know the power of his resurrection and participation in his sufferings, becoming like him in his death.
PHILIPPIANS 3:10

THERE IS A massive difference between knowing about Christ and being captivated by Him. True Christianity isn't a list of platitudes on how to live a better life. Quick-fix advice about how to heal your relationships or become a better leader might seem fine in the short run, but strategies that are man-made won't satisfy your soul.

Be aware that you can have an intellectual knowledge of Christ without ever actually knowing Him. If you want a true and life-shaping revelation of Jesus, you must move beyond head knowledge and experience heart knowledge. It's countercultural to live surrendered to a risen Savior. It means laying down your desires and trusting that there is a God who gives you more than you'd ever ask for or imagine.

Are you eager and ready to know Him? Ready to live a radical life committed to the risen King? When you are, Jesus is ready and eager to reveal Himself to you. He knows that it's only His Spirit and His Word that can complete the longings of your soul.

PRAYER

Jesus, I don't want just the details and the facts, I want a deep relationship and the friendship that comes with walking close to You.

RESTORED, STRONG, FIRM, AND STEADFAST

Cast all your anxiety on him because he cares for you. . . . And the God of all grace, who called you to his eternal glory in Christ, after you have suffered a little while, will himself restore you and make you strong, firm and steadfast.
1 PETER 5:7, 10

PRAYER

God, Your goodness surpasses my understanding. For that, I will worship You with all I have.

FIRST PETER 5:7 is beautiful, and its appeal to cast our anxieties on God is life-giving both in its invitation and its intentionality. When you believe that truth, you not only lay your troubles at the feet of Jesus, but you also learn to love God more because you know that He cares for you. This changes everything.

But have you ever wondered what is waiting for the person who takes God up on that promise? We find the answer a few verses later in 1 Peter 5:10.

When you cast your anxieties on Jesus, the God of all grace gives you restoration, strength, firmness, and steadfast love. He doesn't just remove your anxiety. He empowers you by His Spirit to live a life of purpose, mission, and grace.

He takes your anxiety and gives you awe. He replaces your fears with faith. He carries your burdens and, in doing so, gives you a sense of beauty, wonder, and joy.

YOU HAVE ACCESS TO HIS PEACE

*"Peace I leave with you; my peace I give you.
I do not give to you as the world gives."*
JOHN 14:27

PRAYER

Jesus, I humbly confess my attempts to bring myself joy on my own merit. I realize I cannot do this on my own, but You can, Lord. Do in me what only You can do.

ONE OF THE hardest aspects of wrestling with anxiety is how isolating it can feel. If you can't shake the anxiety you're facing, you might feel alone, forgotten, or like you're the only one who keeps struggling to find joy and peace.

Scripture is full of stories of people who struggled with similar hardships. Through God's Word, you can see that you're not alone. But even more than that, you can find consolation in the truth that you have God's presence, which means you have His peace.

In a world that appears to be crumbling, Jesus is still the Prince of Peace. He is not always looking for the easiest way to get you out of the fire, but He does promise to bring you peace in the midst of whatever uncertainty or trial you are experiencing. As you follow and trust in Jesus, you can expect to know joy again.

GOD DELIGHTS IN
YOUR PRAISE

*Sing the praises of the LORD, you his
faithful people; praise his holy name.*
PSALM 30:4

SEATED HIGH ABOVE the heavens, God is central in a universe that performs His magnum opus.

And somewhere in the midst of it all is you—special among all of creation, made in the very image of God. Stamped with divinity and created in the likeness of God, you were made by and for Jesus. Thus, you have a voice in the chorus. A voice like no other because you have the capacity to know and love the Creator, and the choice to value Him above everything else He has made.

You have been sought after and redeemed. Christ has come for you, dying and rising to life to put life and breath in your lungs again.

As crazy as it seems, your voice is not incidental in a universe as vast as the one we find ourselves in. You are a unique human being, fearfully and wonderfully made by the God of all creation. Your praise makes Him smile. First, because He loves you, and second, because He knows that when you're singing His song, you've touched and tasted the greatest thing in all the world.

PRAYER

God, thank You for loving me intimately and with such powerful intentionality. May my lips never fail to sing Your praise.

UNCHANGING AND EVERLASTING

"This is what the LORD says—Israel's King and Redeemer, the LORD Almighty: I am the first and I am the last; apart from me there is no God."
ISAIAH 44:6

PRAYER

God, let my heart be bolstered by Your unchanging love, set in stone for all eternity. Let me dwell in awe that You are first and last of all things.

WE'RE ALL CONSTANTLY changing and growing, and as a result, relationships can be unpredictable. If you've ever known the pain of a lost friendship, or if anyone has ever walked out of your life unexpectedly, you know the gift of having someone you can depend on. Someone who does what they say they will do.

Have you ever considered the sheer relief of God's unchangeability? He is the same yesterday, today, and forever. We read in His Word that He is everlasting, never altering, and never shifting. He is who He is. Permanently.

This means He has always been loving. He has always been strong. He is stable and holy. His provision does not waver. His grace for you does not fluctuate based on your performance. You can be fully dependent on Him. If you're looking for a safe place to rest your head, if your soul longs for stability, lean into His consistency today. Everything else might change, but hallelujah, He remains the same.

MERCY OVER WRATH

*In his great mercy he has given us new birth
into a living hope through the resurrection
of Jesus Christ from the dead.*

1 PETER 1:3

THROUGHOUT HISTORY, GOD has been motivated by His great mercy toward His people. There is not a single person who hasn't fallen short of the glory of God (Romans 3:23). While our unholiness ought to prevent us from being in His holy presence, God, abounding in love, refuses to allow that judgment to fall on us, and instead sent His Son to bear what we deserve.

God's mercy doesn't eliminate your need to change; rather, it holds back the consequences you deserve. In other words, just because God is merciful doesn't mean He is okay with your sin. But it's critical to be clear on this: your obedience will never save you. Only the resurrected Christ will. Your obedience is a response to God's mercy, not a means to earning it.

Rejoice over this truth: though you deserve the very worst, through God's mercy, you have been given the very best. You are made new and continually being sanctified by the God of the universe. Praise Him for what only He can do!

PRAYER

God, I know it was more costly than I can fully comprehend to offer me Your mercy. I praise You for Your willingness to save me, even when I was far from You.

BY THE POWER OF
THE HOLY SPIRIT

*So he said to me, "This is the word of the LORD
to Zerubbabel: 'Not by might nor by power,
but by my Spirit,' says the LORD Almighty."*
ZECHARIAH 4:6

PRAYER

God, show
me the things
I need to
surrender
and the ways
I can align
my heart with
Yours today.
Guide me and
sustain my
pursuit of You.

HAVE YOU EVER made a bold claim, only later to be
called out by a friend to *actually* take a step toward
that claim? It can be difficult to close the gap between
our intentions and our actions. We have a saying for it:
"Put your money where your mouth is."

When you put your faith in Jesus, you're making a
bold claim with your life. You are saying that you are a
new creation. But you can't stop there. You have to live
it out. It's one thing to believe in Jesus, to acknowledge that He is God, and to say you're a beloved child.
But it's another thing to truly back up your belief by
living out those realities.

If you're truly living in light of your new identity,
then your life will change, and you will lean toward
that change in conjunction with the power of the Holy
Spirit working inside you. By grace, you deliberately
walk in that new direction with your mind and heart
completely and totally fixed on Him.

How can you move from intention to action and
live out your faith in Jesus today?

TODAY AND FOREVER

No, in all these things we are more than conquerors through him who loved us.
ROMANS 8:37

HAVE YOU EVER felt so wrapped up in the future that you've forgotten to live in the moment? Or maybe you live so much for today that you never realize you're in a bigger story.

As a follower of Jesus, you're called to live with a type of spiritual bifocals that help you with both near- and farsightedness, giving you hope and peace both for your present and future moments.

When you live in the moment in front of you, you more desperately depend on God. You worship Him for His grace and His sustaining power. You understand you have all you need today.

But you also get to live knowing the end of the story, where you will hopefully hear God say, *Well done, good and faithful servant.* Knowing how things work out can give you confidence, peace, and a sense of mission to make today count.

God has made you a conqueror, both today and on the final day. Let that spiritual vision fill your heart with celebration and joy, and win today by the grace of God.

PRAYER

God, dial in my spirit so that I would zoom in and out on Your glorious story. Only You can be in the moments and the millenniums today.

THE MEANING OF LIFE

*Ascribe to the LORD the glory due his name;
bring an offering and come before him. Worship
the LORD in the splendor of his holiness.*
1 CHRONICLES 16:29

WHAT WOULD YOU say if someone asked you, "What is life all about?" If you look at Scripture, you'll see pretty quickly that all of our lives ultimately center on the glory of God. Everything in creation—everything on planet Earth—comes back to Him. He's the star of the story. Your job, your family, your church involvement—it's all about Him.

But this glorious God doesn't just stand far off and keep Himself isolated from you. It's the exact opposite. He, in His kindness, has extended radical grace to you. Grace to get you through today, and grace to get you through the valley, and grace to get you up the mountains. He's given you Jesus, the hope of glory.

Because this glorious God has extended radical grace, you are invited to respond with extravagant worship—an all-in kind of worship. One hundred percent, fully maxed-out worship. When you embrace this mindset of extravagant worship, you find joy knowing that you're pursuing the One your soul was made for. His glory is the true meaning of life.

A VICTORY PARADE

*Now thanks be to God who always
leads us in triumph in Christ.*
2 CORINTHIANS 2:14 NKJV

WHEN YOU SLOW down to reflect on your life, what emotions rise to the surface? Maybe you're embarrassed by something you've done, haunted by shame or guilt. Maybe you're exhausted and burned out, knowing you're in need of rest but not sure where to find it. Maybe you're simply disappointed and unsure how you drifted off course; you just want a way forward, but you don't know where to turn.

Whatever your story is, your story joins a larger story. A story of people who have stumbled and fallen, a story of people whose lives were messy, a story of people whose lives were broken and confused, yet they were invited to experience the ocean of God's love. God is eager to provide His redemption to those who need it most, no matter where they have been or what they have done.

Rest easy. God's love for you can override whatever has come before with a new and victorious future. You no longer have to define yourself by the past. You are moving forward in a victory parade, led by Jesus.

PRAYER

Jesus, in Your great triumphal procession, I find joy and peace. I don't have to win the final battle because You have already won it.

87

FROM WORRY TO WORSHIP

To bestow on them a crown of beauty instead of ashes, the oil of joy instead of mourning, and a garment of praise instead of a spirit of despair.
ISAIAH 61:3

IF YOUR STORY has left you mourning over ashes of lost expectations and broken hopes, you can find comfort today through the tide-turning power of worship.

It might sound backward, but worship is the best way to dispel despair. The two cannot occupy the same space; they can't both fill our mouths at the same time. One always displaces the other.

This is why the antidote to fear and despair is faith, and the soundtrack that empowers our faith is our worship.

God encourages us to put on the garment of praise when we feel entangled by the spirit of heaviness. He gives us songs in the night, anthems for the dark night of the soul when worry and stress and fear lurk about. So sing into the face of the uncertainty about a sure and unchanging God.

Today, you get to determine what you choose to speak—worship or worry. When you prioritize keeping Jesus as your lead story—especially when the battle rages—He shows up and transfers beauty and gladness for your ashes and mourning.

FROM THE VERY BEGINNING UNTIL TODAY

"Where were you when I laid the earth's foundation?"
JOB 38:4

WHEN I FEEL myself wanting to be in control and desiring to be in charge, I think about Job and his conversation with God. Job was a righteous man who had a lot of good things going for him. A reputable family, a successful business, right standing, strong health.

You may know the story, but Job went on to lose just about everything, including almost losing his life. Near the end of the story, we see Job crying out to God, essentially asking Him, "Are You still in control of even this?"

God reminds Job—and us—that He's been in control for a lot longer than we have. He was in control from the very moment He spoke and galaxies were born. He was in control when the earth was formed and when the waters were separated from the dry land. And He was in control from the very nanosecond you were brought into this world.

When you begin to trust that God is in control, it can free your heart from the desire of being in charge, because there is another who is stronger, steadier, and far more trustworthy than we could ever be.

PRAYER

God, You are the Creator from the beginning. As such, I rely on You, for You have never changed.

AN IMMEASURABLE WORTH

Day and night they never stop saying:
"'Holy, holy, holy is the Lord God Almighty,'
who was, and is, and is to come."
REVELATION 4:8

PRAYER

God, I never
want to stop
praising You
and crying out
how stunning
You are.
Capture my
heart! Stretch
my soul
toward You.

OUR CULTURE MOVES inconceivably fast. A story
might be breaking news, only to be replaced with
another headline a few hours later. Trends cycle
through at a rapid pace, and there's always a new
expert on the scene with secret tips for how to best
spend our lives.

If you're feeling distracted and disoriented trying
to keep up—unplug and focus on what lasts: God
Almighty. He's not a headline or a blip on the news.
His Word never fails. A million diamonds don't hold
a candle to His value. All the things of this world are
temporary, fleeting, and passing away, but our God
lasts forever. His worth cannot be calculated. And
because of His lasting, immeasurable glory—day and
night, the angels cry, "Holy, holy, holy."

Does your heart echo this cry of heaven? Don't
let your relationship with God become a "breaking
news" story, here today and gone tomorrow. Put your
full attention on Him, and ask Him to stun your heart
again with His majesty.

AWAKE. ALERT. ABLE.

*He who watches over you will not slumber; indeed, he
who watches over Israel will neither slumber nor sleep.*
PSALM 121:3–4

IT'S OF UTMOST importance that you know that
God is a God of love who loves you. When you believe
this, you know He is actively working on your behalf
in every circumstance. And when He works, He is
awake, alert, and able!

The God who is ever before you is always awake.
He's never been tired or weary. The Almighty has
never once closed His eyes in sleep.

God is not only awake but also alert. It's possible
to be fully awake yet not be paying attention. God
is zeroed in on your every need. He knows what you
need long before you do. He sees the whole path ahead
of you before you even take the next step.

Lastly, He is able. What good would it do if God
were awake and alert if He weren't able to do something about the things that are weighing you down?
God is able and working on your behalf—whether
you see it or not. Choose to trust in His great out-
working of love today.

PRAYER

God, You are
aware of my
needs and are
intentionally
focused on
providing for
me in every
season. I'm
humbled
anew that You
love me.

BEING CRUCIFIED WITH CHRIST

I have been crucified with Christ and I no longer live, but Christ lives in me.
GALATIANS 2:20

PRAYER

Jesus,
everything
I am I put
before You.
Purify my soul
and expose
where I've
become too
comfortable.

HAVE YOU EVER experienced a hard workout that was rewarding but left you feeling sore? If you have, you know that discomfort and goodness aren't always opposites.

The cross brought pain to Jesus in the same breath it brought freedom to us. We have eternal life because of Christ's sacrifice. We can fully live because of the rugged cross. This is our story.

People ask, "What does it mean to be a Christian?" It means to put our faith in the work of Jesus. That He came to earth. He lived. He was crucified. He was resurrected. That He sent the Spirit of God to empower us. This is the gospel. This is what we believe, and it all hinges on a very uncomfortable moment.

Somehow as a people of God, if we're not careful, we can sing songs about the "uncomfortable" moment of Jesus while we live in the very comfortable moment of us. We're prone to love His resurrection but shy away from His crucifixion. So today, ask God what area of sin you can continue to put to death. It might be uncomfortable, but it will also bring Him glory.

ALREADY ACCEPTED

Therefore, since we are surrounded by such a great cloud of witnesses . . . let us run with perseverance the race marked out for us.

HEBREWS 12:1

IF YOU LIVE for people's approval, you will die by their rejection.

When we're not careful, we can forget we were created by God for a purpose that He set in motion for our lives. He didn't ask us to compare ourselves to others or run someone else's race. He said, *Run your race.* He didn't want us to work on someone else's timetable. He wants us to work on His time-table. God wants us to know that "he who began a good work in [us] will carry it on to completion until the day of Christ Jesus" (Philippians 1:6). This truth helps us know that God cares for us more than we can imagine.

Whether at school, at work, or with family, we potentially face rejection every day. We move past fear of disapproval by immersing ourselves in the acceptance of Christ. To no longer strive for worldly acceptance because we are already accepted in Him. We can arrive to every situation confidently, knowing we are secure in Jesus' love.

PRAYER

God, I no longer live for man's approval. I trust my identity is secure because You sent Your Son to die in my place. Thank You for accepting me into Your family!

JESUS IS LORD OF YOUR LIFE

But if serving the LORD seems undesirable to you, then choose for yourselves this day whom you will serve. . . . But as for me and my household, we will serve the LORD.
JOSHUA 24:15

PRAYER

Jesus, I surrender my desire to rule my own life in order to embrace Your lordship over my days.

IT'S ONE THING to speak of God's greatness in a general sense—to intellectually acknowledge that Jesus is Lord over creation, over death and the grave, over evil and its consequences. But it's much more vulnerable to recognize Jesus as *your* Lord. Doing so has a major effect on your life, because if Jesus is your Lord, that means you're not the master. You have to acknowledge your lower position. You exist for Him—not the other way around.

For many of us, this is where the rubber meets the road in our spiritual lives. Every single day, our culture hammers us with the idea that we are the masters of our own fates—that we control our own destinies.

We can't proclaim Jesus as Lord and then continue to live as our own masters. Those two realities cannot coexist. Either we are the masters of our lives or Jesus is. The choice of who you serve belongs to you.

APRIL

PERSEVERANCE FORGES STRENGTH

Because you know that the testing of your faith produces perseverance. Let perseverance finish its work so that you may be mature and complete, not lacking anything.
JAMES 1:3–4

PRAYER

God, thank You that my trials are not wasted. You are strengthening me so that I can stand secure in You.

YOU ARE STRONGER than you think. As a follower of Jesus, your strength is not rooted in your own willpower or ability. If it was, no one would be able to stand up to the struggles and temptations of this life. Instead, your strength is based on the perfect power of Jesus given to you through the Holy Spirit.

You will face trials of various kinds. Odds are you might be experiencing hardship right now. No matter what storm comes your way, you are already equipped with all the strength you need to last through it. When you rely on Jesus' strength, hardships no longer destroy you; they can be used to build maturity and perseverance in your spirit. You can cling to God and His power and let the testing of your faith accomplish a great reward for you: God-centered confidence.

Don't waste your hardship. As you tap into the strength available to you, watch how your spirit transforms. Trust that when the next trial comes, you'll be stronger because of this one.

THE ULTIMATE FREEDOM
FROM FEAR

APR 2

For the Spirit God gave us does not make us timid,
but gives us power, love and self-discipline.
2 TIMOTHY 1:7

WE ARE ALL prone to fear. The fight-or-flight response is hardwired into our DNA. In the hunter-versus-hunted lifestyle of our ancestors, fear was a strategic tool that just might have helped keep you alive.

But today, many of us live ruled by fear. We fear nearly everything and everyone, and when that type of living sinks into our souls, anxiety is the natural by-product.

For those of us who follow Jesus, we have the ultimate antidote to fear. When we put our faith in Jesus, we receive the Holy Spirit, who counteracts our innate tendency to fear with power, love, and self-control.

The Holy Spirit prompts and empowers us to live a life of trust and not terror. Do you believe God is able? Do you believe He loves you and cares about you? Do you trust Him to work in and through the circumstances you are facing to do what's best for you? Come to Him in prayer and ask Him to reveal His trustworthiness to you in His Word.

PRAYER

God, my flesh and heart may fail, but You are my strength, my portion forever.

KEEPING GOD IN FOCUS

*Through Jesus, therefore, let us continually
offer to God a sacrifice of praise—the fruit
of lips that openly profess his name.*
HEBREWS 13:15

PRAYER

Lord, when I
keep You in
view, I want
to continually
offer a
sacrifice of
praise to
You for Your
holy and
faithful love.

WHAT DO YOU find yourself fixing your eyes on?
What captures and holds your attention, so much so
that you can't look away?

A more peaceful life begins with keeping your
gaze locked on the Lord. It isn't a onetime thing—it's
a constant activity of recentering your thoughts and
turning your focus to get God in view. Three things
happen as we direct our eyes toward Him.

First, your heart is glad. Your emotions shift,
and fear is replaced by confidence that the Almighty
is with you. Second, you rejoice. Worship displaces
worry as a sacrifice of praise fills your mouth. Third,
your body rests securely. You lie down in the bed
of steadfast hope, and you rest believing God is in
control.

When you keep God in focus, you are able to continually worship Him. This overflow of worship leads
to peace, security, and joy. Make every effort today to
ensure your eyes are always fixed on the King.

SIMPLE PRAYERS OF FAITH

Then he said, "Jesus, remember me when you come into your kingdom."
LUKE 23:42

YOUR PRAYERS DON'T always need to be long or drawn out. On the cross, the thief stretched out beside Jesus simply prayed, "Remember me." That prayer required only a breath, but it was enough to change this criminal's eternity—in paradise with Jesus forevermore.

This man didn't pour out lofty speeches or win intense theological debates. We have no record of any good works he did while on earth. He didn't earn his way into heaven through an upstanding or remarkable life. All we know is that he prayed, and Jesus saved him.

Like that thief stretched out beside Jesus, we must helplessly come to God with a simple prayer of faith. We acknowledge we are powerless. We look at Jesus on the cross and say, "You're God. You're innocent of any crimes. You could get down off that cross if You wanted, but You're there by choice for a purpose. Will You please remember me?" He will remember you. In fact, He could never forget you. And if you put your faith in Jesus, you, too, will be with Him in paradise.

PRAYER

God, would You remember me? Would You remind me that it's not my own goodness that saves me, but it's Your generous love?

A GENEROUS KINGDOM

*Each of you should give what you have decided
in your heart to give, not reluctantly or under
compulsion, for God loves a cheerful giver.*
2 CORINTHIANS 9:7

AS WE COME to life in Jesus, we are invited to become radically generous people. We aren't called to simply give away our leftovers—the few unallocated dollars in the budget or the clothes we've outgrown. Instead, we are called to give our firstfruits. To bring forth our best and give it sacrificially, to the extent that it will actually seem foolish to the world. Why? Because Jesus modeled that kind of generosity. He set the example, and who are we not to follow in the footsteps of our Savior?

Gratitude is the wellspring of generosity. When you receive the grace of Jesus and acknowledge you did nothing to earn His love, the only response you can have is thankfulness that turns into worship.

Pray that God would release the grip you have on your possessions. Ask Him to remind you of His grace, given so freely. The more time you spend with Him in His Word and in prayer, the more grateful you will become.

PRAYER

God, help me to see Your salvation as the foundation of my gratitude. Thank You for Your generous joy, peace, and hope that overflow in my heart.

WE ARE GOD'S WORKMANSHIP

I praise you because I am fearfully and wonderfully made; your works are wonderful, I know that full well.

PSALM 139:14

WE CLOTHE OURSELVES in acceptance when we understand that we are the work of God, reverently and wonderfully made. God doesn't make mistakes. He doesn't produce *rejects*—that word comes from assembly-line lingo. As a "reject" makes its way down the line, a worker will say, "That one's perfect. That one's perfect. Oh, this one's wrong. Throw it out and start again."

The pain of feeling like you don't belong—like you're not acceptable or good enough to those around you—is a lie from the Enemy. You are God's handiwork, and He has a purpose for creating you. David affirmed this, as later in Psalm 139 he declared, "Your eyes saw my unformed body; all the days ordained for me were written in your book before one of them came to be" (v. 16).

When you believe that God created you with beauty and purpose, it changes the way you understand your role on this planet. God made you uniquely and intentionally, and He's inviting you to live out your God-given assignment today.

PRAYER

Lord, my Creator, how wonderful it is that You authored every day I'd live before there was one. I choose to embrace Your plans for me today.

AS YOU WAIT, GOD IS AT WORK

And my God will meet all your needs according to the riches of his glory in Christ Jesus.
PHILIPPIANS 4:19

PRAYER

God, You have met every need and overflowed my joy through Your glorious riches. I surrender my self-sufficiency again today.

IF FEAR IS battling to take over your heart, if anxiety is rising within you—find a quiet space, slow down, and think about the cross. Think about what Jesus has done to ensure that you can be alive with Him. Redirecting your mind away from the spiral of fear takes time, but as you wait, God is at work both in you and through you.

Use these truths to steer you back toward His love.

He is and always will be in full control. Surrender your need to be in charge over to Him.

He is and always will be for you. Find your affirmation in Him and not in the people around you.

He is and always will be present with you. Release your past and submit your tomorrows to Him.

From a place of surrender, you can get out from under the anxiety that's weighing you down and look up to your Good Shepherd. He is there with open arms, ready to lead you to be full of peace.

CONFORMED TO THE LIKENESS OF JESUS

*For those God foreknew he also predestined to be
conformed to the image of his Son, that he might be
the firstborn among many brothers and sisters.*

ROMANS 8:29

ONE OF THE greatest markers of spiritual maturity
is a sense of awakening to who you are and whose
you are.

The more spiritually mature you become, the
more you need to constantly remind yourself of the
truth of your new identity. You are not merely a follower of beliefs about God; you have a new Spirit
thanks to your new relationship with God. He is your
perfect heavenly Father, and you are His beloved child.

Your understanding of your new identity changes
everything for you. By nature, you are not a lost spiritual pilgrim. You are not simply a churchgoer. You
are not trying to be a do-gooder. At your core, you
are born of God. With an understanding of this new
identity, you are given the opportunity and responsibility of being conformed to the image of Jesus to
make much of Him in this dark world.

PRAYER

God, make
me more like
Jesus today.
May I know
with assurance
that my identity
is not rooted
in any other
thing than in
the example
of Your Son.

LIVING OUT YOUR WORSHIP

"In the same way, let your light shine before others, that they may see your good deeds and glorify your Father in heaven."

MATTHEW 5:16

PRAYER

Lord, may
my actions
reflect a heart
that has been
captured by
Your glory
and holiness.

IF YOU'RE GOING to talk the talk of being a Jesus follower, you're going to have to walk the walk. The world is desperate for Jesus followers to live out what they believe. Who else is going to stand up for the marginalized? Who else is going to bring restoration to the broken and dignity to the oppressed? Who else is going to chase back the darkness?

If we've been transformed in Jesus' likeness, we must see people like Jesus saw people. We must engage with those who are hurting, lost, or cast out, not out of pity or guilt but out of love and genuine concern. Our worship must spur our actions to align with the light of Christ. As the world sees our good deeds, they will be moved to worship God in heaven.

Your worship can't be limited to the songs you sing on a Sunday. As believers, we need to live out our worship by serving those in our communities and families, our neighborhoods and workplaces. When you walk the walk, your talk begins to have value and significance.

YOU ARE CHOSEN AS
A CHILD OF GOD

*"You did not choose me, but I chose you
and appointed you so that you might go
and bear fruit—fruit that will last."*

JOHN 15:16

FROM THE VERY beginning of time, God chose you. Long before you knew Him, He knew you. Before you loved Him, He loved you. Before you ever felt the sting of rejection, before someone decided you weren't good enough for them, before the world began, God Almighty, creator of heaven and earth, had already chosen you. Since the very start, He has welcomed you with open arms into His family as a loved son or a daughter of almighty God. That truth cultivates in us a huge sense of acceptance.

Jesus chose us first before we ever did a thing to deserve or merit His choice. Let those words sink in. You no longer need to fill your identity with the things of this world. Your value is already established. You can live today in confidence that you are seen, loved, and valued by a perfect heavenly Father.

PRAYER

God, by Your Spirit in me, I cry out, "Abba, Father," and I receive once again the identity as a loved child of God.

MAKE NO PROVISION

*Put on the Lord Jesus Christ, and make no
provision for the flesh, to fulfill its lusts.*
ROMANS 13:14 NKJV

PRAYER

God, please
place the
right people
in my life
who can help
me pursue
holiness.

GOD IS ALWAYS faithful. He is always true. That doesn't mean you won't come up against the schemes of the Enemy; you most definitely will! God isn't in the business of helping you *avoid* every temptation. But He will always provide you another option when temptation arises.

Rejecting sin starts with not allowing temptations to entice you in the first place. The best way out is to stay out. This means you wisely build safeguards into the way you live so you don't stray near the things that lead you toward sin.

When you "make no provision for the flesh," it means you live with intentional wisdom. You live with discretion. You err on the side of caution. You elevate holiness in your order of priorities.

You will likely find it hard to do this alone. That's why God invites us to pursue Him within the context of community. Consider reaching out to a few close friends today, and start setting up guardrails that will help you resist anything that does not honor God.

THE PERSON AND THE POWER OF JESUS

Through these he has given us his very great and precious promises, so that through them you may participate in the divine nature, having escaped the corruption in the world caused by evil desires.

2 PETER 1:4

THERE ARE SO many voices leading people in the world today, but you really only need to follow one of them—the voice of Jesus. The process of maturing spiritually is often described by the word *discipleship*. As we become disciples of Jesus, we stay connected to Him. We go where He goes and do what He does.

In 2 Peter 1:4, we see that we have everything we need for a godly life. His divine power has given us everything. Everything! We may not have learned how to use everything to the fullest extent yet, but the working parts are already in place. Through His divine power, He's laid out very great and wondrous promises so that we may be like Jesus and that in Him we may have hope in His glory.

Because of this, you can grow in discipleship as you revel and abide in the person and power of Jesus within you.

PRAYER

Jesus, only by Your power and love can I escape the corruption of the world today. I hold on to Your great promises— they are my source of joy and hope!

JESUS FULFILLS EVERY NEED

You make known to me the path of life; you will fill me with joy in your presence, with eternal pleasures at your right hand.

PSALM 16:11

PRAYER

God, You are the most trustworthy and most dependable. Let my heart cry out again, "The Lord is my rock and my salvation!"

WHAT ARE YOU seeking today? Do you have a need for worth? For deeper companionship? Calm in the midst of a storm? Significance? Peace and satisfaction? Maybe you're seeking purpose, love, or acceptance?

All of those needs . . . Jesus fulfills them, and the Enemy does all he can to exploit them. When you feel down, it's usually because some need of yours isn't getting met. That's when the Enemy comes along and whispers, *If you want to feel better, I'll give you a thrill. I can help you meet your needs.*

Those whispers might be enticing, but remember that nothing can satisfy your heart like God. Nothing keeps you from sin better than seeking after Christ. When you begin to learn God's Word, it's a pathway to knowing Him and His character. When you walk with Him in continual prayer, you learn His ways. When you rest in God, you discover your true identity, worth, and purpose. It is by His Spirit alone that you will ultimately find true fulfillment for your every need. You can trust Him to fill your cup today.

HE HAS PROVIDED ALL THINGS

"I am the LORD your God, who brought you out of Egypt, out of the land of slavery."
DEUTERONOMY 5:6

WHEN WE PRAY for our circumstances to change and they don't, it can be easy to feel like God doesn't hear our prayers. Maybe you feel like He might have forgotten about you altogether.

In Scripture, God goes to great lengths to remain faithful to His people. He literally split open the oceans to bring His people out of slavery in Egypt. You would think they would never forget God's faithfulness. But they did. And we forget too.

We far too easily lose sight of the powerful work of Jesus on the cross to reconcile us back to Him, destroying once and for all the power of death and the grave. We forget that He promised to lead us through every circumstance and to fulfill His purpose for our life.

Keeping God in view means you remember His power and rest in His promises. You can renew your mind by remembering His faithfulness today. Fall back on His strength, and watch as His love and power overflow in your heart.

PRAYER

Jesus, help me not to forget Your great love for me. Sear it on my heart and mind.

GOING THROUGH THE VALLEY

Even though I walk through the darkest valley,
I will fear no evil, for you are with me.
PSALM 23:4

IT'S ONE THING to say that you're not alone. It's another to name and know who is walking with you through the valley. When David penned the words to Psalm 23, he was facing life-threatening danger, but instead of fear, we read a stunning account of calm confidence in his Shepherd.

Two lines in this verse are calling out to you with hope:

The first is, "for you are with me." No matter how deep the pit or how dark the night, you can take comfort in the truth that someone is with you. God Almighty is near, and His presence is a catalyst for driving out fear. You may not be able to sense or see Him, but no darkness can hide His presence from you.

The second reads, "Even though I walk through the valley." God is not leading you *to* the valley you're in. He promises to lead you *through* it. This current place of struggle you're in will not be the end, so be encouraged today that God is at work, even if you can't see it right now.

GLORY AND HONOR

What is man that You are mindful of him,
and the son of man that You visit him?

PSALM 8:4 NKJV

IMAGINE THE SHEPHERD David out in the fields at night, tending his flock by starlight. Though he's gazed on these stars a thousand times, this evening is different. He's hit with a powerful and life-changing thought: "What is man that You are mindful of him . . . that You visit him?"

This is the biggest question of all time, isn't it? Why would God be mindful of us? David was looking up into the immensity of God's creation, yet he still knew he had a relationship with the One who made it all—the sun, the moon, the stars, and the heavens. He was blown away by God's indirect answer.

All this, yet the God of the universe knows his name. And He knows your name too. He cares for you and loves you and invites you into His family. Amid the beauty of this world, God cherishes you above it all.

The psalm then talks about how God has crowned mankind with "glory and honor" (v. 5). When you feel low or lonely, think back to those words, take a look at nature's expanse, and breathe in God's affection for you.

PRAYER

Holy God, You love me immensely and intimately. I have no other response but gratitude for Your magnificent love toward me.

TERMS FOR FREEDOM

"You are free to eat from any tree in the garden; but you must not eat from the tree of the knowledge of good and evil."
GENESIS 2:16–17

PRAYER

God, draw my heart toward obedience. I humble myself and submit today to Your authority.

WHEN YOU ACCEPT the invitation to be in relationship with the perfect God of heaven, you must come on His terms. His terms aren't meant to be vindictive or to limit your freedom. In fact, because God loves you, He desires the fullness of life for you, and He knows that without His guidance and guardrails, you're likely to end up off the track of true joy.

Since the beginning, as we see in the garden, the Enemy has been trying to tempt us to believe the opposite—that God's terms are restrictive, unfair, or even harmful. If you buy into those lies, you quickly begin to manipulate God's terms, making your own rules to fit your wants and needs.

Are there areas in your life that you are twisting God's terms and not lining up your heart with Jesus? No one is perfect. But we do have to decide who sets the terms of how we should live our life. There is no half-our-way and half-God's-way Christianity. Commit today to living fully under His terms and flourish in the freedom found in that relationship.

RESTORED AND RENEWED MINDS

To be made new in the attitude of your minds;
and to put on the new self, created to be like
God in true righteousness and holiness.
EPHESIANS 4:23–24

TODAY, YOU HAVE access to the exact same scriptures that sustained Jesus during His earthly ministry. We know from the text that the Word of God fueled Jesus' love for His Father and guarded His mind from temptation.

If you hope to become more spiritually mature, you have to constantly soak your mind in the truths of Scripture. Like it did for Jesus, the Word protects you from the Enemy's attacks. You are sustained as you sow Scripture into your mind and deepen your affection for Him.

When you're planted in the Scriptures, you have truth that protects your mind from intrusive thoughts. You develop the clarity to filter what gets put before your eyes, and, as a result, what ends up in your mind. You possess a promise of perfect peace that comes when your mind is firmly fixed on God.

You are not a product of all of the pathways you've created. You can renew the attitude of your mind today and change the way you think.

PRAYER

God, Your peace is strong enough to guard my mind as I seek to put on my new self, full of righteousness and holiness.

DRAWING NEAR TO LISTEN

"My sheep listen to my voice; I know them, and they follow me."
JOHN 10:27

PRAYER

Jesus, You promise that if I draw near to You, You will draw near to me. Help me cling to this promise today and come close to You.

CALMING THE STORM of our minds is often easier said than done. The noise of fear, discomfort, comparison, and want can bombard our brains. When life gets stressful, it can feel like the noise in your mind is cranked up to a ten. "I just want to turn my brain off" is a reaction to the noisiness that a heavy storm often brings.

But how do we turn down the noise and recenter on the life of fullness and peace Jesus offers? By getting closer to Him and keying in on the voice of our Good Shepherd.

When you listen to Jesus' voice, the cacophony of anxiety starts to fade to the background, and you begin to follow Him more intimately. It's hard to listen to someone who is far off or distant. If you want to listen well, you'll need to draw near. And once you're close, you stay close.

When you listen to your Chief Shepherd, when you are led and guided by His voice, you start to live with eternity in mind and take on a sense of unshakable peace.

LIGHT THAT SHINES IN ANY DARKNESS

In him was life, and that life was the light of all mankind.

JOHN 1:4

IT DOESN'T MATTER how messy life has become—it's never too late for God to do a miracle. It's never too late for God to restore you to Him. Whatever guilt or shame you bear, God stands ready to bring victory over it. There are so many stories in the Gospels that demonstrate how Jesus is always in the right place at the right time to perform miracles.

Just like the people who Jesus helped in the Gospel accounts, we don't need to shine ourselves up before we come before Him. We don't need to have it all together or have a solution ready for every problem in our lives. We don't need to figure out how to become the world's most functional family before we come to Him. We don't need to get well before we meet Jesus.

Jesus is always a light in our darkness. Anyone in any condition can say, "Jesus, I need You. I need a Savior." Whether it's for the first time or the thousandth time, when you confess you need His help—that your life is a mess and that you need a miracle—you will experience His light, and the darkness clouding your soul can and will fade away.

PRAYER

Jesus, You shine in all darkness. I need You and Your light to help the darkness fade away today.

MORE OF GOD

"He must become greater; I must become less."
JOHN 3:30

EVERY ONE OF us has the opportunity to draw near to God. You don't need money, intellect, or a clean past. He doesn't need you to go to seminary or to offer up the largest offering, nor is He wooed by popularity or worldly influence. Instead, the Scriptures emphasize time and again that He has a heart for the lowly and the outcast—the poor, the orphan, and the widower.

So what stands in the way of you and the throne of God? Often, it's pride. To know God deeply, your pride must fall. And the only thing that has a chance of taking down your pride is His love. When you learn that nothing you do can make Him love you any more or any less—that His love is constant, everlasting, and unending—your heart is inspired to draw near to God in prayer, and you truly begin to know Him. When you experience Him in full, your pride won't stand a chance.

He has the power to transform you! Keep drawing near to His majesty, closer to His throne. Keep putting your pride to death by His Spirit and look up in wonder. Watch how He changes the fabric of your soul.

HE FULFILLED OUR RIGHTEOUS REQUIREMENT

Such confidence we have through Christ before God.

2 CORINTHIANS 3:4

LET'S FACE IT, you're not the first person to feel like obeying God requires a lot of work. In the Old Testament, God gave His people the Mosaic law. In part to show them how perfect and holy He is, but also to reveal to them how unreachable His standard of perfection was.

In effect, God laid an impossibly heavy burden on the Israelites and said, *See, you can't carry this on your own. You need a Savior.* That's why God sent His own Son. In doing so, God fulfilled the righteous requirement of the Law for us, who no longer are bound to live according to the flesh and the anxieties that so commonly drag us down.

Renewing your mind might sound like a lot of work. And it is. But remember, it's not yours to carry alone. Because of His perfect love for you, God has given you His Son, and He has also given you a helper, His Spirit.

As you renew your mind, remember that the same power that raised Jesus from the dead is in you. Will it take practice? Yes. But it can be done!

PRAYER

Jesus, You made it possible for me to have a new life, and by Your Spirit I can confidently put to death the deeds of my former ways and renew my mind.

117

THE GREATEST EXCHANGE

"You intended to harm me, but God intended it for good to accomplish what is now being done, the saving of many lives. So then, don't be afraid. I will provide for you and your children."
GENESIS 50:20–21

PRAYER

God, no man-made intentions will ever triumph over Your ordained rule and reign. I find comfort knowing You are always in control.

"YOU INTENDED TO harm me, but God intended it for good." Outside of Jesus' earthly ministry, I don't know whether more powerful words were ever spoken by a human. Joseph, the man who uttered these words, experienced extreme betrayal by his own family year after year. Joseph was a human, like you and me. Even still, in the face of rejection, he was deeply in touch with God's sovereignty and goodness.

How can you come to experience that level of God's power and grace? You have to understand that God is in charge. Joseph never lost sight of God's love and purpose, and he knew God was using him to bring glory to Himself and salvation for many people.

When you comprehend that God is in charge and all-powerful, you, too, can trust that all the evil you see in the world can and will be used for good. God will see you through every darkness, every sin, every pain the Enemy brings, and He will redeem it for His glory.

RIGHTEOUS, HOLY, AND NEW

Watch what God does, and then you do it, like children who learn proper behavior from their parents. Mostly what God does is love you.

EPHESIANS 5:1 MSG

YOU MIGHT HAVE had a hard journey growing up. Maybe your family circumstances were a challenge, and you don't want to grow up to look like your parents. But when it comes to being a child of God, growing up like your perfect Father is the most natural thing you can do. Because of Jesus, you have the access to become more godly, in true righteousness and holiness.

Sadly, there is a strain of teaching in Christianity that goes like this: We're all sinners, and sinners are going to sin. It's who we are and what we do.

Now, while it is true that we all still have the capacity to sin (no one needs to be convinced of that!), we also have the capacity to follow in the footsteps of our Father. We are God's children, and in Christ we are made righteous, holy, and new.

As such, your Father is leading you to change the way you think. As you put off the old and put on the new, you imitate God and His goodness to the world around you.

PRAYER

God, because of Your salvation, I can grow up in faith by imitating You. Empower me today to live as Your dearly loved child.

PROTECTED BY GOD'S ARMOR

Therefore put on the full armor of God, so that when the day of evil comes, you may be able to stand your ground, and after you have done everything, to stand.
EPHESIANS 6:13

PRAYER

God, thank You for Your heavenly armor that I can put on and use to stand firm, protected against the attacks of the Enemy.

WHETHER PLAYING FOOTBALL, renovating a home, or anything in between, we all know the importance of protective gear to one's health and well-being. Even if you're not tossing a ball or tearing down walls, the same remains true for our spiritual walk. If we're to ward off the temptations of the Enemy and live a holy and righteous life, we need the right armor.

Paul told us we have access to the "armor of God," and he didn't mean some rusty, junky metal outfit that can't stop a dull arrow. No, this armor is strong. Durable. Impenetrable.

This armor is held together by the unfailing truth of God's promises. It's the righteousness of Christ over our hearts and the spirit of evangelism over our hands and feet. It's the joy of salvation covering our minds, the shield of faith, and the sword of Scripture. This is the armor of God, and it's yours to put on every day and every hour.

HE CALLS YOU BY YOUR NAME

You created my inmost being; you knit
me together in my mother's womb.
PSALM 139:13

WE ALL WANT to know that we belong to someone. That we aren't an accident or wandering around this planet with no meaning and no purpose.

You weren't born by a random act of the cosmos. God made you with intention and God made you wonderfully. He has redeemed you and knows your name.

You are not the maker; you are made. The good news today: God is not created in your image or how you might think He should be. You are created in His. He decided that He wanted you in His universe. He imagined and fashioned you. You are not accidental. Nor incidental. You are divinely crafted.

When you come to believe this, you have the most powerful truth to combat the lie that God doesn't love you or that you aren't worthy of His affection. He made you, and He pursues that which He creates. The same goodness in Him is alive in you today. His love for you is deep, echoing throughout all time. Unending, immutable, and purposeful love.

PRAYER

Jesus, Your love allows me to live today with joy and purpose. Help me to look on myself with the same kindness and care that You do.

THE HIGHEST GLORY

Humble yourselves before the Lord,
and he will lift you up.
JAMES 4:10

PRAYER

God, who
am I to make
a name for
myself when
all that I have
been given
is from You?
Help me to
elevate Your
name alone.

WHILE SCIENTISTS AREN'T entirely sure just how big the universe is, one thing is clear—we are very small within it.

Our entire solar system is a tiny speck in the midst of the vast Milky Way, which itself is only one of billions of other galaxies in the known universe. When you consider the cosmic grandeur and the glory of God on this scale, it's mind-blowing that the God who created all of this is interested and passionate about being in a relationship with us.

Still, it's easy to forget His invitation to an intimate relationship and instead pour all our focus into making our lives the center of the story. In every generation, we have worked to elevate our names and build things as if we could actually garner fame that lasts. All the while, God is extending His hands— the very hands that hung the stars—and is saying, *I will gladly lift you up, but only if you humble your-self before Me.* He doesn't make it complicated, but it does require surrender. Ask Him today for the grace to humble you as you join creation in worship as someone God created and loves.

GOD'S LOVE FLOWING THROUGH YOU

For as high as the heavens are above the earth,
so great is his love for those who fear him.
PSALM 103:11

THINK ABOUT THE image of standing under a waterfall of God's love.

Can you imagine that? Niagara Falls, Victoria Falls? That's what I'm talking about! A gentle torrent of the goodness, blessing, favor, and love of God. Unending, pouring down every morning, perfect, unconditional. As it washes over you, it makes you brand new. His love saturates your entire being, and it's so ingrained in you—so potent—that it overflows. Like a pipeline of goodness and faithfulness, you simply let the water flow from the source to the people all around you.

This is what it's like to walk with a mindset that understands the reality of God's love. There's joy, compassion, humility, and patience flowing into your life through His Spirit, and instead of keeping it to yourself, you let the Spirit work through you, bringing His blessing to those around you. When you are under the waterfall of God's blessing, you begin to realize that the spiritual life is not ultimately about you—it is Christ in you, the hope of glory.

PRAYER

God, as I stand in awe of You, pour over me Your abundant blessing so that I may bless those around me.

123

A HEAVENLY SONG

"Glory to God in the highest heaven, and on earth peace to those on whom his favor rests."
LUKE 2:14

SINCE THE BEGINNING of time, a chorus of angels has surrounded the throne of God, declaring His glory and proclaiming His holiness. It is only fitting that when heaven came down to earth in the form of a baby, the angels heralded the way, announcing to mankind that God's great and glorious redemption plan was now on the scene.

They heralded a peace that would not come cheaply. Jesus died outside the city wall, bore our reproach, took our sin and shame all so that eternal peace would be possible for us. The perfect Son of God paid the ultimate price so that you—imperfect and unable to make your way to Him—could dwell in the presence of God's glory forever.

Does this reality of God's glory reverberate in your soul? Are you reflecting back to God the angels' chorus with gratitude? When you believe the angels' heavenly refrain, you can walk in assurance that sin cannot bind you. Death cannot hold you. You are alive forevermore—so join in this great song today.

YOUR ROLE IN GOD'S STORY

"For whoever wants to save their life will lose it,
but whoever loses their life for me will find it."
MATTHEW 16:25

HAVE YOU EVER wondered how you fit into God's plan? Before getting into the specifics, it's important to remember that you have been invited into the grand story of God's great glory and grace. It's all about Him. Every aspect and every detail. Yet within this story, you have a seat at His table.

It's no accident that before you were formed in your mother's womb, God knew you. He has always looked out for you, so of course He has a role for you in His larger story.

Your role is to lose your life. Not literally, necessarily, but spiritually. To lay down your "ownership." Your old ways. Your former self.

This doesn't mean you are insignificant. It actually means quite the opposite! You matter to God. But ultimate meaning won't come from putting the spotlight on you. Your life will have the greatest significance when you choose to make it about the One who welcomes you into His never-ending story.

PRAYER

Jesus, if life is on the table, I choose life, even if it means I must die to myself today. Help me surrender and find joy in Your greater story.

MAY

MOVING IN GOD'S STRENGTH

"The LORD will fight for you; you need only to be still."
EXODUS 14:14

WHAT DO YOU think God is doing right here, right now, in your life? Maybe you've been wavering. Or you've been waiting for a long time for all the pieces to line up before you take that next step. What if the answer isn't lining up all the right pieces, but simply pausing and listening to God?

As you look at the decisions before you, slow down and listen. You'll hear Him saying, *I am the God who can bring clarity today. In faith, you can step out of your comfort zone and go where I lead.* There's no guarantee that all the pieces will line up at first. The whole pathway likely won't be revealed. Yet God says, "Not by might nor by power, but by my Spirit" this victory is going to come (Zechariah 4:6).

When you are waiting on God, what matters most is that you understand that you move forward in God's strength. As soon as you grasp that, you're ready to march out in battle and overcome your struggles. From a position of dependency, you can be sure that you will see the salvation of the God who fights for His beloved.

THE RIGHT QUESTION

This is how you can recognize the Spirit of God: Every spirit that acknowledges that Jesus Christ has come in the flesh is from God, but every spirit that does not acknowledge Jesus is not from God.

1 JOHN 4:2–3

HOW CAN YOU practically become free from the weight of worry? You can start by asking yourself, *Where did that troubling thought come from?* Over time, this simple question will help you reject the soundtrack of worry.

When you ask yourself this question, you can count on an answer from one of two places—from God or from somewhere else. But how do you know what comes from God?

First John 4:2 invites you to consider this: Is your way of thinking aligning with the truth of Jesus as the perfect Son of God, who came to earth to die in your place and redeem you?

If the answer is yes, keep that thought. If the answer is no, then you know it's time to replace it. Take the thoughts that are currently weighing you down and do this exercise. Watch how it feels when you off-load anxious burdens and onboard good, gracious, and peaceful truths about God. You'll feel light, at peace, and free.

PRAYER

God, I need a pure mind. Grant me discernment to differentiate my thoughts into that which honors You and that which needs to go.

A HOPEFUL AND HOLY PLAN

But the plans of the LORD stand firm forever, the purposes of his heart through all generations.
PSALM 33:11

PRAYER

God, Your plans are good and unshakable. Thank You for leading me throughout all my days.

GOD HAS A track record of faithfulness. You see, the Bible isn't just a rulebook; it's a written account of God's character, a ledger of His unfailing, pursuing love throughout the span of time, and the story of His plan to redeem the world.

When you read the Old Testament, you'll notice how God's people stray from Him over and over again. (Turns out, humans have a history of thinking we can make it on our own!) Even in their sin, God forgave His people. And every time, they returned to Him with shouts of praise—only to forget and turn their backs on Him once again. God saves, people stray, and so God's mercy cycle goes on and on throughout all time.

If you or a loved one are in a season of distraction or straying from what God says, take heart. He is still working out His plan, and He has an amazing habit of always showing up for His people and offering redemption in the midst of their failures. God is not absent in your story; He is at the helm of it. He delights to offer mercy, and He longs for you to run back to His arms again today.

TRUSTING IN GOD'S HANDS

"My Father, who has given them to me, is greater than all; no one can snatch them out of my Father's hand."

JOHN 10:29

IN THE BOOK of Genesis, we learn that Joseph spent thirteen years in a prison cell abandoned by his brothers before he was brought before Pharaoh. But God didn't allow those years to be wasted. Instead, they were setting up a mighty act of saving power for Joseph, his entire family, and many others.

Fast-forward from Genesis to Luke 23. Nothing ever looked more wrong than the Son of the living God hanging on a cross, but Jesus knew about the bigger plan, and He trusted God with that plan. That's why Jesus said, "Father, into your hands I commit my spirit" (v. 46).

You may find yourself convinced God can't use your circumstances, but thankfully—as we see from Joseph and Jesus—you don't have to figure it all out on your own. All He's asking you to do is to place your life in God's hands, because no one can take you out of His hands once you are surrendered to His story—and He will use your circumstances and hardships for His glory.

PRAYER

Jesus, I trust that no hardship can remove me from the Father's hand. Because of Your example, I live convinced that You can redeem every situation.

JESUS IS GOD

"Very truly I tell you," Jesus answered, "before Abraham was born, I am!"
JOHN 8:58

PRAYER

Jesus, my heart and mind shout with conviction that You are God and You are good. I submit to Your lordship today.

IN EXODUS 3:14, God reveals Himself to Moses at the burning bush, declaring, "I AM WHO I AM." Thousands of years later, when Jesus was teaching in Jerusalem, He used the exact same language, professing to be the I AM. This claim stopped everyone in their tracks. The Jewish people were familiar with the story of Moses and other Old Testament teachings, and they understood the magnitude of what Jesus was asserting—that He was God incarnate, the One they had been waiting for. Jesus was declaring Himself as the Messiah who would save the world.

Jesus claiming to be God is without a doubt the boldest statement ever made or recorded. No one in their right mind would say this, unless it was true. See, Jesus isn't just a good teacher or a helpful friend. He did not come to give you tips for living a good life. He is the King who came to save your soul, the one and only Creator and Sustainer of the universe. You are invited to join Him, but only if you submit to His authority in all areas of your life.

PUT ON LOVE

And over all these virtues put on love, which
binds them all together in perfect unity.
COLOSSIANS 3:14

WHAT THOUGHTS, EMOTIONS, struggles, or victories are you wrapping around your heart today? In the same way that you'll choose an outfit to wear today, you will also choose to put on certain feelings or thoughts.

In Colossians 3:14, Paul encouraged us to clothe ourselves in God's love. It's a garment that works for every circumstance. The garment of love is for all purposes, and the garment of love is ready to be worn by you.

The key to growing in your faith isn't that you grind out the effort by yourself and try really hard to love the person who is not so easy to love. Rather, the key is to remember your new identity as a dearly loved child of God and then proceed from there. God loved you first, even when you didn't deserve it. And because you are loved by God, you can let God's love flow through you and out from you to anyone who's in your life. Make a choice today: You aren't going to hoard the love of God. You're going to release it.

PRAYER

God, I choose right now to put on love. With this garment, help me empathize with and embrace those who need Your loving touch today.

MAY 7

PUTTING PEACE
INTO PRACTICE

*And the peace of God, which transcends
all understanding, will guard your hearts
and your minds in Christ Jesus.*
PHILIPPIANS 4:7

PRAYER

Lord, You have
shown me that
true peace is
only found in
You. Please
help me see
more of You in
the Scriptures
today, that I
may live more
like You.

IF YOUR GOAL is to be transformed and fully take up your identity as a new creation, a loved child of the King of the universe, you'll need to start by renewing your mind (Romans 12:2).

As you renew your mind, you will begin breaking away the old stones and strongholds that made up your sinful foundation before you were in Christ. You submit your fears and surrender your misaligned desires to Christ. You begin to take what you've seen modeled in Jesus and you put it into practice.

Paul told the Philippians that to not be anxious about anything, they needed a new story. A new narrative. New thoughts. That's what you need today. You need to replace the nightmare of sin with things that are noble. You're invited to replace the old ways with things that are right and true. As you grow in your wonder of the One who saved you, the peace of God will be with you.

GOODBYE GUILT

For God did not send his Son into the world to condemn the world, but to save the world through him.

JOHN 3:17

THE STORIES WE tell ourselves have the power to build us up or tear us down. Unfortunately, one story we repeat far too often is that of our guilt. Our failure. The Enemy loves nothing more than to hurl accusations and whispers of condemnation into our heads and our hearts. And once that story of guilt starts flowing, it can be difficult to turn it off. Like a movie on an endless loop, we replay our shame until we start to believe it's our reality.

But Jesus has a better story, and it is this: In Christ, your guilt is gone. Radical grace overwrites everything—your pride, your selfishness, your sin. Whatever you've done, grace can overcome it. If guilt has a stronghold on your life, you have the power in Christ to overcome it for good.

You can live forgiven and free because Jesus came from heaven to earth and did what you could not so that He could give you the grace you did not deserve. Embrace His majesty and praise the God who has set you free.

PRAYER

God, through Your blood I declare that guilt no longer has a hold on me!

135

A DELIBERATE PLANTING OF GOOD SEEDS

Do not conform to the pattern of this world, but be transformed by the renewing of your mind.
ROMANS 12:2

PRAYER

Lord, You know the state of my mind better than I do. Spirit, illuminate the weeds I should uproot today, and spread Your seeds of goodness.

IMAGINE THAT YOUR mind is a garden. You as the gardener are responsible for what grows there. You have the power to water and cultivate the good seeds and pull out any weeds that come from seeds you don't want.

How do you cultivate, weed, and water the garden of your mind? Whatever you give shelter, light, and sustenance to will grow. You're going to reap what you sow. The way you renew and cultivate your mind is by wrapping your thoughts around Scripture. You can take control of what you think about. Deliberately plant thoughts of God in your mind.

You can start by taking a small step today. The process of realigning your thinking with God's will take time. Take one thought: something that is weighing you down, something that is stressing you out, or something leading you to fear. Write that thought down and submit it to the Lord in your prayers to Him today.

DROWNING OUT THE DISTRACTIONS

Whoever dwells in the shelter of the Most High
will rest in the shadow of the Almighty.
PSALM 91:1

DO YOU FEEL constantly bombarded by waves of alarms, texts, questions, to-dos, or interruptions? If so, how can you mute the distractions that seem to continuously come up? Start by holding on to Jesus and abiding in Him.

Scripture is full of powerful promises for those who abide in Jesus. We are able to dwell in the shelter of the Most High and rest in the shadow of the Almighty. Through Jesus, we have been given everything we need for a life of godliness, and when we remain in Him, John 15 tells us that we will bear much fruit.

Today, listen to His voice and follow where He guides. Cling to Him and watch in wonder as He leads you toward life to the full. Rejoice as His eternal life becomes yours, and depend on Him not just to protect you but to provide for you. Then, no matter your circumstances, you will be able to truly say, "The LORD is my Shepherd; I shall not want" (Psalm 23:1 NKJV).

PRAYER

Lord, I prioritize resting in the shadow of the Almighty today. I stay, remain, linger, and wait for You to lead me in Your grace and into Your glory.

THE POWER OF THE CROSS

For the message of the cross is foolishness to those who are perishing, but to us who are being saved it is the power of God.
1 CORINTHIANS 1:18

WE ALL HAVE hurts and pains we are carrying around—some big, some small. Regardless of the size, it can be difficult to surrender your pain, and even harder still to feel like you can truly ever heal from it.

But when you begin to grasp the power of the cross, radical grace invades your story. You realize that through faith in Jesus you are made new—you get a fresh start. There's no one-size-fits-all bandage that can make sense of your hurt and pain. But there is a history-shaping cross standing in the middle of your story.

Jesus' cross is real. And immovable. And gritty. And glorious. And it's the only place you can truly find healing in the midst of deep, heart-shattering pain.

So run to the cross. Lean into Christ as the One who knows everything you are feeling. He has walked the road of lows and suffering before. He understands your pain. You can depend on His strength and power. Let Him comfort you with His strong arms today.

PRAYER

Jesus, You know what I'm walking through, and You know my story. I put it all, once more, before Your cross and surrender to You.

SEEING GOD CLEARLY

"Blessed are the pure in heart, for they will see God."
MATTHEW 5:8

IF YOU'VE EVER worn glasses, you know how much your lenses determine your ability to see. If you have the wrong prescription, things can get pretty blurry. Likewise, the perspective you use to look at your life matters. You can take your hardships and hold them up in front of your line of sight, effectively blocking your view of God. Or you can look at adversity through the lens of heaven, letting God's eternal perspective inform your thinking.

When you take on the lens of heaven, you'll see God's faithfulness where others may not. You'll see His purpose where others see meaninglessness. You'll gain a clear-sighted hope for the future, knowing He is your God and He will not forsake you.

Changing your lens changes the view of your life. As your understanding of His glory comes into focus, you will follow His commands with newfound confidence. You will be unashamed in obeying His Word, no matter what you endure, because you are seeing your circumstances with the eyes of eternity. Ask the Lord to purify your heart so that you can see Him with new clarity.

PRAYER

God, I want to see You clearly. Purify my heart, remove sin far from me, that I may experience seeing that leads to singing your praise.

REFLECTING GOD'S LOVE TO OTHERS

And walk in the way of love, just as Christ loved us.
EPHESIANS 5:2

PRAYER

Jesus, would
Your love
for me flow
through my
soul and into
the people
all around
me who You
desire to touch
today with
Your generous
grace?

THERE ARE DOZENS of motivations for us to love others. We see needs. We want to look good. We want to give back. But nothing ought to inspire us more to love people than knowing that we ourselves are loved by God.

When you know you are fully loved by Jesus, you don't just want to offer any old love to others; you want to offer God's love. We are to "walk in the way of love, just as Christ loved us."

As children of God, we get the joy of imitating God by doing what Jesus did. We don't start imitating God by deciding one day we're going to become more spiritual. We don't start imitating God by reading a book of character traits and trying to hammer our habits into new shapes. We start imitating God by knowing we're born spiritually into a new relationship with God, where we know we're the beloved children of God. From there, we look to Jesus. We live a life of love that reflects how Jesus loves us. And, having received His love, we seek to reflect that love to others.

GOD NEVER LEAVES

But You, O LORD, do not be far from Me;
O My Strength, hasten to help Me!
PSALM 22:19 NKJV

IF YOU'VE EVER experienced prolonged or significant hardship, you may be tempted to believe God has forgotten you. Maybe you tell yourself that if God was *really* with you, then your life would be better by now.

A disservice is done by any version of Christianity that promises there's always going to be a better road ahead, or insists that your circumstances will change, or claims everything is going to work out right and all your wildest dreams will come true *every* time. That's not how it works, because we live on a broken planet. We're in a fight for our lives in a dying world. And we follow a Savior who was crucified in the middle of it all.

Sometimes our circumstances don't add up to the dream we envisioned, but that never means God isn't with us. God never leaves us nor forsakes us, and that truth alone—that's a game changer. Let your petition turn to praise in prayer, thanking Him for the support and shepherding He is doing for you.

PRAYER

God, I remind my heart today that I am not the lord of my life—You are. Help me refute the lies of the Enemy and say, "I am not but He is!"

THE EASY YOKE

Come to me, all you who are weary and burdened,
and I will give you rest. Take my yoke upon you
and learn from me, for I am gentle and humble
in heart, and you will find rest for your souls.
For my yoke is easy and my burden is light.
MATTHEW 11:28–30

PRAYER

Jesus, I come to You. I want to exchange what is burdening me for Your light and easy yoke today.

WORRY CAN WREAK havoc on our hearts and minds. It can trap us in a cell with bars of fear and anxiety, filling our heads with thoughts of *What if? What if I don't get the job? What if my kids get sick?* We wonder, *What if . . .* , and before we know it, we are constantly burdened by worry, living out of weariness instead of the peace God has provided for us. God did not give us a spirit of fear or anxiety. He gave us a Spirit of adoption—His Spirit (Romans 8:15). Jesus can lead you into the fullness of peace.

It's difficult to cast off your cares unless you realize that through Christ, you have the power to do all things. Through Christ, you are a resurrected, new creation. You are free and perfectly loved, and as such, you can claim victory over darkness, eliminating worry by accepting the easy and light yoke of your good and gracious Savior.

FULLY EMPOWERED

To this end I strenuously contend with all the energy Christ so powerfully works in me.
COLOSSIANS 1:29

EVEN IF YOU can recite the commands of Jesus word for word, when the time comes to put them into practice, it can suddenly feel like following Jesus requires a supernatural kind of strength.

And that's because it does! Mere human power cannot yield a supernatural result.

If you pressure yourself to perform a perfect version of Christianity, you may try to tackle your problems apart from the power of Jesus. You might have some initial success. As you double your efforts, you could find a burst of enthusiasm. But it won't last.

Scripture teaches that you are not sufficient to live a holy life on your own. You can't win your own battles, slay your giants, or take up your cross daily without the shed blood and death-defeating power of Jesus.

He is the One who fights the battles for you, who stares down the face of impossible odds. He gives you His supernatural strength to walk with Him, to follow His leadership and align yourself with the direction He's going. He empowers you to do all that He commands you to do.

PRAYER

Father, I surrender trying to live my life through my own efforts. You and You alone are sufficient and worthy.

143

BE IMITATORS OF GOD

Therefore be imitators of God as dear children.
EPHESIANS 5:1

AT ANY MOMENT you can call on your heavenly Father and He will hear you. From anywhere on earth, you can approach the throne of thrones. With one breath you can be in conversation with God.

The access we have to God as His children is incredible. Yet, simply having access isn't the main goal. Instead, we should aim to grow into the likeness of our heavenly Father—to grow up and reflect Him.

Scripture invites us to be imitators of God. This means we are to follow God's example and do what God does. We're to think what God thinks. We're to care how God cares. We're to imitate our perfect heavenly Father the same way children imitate their earthly fathers. We have a responsibility and an opportunity to grow up and act like God.

At first glance, you might think this is impossible. How can we imitate the divine? But imitating God is not out of reach for anyone who follows Jesus. He has equipped you with everything you need, and if He calls you to it, He will help you fulfill it.

PRAYER

God, would You help me to think, act, and love like You do today? I want to look like You, so bring forth Your likeness through my living.

THE WEIGHT OF GLORY

And they were calling to one another:
"Holy, holy, holy is the LORD Almighty;
the whole earth is full of his glory."
ISAIAH 6:3

AT TIMES IT may seem like it's in your best interest to focus on your name or reputation or success. It's tangible. That's what seems to matter to the world. So why are you called to leverage your whole life for God's glory instead?

It falls short to think of glory as fame, or as the glory of a city, or as making it on the cover of a magazine. That's tinfoil praise. God's glory is far different. God's glory isn't fleeting. His glory isn't measured in a headline. God has incalculable substance and incalculable value. He is full of magnitude, and He is priceless. That is God's glory.

His glory is His holiness on display, and the more we see of His glory, the more we come to understand who God is and what He has done for us.

When you see God's glory and understand His worthiness, you joyfully lay down any interest you have in making much of yourself. Pride vanishes. Prayer deepens. Praise never ceases. Let this holy and glorious God become the center of your world.

PRAYER

God, how majestic and otherworldly is Your glory! I exalt Your holiness and desire to see more clearly Your infinite worthiness.

145

HIS WAYS ARE HIGHER

"For my thoughts are not your thoughts, neither are your ways my ways," declares the LORD.
ISAIAH 55:8

IF YOU'VE EVER looked out the window of an airplane, you know that your perspective shifts the higher you ascend. You don't see things in the same way as when you are on the ground.

This is a helpful way of understanding Isaiah 55:9, which says God's ways truly are higher than our ways, and His thoughts are higher than our thoughts. Instead of this being something to fear, it should drive us to praise God! God isn't small like we are; He's higher. He sees bigger, He knows more, and He's doing more—all the time.

Nothing gets in the way of God's great plan. Nothing blindsides Him. He doesn't fret for one second over the chaos we feel unfolding. He's seen dictators come and go, empires rise and fall, decades and centuries and millennia fly by. He's sovereign over it all. He's working in and through all of it.

When we aim to live surrendered to God's great plan and power, our lives become filled with purpose. We can find contentment and peace while loving those around us and bringing glory to God.

PRAYER

God, thank You for allowing me to play a part in Your grand story today. I don't have to know it all to know that You are my ultimate joy.

THE JOY OF YOUR SALVATION

I will give thanks to you, LORD, with all my heart; I will tell of all your wonderful deeds.

PSALM 9:1

SO MANY BELIEVERS desire to live a life characterized by joy. We want to be content and grateful people. And there's nothing wrong with that. But sometimes we can forget our greatest calling—to go and make disciples. When was the last time you told your story of how Jesus saved you? When we recall God's grace to us and share our journey to faith, something in our hearts comes alive. It's your story of redemption and restoration that reminds you that gospel blood is still flowing through your veins. It's as real today as it was the day you put your faith in Him.

Every time you share your testimony, you declare hope and faith that God will continue His salvation work in the lives of those around you. The same God who saved you stands poised and ready; there is not a single person outside of His reach. If you want to experience the fullness of praise and joy, commit to going public with your story and watch as you plant seeds of faith in the lives of others. There is no greater calling, so rejoice in your faith and tell someone else about what God has done!

PRAYER

Lord, may the story of Your saving grace be forever on my lips.

TAKE EVERY THOUGHT CAPTIVE

The weapons we fight with are not the weapons of the world. On the contrary, they have divine power to demolish strongholds.
2 CORINTHIANS 10:4

YOU HAVE THE power through Christ to identify and bind the power of every lie that comes into your mind. You can take every thought captive! When you commit to this and put it into practice, you begin tearing down every lie—brick by brick and thought by thought.

Demolition can be fun, but don't expect it to be a walk in the park. Whenever you set out to make a change, to start tearing down bricks and demolishing strongholds, the Enemy is likely to rise up and attack with even more vengeance.

But Scripture doesn't leave us to battle this alone. It gives us great comfort and confidence that not only do we have mighty and eternal weapons to overcome the darkness, but as the prophet Isaiah said, "No weapon forged against you will prevail" (Isaiah 54:17). You have all you need, offensively and defensively, to start this process of taking your thoughts captive and demolishing the strongholds of sin in your heart.

NEW SPIRITUAL DNA

And this is how we know that he lives in us:
We know it by the Spirit he gave us.
1 JOHN 3:24

WHAT ARE SOME characteristics you have that resemble your parents or family? Maybe you have your mom's eyes? Or your dad's laugh? Most of us begin to look and act like our parents as we grow up.

The same is true of our relationship with God. He is our perfect heavenly Father. That means we have His nature, a new spiritual DNA, coursing through us.

When we receive this new spiritual DNA, it means whole new possibilities open up. Our old nature was crucified with Jesus, done away with. True, our parental, biological DNA is still part of us, but thanks to Christ, we can resemble Him above all else.

That doesn't mean we become divine. We're not "little gods," and we're not equal to God in any way. Yet Scripture tells us a new nature has been given to us by God. We actually have the Spirit of Jesus living inside us. We have a new nature, new freedom, and a new source of power to live out our lives in accordance with His Word.

PRAYER

God, You have grafted me into Your family, and I will never be the same. May my soul rejoice in my new spiritual heritage!

149

MORE OF JESUS

Then he said to them all: "Whoever wants to be my disciple must deny themselves and take up their cross daily and follow me."
LUKE 9:23–24

God, I want to decrease so that You may increase in my life in every way. I deny myself and take up my cross for Your glory!

HOW CAN YOU ensure that your life will count, both now and for eternity? It may just begin with a simple prayer similar to this:

Jesus, I want my life, my words, my actions, my thoughts, and all I hold dear to reflect Your glory today. Help me to take up my cross and follow You. I'm less interested in people seeing me and desire far more that people will see You in me.

Scripture says that you are prized by the God of all creation, more valuable to Him and more deeply loved by Him than you can fully know. As such, you can have a relationship with and know the One who has breathed out the stars. Who is faithful and true. Whose power knows no end. Whose voice brings forth the morning. He is what makes your life count for now and eternity.

In the end, taking up your cross is simply less of you and more of Jesus. Less trying. Less striving. Less strutting. More trusting. More surrender. More of His power, doing in and through you what only He can do.

AT THE END OF YOUR ROPE

I pray that out of his glorious riches he may strengthen you with power through his Spirit in your inner being, so that Christ may dwell in your hearts through faith.

EPHESIANS 3:16–17

WHEN LIFE FEELS overwhelming and out of control, we're prone to bear down and turn inward. We try to muscle through whatever obstacle is in front of us. We grab on to whatever we think we can control, believing the lie that our own might and self-sufficiency will save us.

When you're at the end of your rope, you *are* supposed to turn inward. Not to your own strength but instead to the Spirit that God placed in you—the same Spirit who raised Jesus from the dead is who empowers, encourages, and helps you endure any and every hardship.

When you turn to the Spirit of God in you, you can let go of the things you are clutching so tightly in your hands. You can breathe in the miracle of grace that triumphs over all forms of self-striving. You can let God carry your burdens. He can handle everything that is weighing you down.

When you let God be your source of strength, He will sustain you and show you His gentle and tender grace.

PRAYER

Lord, I unclench my fists today and surrender what I've held to so tightly. Thank You for Your grace that lives in me.

A LEAGUE OF HIS OWN

*Who is like you—majestic in holiness,
awesome in glory, working wonders?*
EXODUS 15:11

PRAYER

God, open
my heart and
stretch my
mind to more
fully embrace
Your holiness,
that it would
inspire me to
worship You
more rightly.

IF YOU'VE WATCHED a professional athlete up close, or listened to a world-class symphony perform live, you've likely seen how they operate on a different level from the majority of the world. They are clearly in a different league. The same is true for God's holiness, except the gap between God and the next competitor is infinite and unmeasurable.

Holiness is the perfection of God, the purity of God, the sinlessness of God. But even those words don't fully convey what holiness is. The word *holy* comes from the Hebrew word *qadash* (pronounced kah-DOSH), meaning "sacred" and "set apart."

God isn't running a race with anybody else. He is holy, sacred, and set apart. And because He is holy, He is powerful enough to rescue you and to bring you into His family.

When you've been rescued and redeemed, worship shifts from the theoretical, "I hope God can help me," to the confident declaration, "God has changed my life!"

GOD CAN CARRY
THE WEIGHT

I will say of the LORD, "He is my refuge and my fortress, my God, in whom I trust."

PSALM 91:2

AT SOME POINT everyone faces headwinds in life—difficulties, challenges, situations that cause us pain or fear. What might be weighing you down may vary from relationships to health challenges to difficult work circumstances. But what never varies is the faithfulness of God. He always has your back. As a child of God in Christ, you can rest assured your heavenly Father is always looking out for you.

No evil plan, attack, or fear can stand up to your Shepherd, Jesus. Even while you are sleeping, He watches over you. He doesn't just leave you in a dark valley to fend for yourself; He leads you through it with a rod in one hand and a staff in the other.

As you come to know and see that God has your back, you'll start to trust Him more to lead, guide, and protect you. You'll start to turn to Him first, to call out His name, and to depend on His strength. And you'll give Him what's weighing you down because He's proven time and again that He can carry it.

PRAYER

Lord, Your arms are stronger than my arms, and Your hands can hold what mine cannot. I release my burdens to You and, in exchange, I take on Your light yoke.

THROW YOUR NET OVER THERE

He said, "Throw your net on the right side of the boat and you will find some."
JOHN 21:6

PRAYER

Jesus, I am prone to wander back to my old ways. Show me that my life is more abundant when I am walking with You.

AFTER JESUS WAS resurrected, He showed up early in the morning on the shore of Galilee. Led by Peter, the disciples had gone back to doing what was familiar, what made them feel comfortable—fishing. But at the end of a night of returning to their old ways, guess what? All they had was a long night of nothing. No fish.

When Jesus arrived, He already knew how poorly their night had gone. Similarly, whenever you return to your old ways, He knows where it leads you—empty. But He needs *you* to see your emptiness, because knowing your need is one of the catalysts for God's restoration.

The moment you confess to Jesus, "Actually, what I'm doing isn't helping at all," is the moment He will start transforming your life. He already knows exactly what you're looking for; you'll find all you need when you surrender your own ways and follow His. Be honest with Jesus about where you really are. He can handle it, and He wants to step in and support you.

CONTINUOUS PRAISE

And do not forget to do good and to share with others, for with such sacrifices God is pleased.

HEBREWS 13:16

WORSHIP IS A lifestyle that cannot be confined— your ongoing expression of gratitude to a holy Father. You worship when you live confidently, knowing God is in charge, trusting that He is working out His plan. You worship when you reject the rush of life and choose instead to pause and admire the beauty of creation. You worship when you direct your thoughts to the chorus of His grace, even quietly during a meeting or while preparing dinner. You worship with every silent praise that the great I AM wants a personal relationship with you.

Worship can become the undercurrent of your entire day. The more you remind yourself of God's majesty, the more you'll live according to His righteousness. When thoughts of His love fuel you, you'll find delight in the good works He's set before you. When you live with a continuous stream of God-praise, you realize that you're not the hero of your story. You become equipped to live humbly, sacrificially, and lovingly toward others.

Worship is the wellspring for good works, so don't relegate it as an activity to check off. Let it infuse your every breath.

PRAYER

Lord, would You help my soul rise in continuous chorus of worshiping You today?

AT THE CENTER OF GOD'S PLAN

"So do not fear, for I am with you; do not be dismayed, for I am your God. I will strengthen you and help you; I will uphold you with my righteous right hand."
ISAIAH 41:10

GOD HAS A specific plan for your life. This is what we read throughout the entirety of Scripture. If you need some reminding today, here are some verses you can stand on:

He knew you even before you were born, and all the days you'll live were chronicled in His book before one of them came to be (Psalm 139:16). God began a good work in you, and He'll finish what He started (Philippians 1:6). God has prepared an incredible future for you. It's so amazing that no mind has ever conceived it (1 Corinthians 2:7–9).

This is why He will never back down from any threat that comes against you, His child. He's already overcome the greatest dangers you'll ever face—sin and death. And He won't stop now. He is your perfect Father. He will protect you as you go because He has a purpose and plan for your life.

Pray that God would imbue His purpose into your heart, that He would help you trust Him as He guides you on.

EMBRACE THE DISCOMFORT

*Now if we died with Christ, we believe
that we will also live with him.*

ROMANS 6:8

IN FOLLOWING CHRIST, you are called to turn away from idols and sin patterns that are all too celebrated in this world. Living counterculturally is not easy. It's often at this crossroads of discomfort where you let go of your desires and embrace God's desires for you.

Our desires become merged with Christ's when we remember that death and life are both part of Christ's work. This is what Paul meant in Romans 6:8. We are intended to both die with Christ and to live with Him.

Can you name anything in the life of faith that's completely comfortable? Resisting sin? Nope, not comfortable. Being transformed into the image of Christ? No, not comfortable either. Joining with Christ on His mission? No. Wondrous, but not always comfortable. It's no wonder Paul wrote in 2 Corinthians 12:10, "That is why, for Christ's sake, I delight in weaknesses, in insults, in hardships, in persecutions, in difficulties."

You might be tempted to despise the discomfort, but God is inviting you to embrace it, as He continues to strengthen you to make you more like Him.

PRAYER

God, I want to live with You and desire what You desire. I trust Your Spirit to strengthen my soul.

157

GOING DEEP

Oh, the depth of the riches of the wisdom and knowledge of God! How unsearchable his judgments, and his paths beyond tracing out! . . . For from him and through him and for him are all things. To him be the glory forever! Amen.

ROMANS 11:33, 36

PRAYER

Oh good and glorious God! Thank You for inviting me to explore the depths of who You are because I know that the more I know You, the more I will become like You and find everlasting satisfaction. I want to know You more!

WHEN IT COMES to knowing God, He doesn't want you to settle for surface knowledge. He invites you into a deep and personal knowledge of Him where you can explore His grace, His love, His mercy, His immensity, His purity, His holiness, and His omnipotence.

You can know how He helps you. How He cares for you. How He provides for you. How He never fails you. How He works things out for your good. How He's full of wisdom. How He's rich in counsel. How He never changes. How He is always everywhere . . . yet can love you individually. How He's full of justice.

Yes, you can know how God is kind. How God is gracious. How God is infinitely beautiful and powerful and glorious.

God wants to be known . . . by you. And you can know as much about Him as you have the appetite and desire to know.

JUNE

THE GRAND CANYON OF INFINITE LOVE

Worship the Lord in the splendor of his holiness.
PSALM 96:9

PRAYER

God, I want to
delve deep into
the depths of
Your love and
put my hope in
the One who
never changes.

TAKE A MOMENT today to sit in silence and reflect on the reality that you can talk to and rely on the one true and holy God, who is set apart from everything else in creation.

If you don't acknowledge how holy God is, you won't fully understand the other attributes of His character. You can sing all the well-known worship songs about God, but if you don't stop and realize that you are singing about a holy and loving God, then you might need to take a step back and get the God of the cosmos back in your view.

We are too easily content sipping from a little tea-cup of theological understanding, while we're standing on the Grand Canyon of the infinite goodness and beauty of God. You were made for more. You have access to more. If you want to find freedom, peace, rest, love, and joy, then journey down into the canyon of His love and discover the unmatchable holiness, majesty, and mightiness of our God. In the canyon is where you can trade your superficial ideas about Him and begin to discover the depth of His unshakable glory and love.

THE LOWLY ARE LIFTED

God sets the lonely in families, he leads out the prisoners with singing.
PSALM 68:6

WHEN DARKNESS CONTINUALLY pushes in, and you can't seem to catch a break, it can feel like you're living in the worst-case scenario. It's as if hope has fled and no light remains at the end of the tunnel.

In the culture in which Psalm 68 was written, the worst-case scenario for anybody was to be fatherless or to be a widow. You were basically left to fend for yourself. In these particularly difficult scenarios, God reaches down to people who are feeling low and living low. He sets the lowly within families. He rejoices over them with song.

Today, He is reaching with strong arms to pick up any who are lost, broken, or hopeless. He is announcing to all who will listen that He is close and He is working.

Do you believe that His eyes are on you? He's the perfect Father, the One who is loving and good and in control. The One who will provide everything you need. He's the Father who set you back into the family of God and who leads you forth out of the prison of spiritual death.

PRAYER

God, I am no longer isolated, because You have rewritten my story. No longer alone, I am adopted into Your family.

HE SERVES US IN
OUR EMPTINESS

Jesus said to them, "Come and have breakfast."
JOHN 21:12

IF YOU'RE IN the middle of a long season of wrestling and doubt, remember that you follow a God whose mercies are new every morning. He invites you to breakfast and promises to sustain you. He doesn't give you a lecture about the rough night. No condemnation. No rebuke. There's just acceptance, provision, and a kind of familiarity only Jesus can provide.

That tenderness is mercy on display. It's the gospel, and it's the gospel repeated. It's the gospel when we need it the first time, and it's the gospel when we need it the second time, and the fiftieth time, and the three hundredth time. Jesus serves us in our emptiness. Jesus feeds us after we've let ourselves and Him down. Jesus welcomes us near and says, *Hello, you look tired and scared and bewildered and beat down and exhausted and burned out and like you're about to go under. Would you like some breakfast?*

Jesus is alive and loves us and has a purpose and a plan for our lives, no matter what. He doesn't run from our mess; He runs toward it.

PRAYER

Jesus, You meet me where I am with comfort and truth. You lead me up and out of my circumstances toward Your great and marvelous light.

GOODNESS AWAITS US IN THE END

For I am convinced that neither death nor life, neither angels nor demons, neither the present nor the future, nor any powers, neither height nor depth, nor anything else in all creation, will be able to separate us from the love of God that is in Christ Jesus our Lord.
ROMANS 8:38–39

WE LIVE ON a broken planet. Perhaps you or someone you know is currently walking through very real and very difficult circumstances. In spite of challenge and trial, you can take courage and know that victory is coming in the end. When the final curtain falls, when the last bell is rung, you know what you can expect?

Goodness. Joy. Salvation.

God is committed to working all things out for the good of those who love Him. He's proven it by not sparing His only Son but sending Him as the ultimate sacrifice. And when you come alive in Him, nothing will ever be able to separate you from that love.

Do you believe God loves you? Not just that He likes you when you do good things or tolerates you even though you occasionally slip up. But that He loves you and that nothing—absolutely and unequivocally nothing—can separate you from that love?

PRAYER

Lord, thank You for keeping me and carrying me through every void and valley with an everlasting goodness.

LIVING LIKE JESUS

But if anyone obeys his word, love for God is truly made complete in them. This is how we know we are in him: Whoever claims to live in him must live as Jesus did.
1 JOHN 2:5–6

AT SOME POINT, most of us have bought into the lie that Christianity should be easy. That somehow once you get saved, everything else will just line up and level out. But ask any Jesus-follower who's gone through the fire, and they'll tell you that's not always the case.

Once you say yes to Jesus, the real work begins. Your old ways must be put to death as you seek to obey God and align with the Holy Spirit inside you. If you claim to be alive in Jesus, you're going to have to walk out your faith just like He did, especially when the going gets tough.

The best news is that you're not left to do this alone. God is always at work for you and in you because He wants you to know with outright certainty how loved and adored you are. Then from that love, you can live like Jesus. Commit to the work with Him today as you aim to become more like Christ.

PRAYER

God, work in me until I walk as Jesus did. Strengthen me to the task at hand—holy obedience inspired by Your love.

FIRST THINGS FIRST

In vain you rise early and stay up late, toiling for food to eat—for he grants sleep to those he loves.

PSALM 127:2

WHEN YOU'RE IN quiet moments, what occupies your thoughts? When you're making your schedule for the week, what gets first priority on the calendar? When you wake up, what's on your mind? These are all strong barometers of what your priorities are, and if your attention is consumed by work, errands, or personal goals, then it's a telling sign your priorities may be out of alignment.

It's good to work toward admirable goals, but when what you desire supersedes your affection for your Creator, even the most holy acts can become corrupted. Whose glory are you working for today? Before you pursue your earthly ambitions, reorient your thoughts and priorities around God's love. Living in constant prayer and admiration, you'll find that all other tasks fall into place. As you deepen your trust in Him, you will feel confident walking away from a lifestyle of over-achieving and learn to move toward a lifestyle of rest.

Without Him, all work is in vain. With Him, you'll find eternal purpose with everything you do. Surrender your time and thoughts to Him and learn a new definition of *abundance*.

PRAYER

God, before I take another breath, I put You first. More than anything else, You are my top priority.

ALL ACCESS

We have confidence to enter the Most Holy Place by the blood of Jesus, by a new and living way opened for us through the curtain, that is, his body.
HEBREWS 10:19–20

WHEN ANGELS ANNOUNCED Jesus' birth, they proclaimed, "Glory to God in the highest heaven" (Luke 2:14). The greatest weight and the greatest value have come to earth in Christ. This is a staggering truth for us today. Jesus opened the way for us to come into the very presence of God. And when Jesus died, "the curtain of the temple was torn in two from top to bottom" (Matthew 27:51). Thanks to Jesus, the separation between God and man does not need to exist anymore. We have access to the Father!

God is inviting you to climb all the way up His mountain with humility and confidence. And as you do, you'll find God's infinite power. Infinite love. Infinite beauty. Infinite majesty.

Saint Augustine said, "Thou hast made us for thyself, O Lord, and our heart is restless until it finds their rest in thee." Today as you dwell in the presence of God, let your restlessness fall away to His great and glorious peace.

PRAYER

Jesus, You have torn down every dividing wall, and in You, we have boldness to approach the throne of grace.

HEALING COMES WHEN WE LIFT OUR EYES

A father to the fatherless, a defender of widows, is God in his holy dwelling.
PSALM 68:5

IT CAN BE hard to join God's song when you're hurting inside. When you are suffering, you are likely looking for comfort and care before you are looking for a song. But the invitation to lean into God's care begins with worship. This is the primary way you are reminded that He alone is worthy and able to step into your story.

God is singing over you, and sometimes all you can do is breathe in His words of love, and that is enough. If you're feeling pain or heartache, turn toward Him, and rest knowing that He's caught you and is holding you close. Perhaps today you need to simply linger in that posture for a while—in the healing and loving song of a good Father.

At some point within your healing journey, you'll sense the invitation to sing praise back to God and join in His song. Your eyes will be lifted off yourself as you gaze lovingly at your flawless Father, who isn't afraid of a dark night or a hard circumstance. There, you'll sense His nearness and compassion flowing over you.

PRAYER

God, You aren't just working on my behalf; You are defending me from darkness with Your songs. I rest here, in Your arms, today.

JUN 9

FINDING RELIEF IN THE PRINCE OF PEACE

For to us a child is born. . . . And he will be called Wonderful Counselor, Mighty God, Everlasting Father, Prince of Peace.
ISAIAH 9:6

Father, I accept the promise of peace today through the blood of Jesus. May I be an ambassador of peace to those around me.

THE PROPHET ISAIAH referred to Jesus as the Prince of Peace. This is good news for what is all too often an angry world.

Jesus Christ is in the world, and He comes as a Wonderful Counselor. Jesus is coming to the negotiating table and saying, *I have authority from heaven to broker a peace treaty. I have all authority to sit at the table and talk about your wrongs, but I'm not going to do that. I'm here to offer you a deal, to offer you peace, to offer you what no one else can offer you: salvation.*

In Ephesians 2:14, Paul described Jesus as "our peace." Jesus comes before God the Father and makes peace for us. How does Jesus do that? He does it through His shed blood poured out on the cross.

All the righteous anger and holy wrath of God landed on Jesus at the cross. God's anger has been satisfied. We can run to Jesus and find relief. We have a new relationship with God, kept by Jesus, the Prince of Peace.

GOING UP THE MOUNTAIN OF GOD

When Moses came down from Mount Sinai with the two tablets of the covenant law in his hands, he was not aware that his face was radiant because he had spoken with the LORD.

EXODUS 34:29

PRAYER

God, I want to go deeper with You. Strengthen my resolve to pursue You intimately, that I may come to experience Your love more richly and renew my mind in Your presence.

THE CHOICE TO know God more fully is yours. Thanks to Jesus, there are no barriers to you knowing God. But it wasn't always this way. In the Old Testament, there were barriers. People had to look ahead in faith, trusting the promises of God and believing that the barriers would be broken down by a Savior.

When Jesus came, He made a way for us to come into the presence of God. To actually know God without limit. The result? We all, with unveiled faces, can behold the Lord's glory and be transformed into His image. The cross and the Spirit have brought us freedom.

And what is this freedom? To come boldly into His presence. To come as high as we want on the mountain of God. That's what Christ has accomplished, but how you embrace that invitation to grow deeper with God is up to you.

LINGERING LEADS TO KNOWING

My heart says of you, "Seek his face!" Your face, LORD, I will seek. Do not hide your face from me, do not turn your servant away in anger; you have been my helper. Do not reject me or forsake me, God my Savior.
PSALM 27:8–9

PRAYER

Jesus, I push pause on all my hurrying and hustling. I breathe in Your grace and mercy, and I breathe out my praise and affection for You. Let me linger with You today.

GOD IS OF infinite greatness, and He has invited you to know Him deeply and closely and richly. The invitation is to sit with Him. To be in His presence. When you realize the magnitude of this possibility, you see there is nothing in your life more valuable or rewarding than your full-on pursuit of knowing Him.

But to truly know God, you have to learn to linger with Him . . . not to be in a rush to end your times with Him . . . to enjoy His presence.

Lingering with the Almighty invites an intimacy into your heart that breeds confidence, poise, and strength. This intimacy fuels your defense against the Enemy. It is the foundation of your offense, or your love, toward God. That which has most captured your affection is that which you most love.

So linger with Him today. Slow down. Take your time and watch as your heart begins to bloom in the presence of the everlasting spring of life.

HIS JUSTICE WILL MAKE THINGS NEW

You, dear children, are from God and have overcome them, because the one who is in you is greater than the one who is in the world.

1 JOHN 4:4

THE AMOUNT OF injustice in the world today can be overwhelming. So much heartache from poor choices and selfish ambition. God, in His infinite wisdom, has given people freedom of choice. Some people choose to bless others with their freedom of choice. Sadly, others choose to hurt people.

Fortunately, the Bible says that one day, all things will be made new. One day, everything will be made right. One day, justice will "roll on like a river, righteousness like a never-failing stream!" (Amos 5:24).

But even today, despite all the pain in the world, God is greater than all our greatest wounds and hurts. God is always near for us to turn to, and when we do, God takes us in and holds us close. He draws us into His arms as a loved child of the Creator of the universe.

If you're surrounded by pain, take heart that the perfect Father is loving and good. He is in control and will provide everything we need.

PRAYER

God, nothing is a surprise to You. You have never been shaken or confused. I cling to Your stability today when things around me seem shaky.

171

FIXING YOUR EYES
ON THE ALMIGHTY

So we fix our eyes not on what is seen, but on what is unseen, since what is seen is temporary, but what is unseen is eternal.
2 CORINTHIANS 4:18

YOU HAVE THE power, no matter how helpless or broken down you feel, to choose what you set before you today. You may not even realize it, but the eyes of your heart are always looking at something.

If you set the Almighty in view, your temptations will be resized, demoted, reduced, diminished, and weakened by God's greatness. It all comes down to what the eyes of your heart are fixed on.

When the eyes of our hearts are enlightened, we can know the hope that God has called us to. We can bask in the glorious promises given to the people of God and live with incomparably great power—the same power that raised Jesus from the dead!

Where we fix our eyes matters. We can spend our days looking at the things of this world, and if we do that, our fixation will likely only grow bigger and bigger. But if we look up, if we gaze at the One who is seated at the right hand of God, the eyes of our heart will expand.

GATHER

"I will consider all your works and meditate on all your mighty deeds." Your ways, God, are holy. What god is as great as our God?

PSALM 77:12–13

WHY IS IT important that we come together and worship shoulder to shoulder with other Christ followers? Wouldn't it be enough to worship God in our own personal and private ways?

Yes, worship begins with an intimate relationship between you and God. It must start from a place of awe and wonder at what God has done for you and in you. But worship is never truly finished until what has been placed in us—joy, gratitude, celebration—moves through us to fellow believers and those who don't yet know Jesus as their Savior.

When we gather as believers, collective hope rises. Our trust is strengthened as our faith is anthemed. This is where the weary get lifted, the fearful get emboldened, and the downcast get rejuvenated. This is the power of a worship gathering, and all it takes to unlock it is for you and other believers to show up with open hearts. Make gathering together a priority, and watch what God does.

PRAYER

Lord, point me back to my first love, a pure devotion to You rooted in a holy awe at Your salvation power and work.

LEARNING TO BUILD ON HIS FIRM FOUNDATION

"The rain came down, the streams rose, and the winds blew and beat against that house; yet it did not fall, because it had its foundation on the rock."
MATTHEW 7:25

WE PUT OUR trust in a lot of places—bank accounts, relationships, our jobs—but Jesus is reminding us today that He is the only One who will always have our back and will never let us down. Throughout history, He has a 100 percent success rate of being trustworthy and dependable.

Matthew 7:25 reminds us that when we trust in Jesus, He will help us find freedom. When we depend on Him, we can live in a state of perfect peace.

Doesn't that sound appealing? Imagine what your life would look like if it were characterized by perfect peace. No circumstance could shake you. No hardship could crush you. No minor or major storm could overcome your resting in the mighty hands of God.

How do you move toward that? You learn to trust in Jesus. You learn to build on His firm foundation so that when the waves and the winds of life inevitably crash onto your shores, your life stands firm.

PUT YOUR HOPE IN GOD

Why, my soul, are you downcast? Why so disturbed within me? Put your hope in God, for I will yet praise him, my Savior and my God.

PSALM 42:11

WHEN LIFE GOES awry, we become more vulnerable to allowing our mind to spiral into negative thoughts. *I don't know if I can trust God. I don't know if God has my best interests at heart.*

If you find thoughts like these bouncing around in your head, stop for a moment and ask: Where did this thought come from? God didn't put those thoughts there. The Enemy is a liar, always working to flip the narrative and convince us that God isn't trustworthy. He tells us that full surrender to Jesus equals less in our lives, not more.

From the very beginning, God has put all of His cards on the table. He promised, *I'm going to come down and deliver you. I'm going to set you free.* And He did; His saving grace is still true. His plans and purposes haven't changed even if your situation looks bleak. His light shines brightest through the darkness. Pray that the Spirit would guard your mind today, and that you would be assured of the good and perfect will of God for all eternity.

PRAYER

Lord, when my soul is downcast, help me to remember Your faithfulness. You are my Savior and my God.

ALL THINGS

We know that in all things God works for the good of those who love him, who have been called according to his purpose.
ROMANS 8:28

DO YOU EVER feel like God is holding something back from you? True, He's saved you, but will He also give you strength to get through that hard relationship? Will He give you wisdom for that tricky work situation? How about grace when you're at your wits' end and feel broken or pressed down?

Romans 8:32 says, "He who did not spare his own Son, but gave him up for us all—how will he not also, along with him, graciously give us all things?"

Did you catch those last two words? *All things*, which references back to today's verse, Romans 8:28.

Because God's already given you Jesus, granting you salvation, He is also willing to give you everything else. And all those things that He gives you, He works out for your good and His glory.

God is not holding back on you today or any day. Turn to Him. Ask Him for what you need. He already knows, and He is ready to provide and work on your behalf.

JESUS IN ME

"But very truly I tell you, it is for your good that I am going away. Unless I go away, the Advocate will not come to you; but if I go, I will send him to you."
JOHN 16:7

WHILE JESUS IS not physically with you, He has given you another, "the Advocate," who is with you forever—the Holy Spirit. And you can know that He is not just *with* you but is *in* you in a powerful way.

A shift happens when you put your faith in Jesus, and you understand that life is not so much "Jesus and me" as it is "Jesus *in* me." As the Spirit fills us, we grow to know what it means to sense that He is near on sunny days and stormy nights.

He is in you and with you at all times. The Counselor has come in the person of the Spirit and He intercedes for you on behalf of the will of God. Those words aren't a prescription for a magical happy pill. The truth in those words is what allows you to develop real faith, a raw faith, a faith where you acknowledge the Lord as the King of your life.

PRAYER

God, Your Spirit empowers me to live with real and confident faith today because He bears witness to Your unchanging character. Holy Spirit, guide me into truth today.

KNEES TO THE EARTH

"You shall have no other gods before me."
EXODUS 20:3

HOW LONG HAS it been since you were stunned by the radical grace of God? When was the last time the wonder of the goodness and glory of Jesus overwhelmed your heart and put wind in your sails? If you are looking for a mighty move of God, you won't find it by trying harder or running faster after the things of this world. If you long to experience Him anew, you may need to embrace His invitation to surrender, kneeling down intentionally before your risen King.

Where you put your time and energy matters. You can't experience a mighty move of God if you worship the little gods of this world—money, influence, intelligence, and beauty, to name a few. God isn't satisfied with a half-hearted relationship with you. He wants all of you. He's reaching out to you, saying, *Put your faith in Me. I'm your one shot. When you trust in me again and obey, watch how I come through for you.*

Nothing or no one will satisfy or give you rest for your soul except the God of heaven. Prioritize your time with God and kneel before the one true King.

PRAYER

God, I surrender all the ways I go about putting my trust in false hopes. I put my full trust in You.

EVERYDAY GRACE

"Give us today our daily bread."
MATTHEW 6:11

THE GOSPEL IS not only about a decision you make once and for all—it's about a decision you make every day.

That doesn't mean that you lose your salvation and need to get saved all over again. It means that the gospel is not simply about walking down an aisle or praying a certain prayer or getting baptized. The gospel is about living in the light of Jesus' resurrection power every day.

We need God's *saving* grace to be made alive. And we need God's *transforming* grace to be made alive every day. The grace is the same grace. The gospel is the same gospel. We need grace to come up out of our graves for the first time. We need grace to stay out of the grave if it ever beckons us back.

That's the beauty of Christ's work on the cross. Jesus' work raises us to life and sustains that life each and every day. How does He do it? By giving us today our daily bread. Every day, He provides and sustains you for your spiritual life.

PRAYER

God, I need Your daily bread to flourish today. I need Your new mercies to wash over me right now, that I would know the power of Your salvation anew.

179

A KIND AND GENEROUS RESTORATION

When they had finished eating, Jesus said to Simon Peter, "Simon son of John, do you love me more than these?"
JOHN 21:15

PRAYER

Jesus, I do not deserve Your loving-kindness, but I accept Your grace as You invite me to continue to walk forward with You.

HAVE YOU EVER felt like you've fallen so far, or done something so off the mark, that even Jesus wouldn't want to lift you back to your feet? If so, the way Jesus responded to Peter is key for you today. Peter denied Jesus, even as Jesus was staring down death. After Jesus resurrected, He had every right to shame Peter.

But Jesus chose grace, and He didn't hold the record of wrong against Peter. He simply said to Peter, "Come and have breakfast" (John 21:12). In other words: "Sit with Me. I bet you're hungry. Here's some freshly baked bread. Let this fire warm you. Rest awhile."

What do you think Jesus would say to you after you've fallen or stumbled? Romans 8:1 says, "There is now no condemnation for those who are in Christ Jesus." Jesus gave us a perfect picture of that verse in His invitation to Peter, and you can be sure that Jesus will offer you the same mercy and kindness.

A NEW NAME

Jesus said, "It is finished." With that, he bowed his head and gave up his spirit.
JOHN 19:30

NO ONE LIKES to be defined by their worst mistakes, forever labeled by something they did during a moment of weakness. We all yearn for the possibility of redemption and grace to write over our wrongs.

When Adam and Eve fell in Genesis 3, sin and death entered the world. There were consequences to their actions, but even then, God was setting in motion a redemption plan. He promised that even though death looked as if it had won, God would have the final victory.

Even in the garden, God knew that one day, His Son would hang on a cross at Calvary. That with His last breath, Jesus would cry out, "It is finished." What is finished? The work of God to break the power of sin over your life. You are no longer defined by your brokenness. Rather, you are called. Loved. Adopted. Holy. Chosen. Embrace this identity today. God executed the greatest rescue plan the universe has ever seen, and you are invited to step into this grace and live free.

PRAYER

God, You don't label me by my shortcomings, so I won't either. I choose to see myself how You see me, as Your loved child.

181

GOD'S LOVE DOESN'T EBB AND FLOW

The LORD appeared to us in the past, saying: "I have loved you with an everlasting love; I have drawn you with unfailing kindness."
JEREMIAH 31:3

PRAYER

Lord, how radical is Your unconditional love! Your faithfulness and consistency lead me to awe and wonder.

GOD HAS LEFT you a stunningly powerful message of love. He hung the greatest "I love you" of all time on a tree at Calvary through the death of His Son. You can see His message from wherever you are today if you just turn and look toward the cross.

God loves us. Perfectly. I know that sounds simplistic, as it echoes the song so many of us sang as young children, "Jesus loves me, this I know, for the Bible tells me so." Even though this sounds elementary, many of us still wrestle with how to embrace this foundational, life-shaping, worry-conquering truth.

Jesus loves you.

His love for you does not ebb and flow based on your position or performance. He is not carefully calibrating His love for you based on your potential. He is not reserving some of His love for when you prove your dedication and commitment to His mission. You can anchor your deepest hopes in the love of Jesus. He won't let you down.

OUR COMPASSIONATE AND MERCIFUL GOD

He saved us, not because of righteous things we had done, but because of his mercy.

TITUS 3:5

GOD IS A God of wrath, but that's only part of the story. We need His wrath to judge the evil in the world. But whenever we consider His wrath, we must remember that it is deeply intertwined with His mercy.

Every human has fallen short and deserves the judgment of God. But God isn't in heaven folding His arms saying, *You blew it*. He's not shaking His finger at you as a disappointed Father. No. Compassion is at the core of God. It's not a mood that swings; it's an attribute.

Praise God that He is rich in mercy! He's not searching His pockets or scouring underneath the couch cushions for some spare grace to give. He's offering an unending amount of compassion and kindness to you, freely, without charge. Because of His great love for you and because you follow Jesus, you are no longer under the wrath you deserved. You are saved by mercy because of who He is and what He's done.

PRAYER

God, when I could do nothing to help myself, You brought me mercy and grace. You not only held back Your wrath; You also gave me Christ. Hallelujah!

GOD'S SOVEREIGNTY LEADS TO GREAT CONFIDENCE

"I know that you can do all things; no purpose of yours can be thwarted."
JOB 42:2

WHAT DO YOU put your confidence in? Honestly, what is the ultimate source of power that you think has the most control in and over your life? Maybe it's your wealth or your family. Maybe it's even yourself.

Scripture lays out a clear answer to the true source of ultimate power. Over and over the Bible points to the truth that God is sovereign. His sovereignty means He is the greatest force in the universe. He sees everything. He understands it all. He stitches together generations and millennia and galaxies and time into a story of His love and grace. He is omniscient of past, present, and future. There is nothing you can say or do that will surprise the Almighty.

God is not only ultimate in knowledge and power. He is also ultimate in love. His love invades and conquers every darkness. There is no place His love can't reach. And today, the omniscient God above all offers His limitless love to you. Place your confidence in the God of the universe, and trust His loving plan for your life will come to pass.

FROM FAILURE TO FAMILY

See what great love the Father has lavished
on us, that we should be called children
of God! And that is what we are!

1 JOHN 3:1

WHEN YOU'VE FALLEN short of an expectation, a goal, or a personal conviction, that mistake can loom over your head. It might bring with it shame, frustration, and even doubt about whether things could ever get better.

That's where grace comes in. Grace not only cancels your guilt and shame but also redefines you. The biggest change caused by grace is shifting the definition of who you are, from "failure" to "family."

God transforms your identity. The Enemy wants to define you by your scars, but Jesus wants to define you by His scars.

You are a son or daughter of God. You are a child of the King. You are written into God's will, and you are an heir of everything God has. You are a beneficiary of the lavish love of God.

How powerful! Guilt and shame are canceled, and you are restored by grace. You are a beloved family member of God, and because of that you are given a seat at the table with Him.

PRAYER

Lord, You have lavished us with love, over and above what I thought possible. You have made me new in Jesus, so I will live today as a child of God.

SUSTAINED UNTIL THE END

*I have fought the good fight, I have finished
the race, I have kept the faith.*
2 TIMOTHY 4:7

PRAYER

Lord, I want
my story to
be defined by
faithfulness to
You. Sustain
me as I share
Your Word
with others.

WHAT DO YOU want your legacy to be at the end of your days? Will you be remembered as someone who persevered through all the ups and downs? Will they recall your soft, steady, and sacrificial heart? Will you be remembered as someone who continued in the work God put before you, even when things got tough? How about that you lived for Him more than for yourself?

Keeping the faith is a lifelong commitment, and the Bible offers us examples of those who have endured much to follow Jesus. Under all kinds of pressure, adversity, and temptation to bail, the apostle Paul confidently stayed the course. When his time came to an end, his final moments were marked with confidence and hope. He knew the crown of righteousness was awaiting him in heaven.

That same crown is offered to you. If you want a similar legacy of faith at the end of your story, you'll similarly have to endure adversity. But like Paul, you know how the ultimate story ends. Jesus wins. Death loses. You get resurrected, crowned, and redeemed. So stay steady today. Renew your commitment to last. God is at work in you.

A STORY TO SHARE

*This news about Jesus spread throughout
Judea and the surrounding country.*
LUKE 7:17

WHEN JESUS BROUGHT a young man back to life, the people around who saw it erupted and worshiped God. They couldn't stay silent. They'd just seen a miracle happen right before their eyes. Some clapped. Some cheered. Some shouted for joy. Some fell on their faces in worship. That's what happens when the Son of God is in your midst and He's calling off a funeral procession.

Then what happened? The news of Jesus spread everywhere! When we're worshiping God, we're seeing Him for who He truly is—a God who has power over everything, even death. When you get that view of God in your mind, you can't just quietly go on your way, doing business as usual. Seeing God's resurrection power shifts everything, and you suddenly become eager to tell everyone, "I've seen God raise a person from the dead!"

You may not feel like you have a story worth sharing, but if God has raised you from spiritual death into spiritual life, you have a story to share.

PRAYER

God, when I think about how You have changed my life, I rejoice and recognize Your great faithfulness. Embolden me to share Your gospel with those around me.

PROPELLED TO PROCLAIM JESUS

"As long as it is day, we must do the works of him who sent me. Night is coming, when no one can work."
JOHN 9:4

PRAYER

God, You've invited me to participate in Your rescue mission on planet Earth. Take my gifts, my strengths, all that I have, and leverage it all for Your kingdom.

HAVE YOU EVER talked yourself out of remaining obedient to God? Maybe it seemed too hard or too costly in the moment. Any of us can rationalize following the world's message. But the invitation for each of us is not to obey and follow our neighbor. It is to follow Christ. We have to be diligent about who and what we align ourselves with. Because it is going to determine where we arrive months and years from now.

A meaningful, lasting life is the by-product of walking closely with the Father, Son, and Spirit. When the Spirit fell on the early followers of Jesus, His power propelled them into the world to proclaim the goodness of the gospel, regardless of the cost.

God doesn't call you to avoid hardship. Rather, He leads you into the darkness with the sword of the Spirit in your hands, and He invites you to carry out His tasks in the time you've been given.

SINGING IN THE STORM

*Therefore my heart is glad and my tongue
rejoices; my body also will rest secure.*
PSALM 16:9

LIFE CAN BE stormy. A simple glance at the headlines, a look at your bank account, or an unexpected emergency can disrupt your day in a moment. It can seem like hardship is everywhere, threatening to thunder its power over you.

But with Jesus, worship can flow unobstructed from our mouths. A song of praise can be on our lips. Seeing Jesus makes our hearts glad and restores rest. Seeing Jesus causes us to sing.

You may be thinking, *Why would we sing when the outcome of this struggle is not yet decided?*

No matter how stiff the headwinds of life become, you can sing because you know God is with you. You see His might and are reminded of His love. He has always come through for you, and His mercy has never failed. You don't lose sight of Jesus because of the raging seas. With your eyes firmly fixed on Jesus, you cry out, "You are in control!" Not ignoring the presence of danger but declaring the presence of God. When you surrender, you open yourself up for gladness, rejoicing, and peace.

PRAYER

Lord, in You my heart is glad. The storm may rage, but I know I am secure and at peace with You.

JULY

STAYING POWER

*He will wipe every tear from their eyes. There will
be no more death, or mourning or crying or pain,
for the old order of things has passed away.*
REVELATION 21:4

THINK FOR A moment how everything beautiful in life has an expiration date—that point in time when even fine things wilt and decay and die.

But you don't have to worry or fear today, because every step of the way your perfect Father will be *good*. And when the end comes, He will take you to a new forever with Him where every bad thing that sin has brought into this world will be vanquished. Until then, you can be sure that everything that happens to you will pass through His goodness and His love.

God says, "For I know the plans I have for you . . . plans to prosper you and not to harm you, plans to give you hope and a future" (Jeremiah 29:11). And He promises "that in all things God works for the good of those who love him, who have been called according to his purpose" (Romans 8:28).

Anchor your hope in the cross, the place where your perfect Father placed every evil thing on His innocent Son so that you can know His love, experience His forgiveness, and know He is good.

PRAYER

Jesus, I look eagerly toward the day when You will restore all things in newness. May that future truth fuel me to fight back the darkness today.

REPENTANCE LEADS
TO GRACE

"Woe to me!" I cried. "I am ruined! For I am a man of unclean lips, and I live among a people of unclean lips, and my eyes have seen the King, the LORD Almighty."
ISAIAH 6:5

WE CAN SEE hints of the grace Jesus followers live under—even in the Old Testament. For example, Isaiah 6 records the prophet Isaiah having a vision of the Lord and of heaven. It was a beautiful and powerful vision, and when he saw it, he was guilt-struck because he immediately recognized the gap between who he was and who God is.

Isaiah's response points us to the finished work of Jesus on the cross. You can step into that finished work by the act of repentance when you say the equivalent of Isaiah's words: "Woe is me. I've fallen short of God's holy standard. I admit it. I take responsibility for it. I realize that I am accountable for my choices and my sin before God Almighty."

Repentance is not a negative thing. Your act of admitting guilt opens a doorway called *grace*, and God comes to you through that doorway and does for you exactly what your heart most deeply desires: He reunites His Spirit with yours as a new creation.

PRAYER

God, I repent of my sin today. I lay it at Your feet, and I trust that You, in Your grace, redeem me.

193

UL 3

GOD'S ALREADY GIVEN US HIS BEST

He who did not spare his own Son, but gave him up for us all—how will he not also, along with him, graciously give us all things?
ROMANS 8:32

RAYER

God, I'm humbled and grateful anew that You gave Your greatest treasure, Your Son, so that I can have everlasting life in You.

PAUSE AND THINK about what you need from God right now. Encouragement? Peace? Grace? An answer to prayer?

The stunning news is that God can provide all you need because in His infinite love, God has already sent His Son for you. He didn't spare Jesus but instead sent Him to show you how perfectly and how much He loves you. And to give you concrete proof of how far He was willing to go to make a way for your salvation.

If God was willing to do that, how will He not also help you overcome every fear and source of worry in your life?

Can God grant you peace? He gave His only Son for you, so yes. Why wouldn't He also give peace? Can He give you comfort? Assurance? Freedom? Joy? Hope? Yes, yes, yes, yes, and yes. Do you see that logical reality? If God already gave you His best, He has no reason to withhold the rest from you.

94

A HOLY AND LOVING GOD

For Your lovingkindness is before my eyes,
and I have walked in Your truth.

PSALM 26:3 NKJV

GOD IS HOLY and righteous—set apart from sin and entirely perfect. And because He is holy and righteous, He enacts judgment. When we sin against the Lord, we deserve no less than to bear the Lord's wrath. Our choices aren't just bad; they put us in direct opposition to a holy God.

But thankfully, though He is a God of judgment, He is also a God of love. These are not opposite characteristics but two sides of the same coin. You'll never encounter anyone more loving or more sacrificially generous than God. He was willing to give up His greatest treasure, His Son, to ransom you because He *so* loved you.

God isn't looking to punish people unjustly. That's not His way. In kindness, He is eager to forgive you. He loves you enough to provide you a way of salvation, but He desires for you to turn to Him and trust in the righteousness of Christ. When you do this, you get all the benefits of Christ's life—His freedom, grace, and peace—while God's standard of holiness gets met by the perfect life of Jesus.

PRAYER

Jesus, thank You for loving me in such a way that I can walk according to the holy and righteous standards of Your truth.

MORE AT STAKE

Shout for joy before the LORD, the King.
PSALM 98:6

WHEN YOU DISCOVER good news, it can feel like you're going to burst from the excitement of getting to tell people. That's because when you have amazing news, you want to spread it everywhere and to everyone.

Likewise, it should be hard for our worship to stay quiet for too long. When we experience the unfathomable presence of Jesus, emotions overtake us. We stand. We sing. We kneel. We cry. We shout. We dance. Jesus is alive! Jesus has all power over death!

If you are captured by the joy of the good news of Jesus, it doesn't matter where you are or who you are with; the news of Jesus can spread far and wide. It spreads among friends and families, from dorm rooms to boardrooms, from conferences to conversations over coffee. Even the stranger you pass in the street!

When Jesus changes your heart, don't make the mistake of thinking that your resurrection story concludes with you. It doesn't. You now have a story to share, so go out and tell some people today about what Jesus has done in your life. You'll never regret sharing the good news with those around you.

PRAYER

God, You have planted praise in my heart and invited me to worship You with my every moment! I rejoice, for You have freed me. Hallelujah!

BREAK FREE FROM THE ROUTINE

After a long time, in the third year, the word of the LORD came to Elijah.

1 KINGS 18:1

WE'VE ALL BEEN in seasons of life where it feels like we're on autopilot. Our work, relationships, even our time with God—they all start to lose their luster. Life becomes mundane, we disengage our hearts, and we lose the passion that once fueled our interactions.

If you feel like that's true of your faith, maybe you're in a season as a believer when you need the joy of your salvation refreshed. Perhaps, like the prophet Elijah wandering the desert, it's been a long time since you've sensed God or experienced His power or felt assurance of His plan. You need God to show up in your life in a powerful way.

Rest assured, just because it's been a while doesn't mean that the Lord has checked out of your life. In fact, He's just as close to you as He's always been. There will be seasons where you might feel closer or further from God, but you can have peace knowing that He never leaves your side. His love and care for you abounds, and whether you know it or not, you are always on His mind.

PRAYER

God, draw me out of complacency and bring a freshness into my relationship with You.

197

EXCELLENT AND PRAISEWORTHY

Finally, brothers and sisters, whatever is true, whatever is noble, whatever is right, whatever is pure, whatever is lovely, whatever is admirable—if anything is excellent or praiseworthy—think about such things.
PHILIPPIANS 4:8

PRAYER

Jesus, help me identify the lies I need to uproot today. By Your Spirit, plant Your truth in the open soil of my heart.

IF YOU'VE EVER cultivated a garden, you know how easy it is for weeds to sprout up. The same is true for your mind. If you're not watchful, negative thoughts about your worth, your status, or your stability might begin to grow. Like weeds in a garden, negative thoughts can destroy good thoughts.

But just because a negative thought pops up doesn't mean it has to stay planted in your mind.

By God's grace, you can root *out* the lies of the Enemy. And that's not all. You can also reseed, or put *in*, truths about God.

Paul told us in Philippians 4 that we're to use prayer and supplication to dismantle anxiety. Whatever is true, noble, right, pure, lovely, admirable—dwell on those things. As you plant those truths in your mind, you'll experience more righteousness. Your thoughts will begin to echo the words of God—that you are loved, highly valued, and secure.

A SUN AND A SHIELD

For the LORD God is a sun and shield;
The LORD will give grace and glory;
No good thing will He withhold
From those who walk uprightly.

PSALM 84:11 NKJV

GOD INVITES YOU to taste and see that He is good, to experience Him in the fullness of your senses. He wants His love to be palpable, not just studied.

God desires you to encounter His character through the pages of His Word and the person of Christ. He wants you to ponder His attributes and dwell on who He is. He doesn't want to be reduced to information you read on a page. God wants you to look up from the pages of Scripture with the eyes of your heart and realize He is right there with you.

To say that God is good speaks to His motives, to His intent, although not everything in life is good. In fact, the world is badly broken. But in a world filled with wrong, your Father is still good and right. As you come closer to Him, you begin to realize that He not only provides for His children; He also protects them. As the psalmist in Psalm 84 assured us, "the LORD God is a sun and shield" (v. 11) to those who are His.

PRAYER

God, You go before and behind me, giving me everything I need for today. You will guard me from darkness and steer me toward life.

POISED TO FOLLOW

Then I heard the voice of the Lord saying, "Whom shall I send? And who will go for us?" And I said, "Here am I. Send me!"
ISAIAH 6:8

PRAYER

God, knock down the barriers that are keeping me from following You fully.

WHEN GOD STIRS your heart and calls you into a new mission, stop everything and follow. Will it be easy? Likely not. But will it be worth it? Guaranteed.

When the Lord was looking for someone who would go and proclaim His name, without a second thought, Isaiah replied, "Here am I. Send me!" Isaiah didn't care where he'd go or for how long he'd be away. He didn't ask to see a road map. He didn't even know exactly who he'd be going to witness to. He had no details. But he had seen God's goodness and experienced His holiness, and he trusted God enough to say, "Here am I."

God is inviting you to play a role in His story, so when the Spirit nudges your heart to step out, speak up, or set off in the work He is calling you to do, don't hesitate. Remember that the sovereign God of all the earth goes with you. Hardship may come, but when you follow His lead, you'll see His glory at work. So put your yes on the table before God and let Him use you.

GOD'S GLORIOUS RESCUE PLAN

For the grace of God has appeared that
offers salvation to all people.
TITUS 2:11

THE PATHWAY TO spiritual freedom is open to all people through the covering of grace. Grace isn't some ethereal, flimsy, milquetoast kind of thing. Grace has grit, backbone, and muscle. Grace is the left hook that destroys the power of sin.

To prove this, let's look at how grace destroys shame. Shame is a powerfully destructive force. It causes you to feel as if you're unworthy of God's love, acceptance, purpose, or plan. When you feel shame, you're prone to hide. You try to hide from God behind denial or by trying to keep out of His way.

Fortunately, even back in the very beginning, God formed a rescue plan. He knew you couldn't "hide" your way out of sin. So He pointed to the future and to the cross, where God crushed shame with His grace. He created the way that allows you to live a new and worthy life of freedom. This grace can transform all things for you.

PRAYER

God, You took away my shame when You died for me on the cross. I step into the fullness of grace today. Let it wash over me and lead me into freedom.

THE WAY OF WONDROUS JOY

The mind governed by the flesh is death, but the mind governed by the Spirit is life and peace.
ROMANS 8:6

PRAYER

Spirit, control my mind, that I would see the joy of Jesus as something worth my pursuit. Guide me into the life and peace offered when my mind is led by Your Spirit.

WHEN WAS THE last time you sensed the joy of God? As followers of Jesus, who have access to the best news on planet Earth, our lives should be anthems of joy, mirroring the wonder and worship of creation as we adore our Creator and King.

But as we know, it's too easy to get sidetracked. Instead of looking up and setting our minds on our God in heaven, we start to look around. We let comparison become our source of worth and identity. Or we start to look inward, fixating on ourselves as our own minds become consumed with a me-centric way of living. Everything becomes about us, which derails the joyful death-to-self spirit of the gospel.

True joy isn't found in comparison or egotism. It's found only in Christ. His sacrifice and resurrection changed everything because it freed you from the chains of every other counterfeit path to satisfaction. You can now put Jesus at the center and always have access to perfect joy, life, and peace. When you set your mind on Him, everything else fades away.

HAPPY TO BE A DOOR HOLDER

Better is one day in your courts than a thousand elsewhere; I would rather be a doorkeeper in the house of my God than dwell in the tents of the wicked.

PSALM 84:10

REST ASSURED: GOD doesn't just love you with a love that looks good from a distance. Your heavenly Father is a good Father, perfect in every season—so goodness is who He is.

But how can you know that He is good? For one, you can draw close and examine His character and actually experience His goodness. The psalmist declared in Psalm 34:8 to "taste and see that the LORD is good; blessed is the one who takes refuge in him." God is not afraid to invite you for a close inspection. In fact, He wants you to be near to Him. He knows that it is better to be in His house than anywhere else in the world.

God's altar is holy, surrounded by awe and wonder. Yet even in that holy place you will find a welcome mat for all looking for a home—for all seeking to be close to their Maker. Because He is good, He's done all the work to ensure that you can walk closely with Him. That's why you can find peace and refuge near the very throne of the holy and good God.

PRAYER

God, You aren't pushing me away; You're calling me closer, to see You more fully and to love You more intimately. Draw me nearer.

THE VOICE THAT RAISES THE DEAD

Everything that is made easy to see can become light. This is why it is said: "Wake up, sleeper! Rise from death, and Christ will shine on you."
EPHESIANS 5:14 NCV

PRAYER

Jesus, I hear You calling me. "Wake up; rise from the dead!" Shine Your light on my heart and make Your love visible in me today.

MOST PEOPLE WAKE up by using an alarm of some fashion. When we're deep in sleep, we need a blasting noise to help pull us out of that slumber and get us up and going.

The same can be true of Jesus' voice when we are spiritually asleep, dead in our sins. You could have been asleep for a day or for seventy years. Either way, when you hear the voice of Jesus saying, *Wake up, sleeper!* Something within your soul stirs and you begin to awaken into new spiritual life.

God wants to touch your life and use you to raise up hope for your generation. It's time to let Jesus' voice lead you into the fullness of grace and joy and healing. In Jesus' hands, funerals turn into worship celebrations. He called your name when you were dead in your grave and told you to live again.

Listen to His voice today, and thank Him for His powerful love that changed your spiritual destiny.

CRYING OUT IN HARDSHIP

I called on your name, LORD, from the depths of the pit. You heard my plea.
LAMENTATIONS 3:55–56

NO MATTER HOW worn or weary we become, no matter what we're going through, we are never out of reach of our heavenly Father. God knows your situation, knows your loss, and knows your pain.

Whenever you face adversity, God's question for you isn't about how you plan to get yourself out of the depths of this pit. Instead, He wants to know if you believe in Him. That's all. If you do believe, He's inviting you to tell Him. He wants you to say, "God, in the midst of it, in the dark, in the uncertainty, I choose to cry out to You, my only hope of salvation."

God hears when you call, and He is moved by your cries. You are not forgotten, and you are never left to fend for yourself. God has a track record of coming through. He is a good God, and when you cry out to Him, He's ready to answer you with goodness and grace. He delights to bring relief, and you can trust that whatever iniquity you face, God will conquer it in the end. Evil will not stand. Turn to God and rest assured your eternity is secure.

PRAYER

God, from my depths I call on You. Answer me and come to my relief.

WORSHIP BRINGS
FAITH ABOVE FEAR

I will be glad and rejoice in you; I will sing the praises of your name, O Most High.
PSALM 9:2

PRAYER

Father, when life is pressing in with fear and worry, give me a song to sing in the night and I will praise You.

WHEN YOUR HEART is tired and your soul is weary, pause and look up at the One who made you. As you turn your eyes and heart toward Jesus, you can reflect on who He is and what He's done. You can worship Him. It's our worship that keeps the eyes of our heart on God and drives away the shadows that press all around.

With God is in view, worship is possible regardless of your circumstances. When worship flows, things change, because worship is one of the greatest weapons that pierces the darkness. Songs of praise in the darkest of nights have the power to pierce through the shadows and lead you back into the light.

When you worship, faith rises above fear. Wonder rises above worry. The more you reflect on the person of Jesus and the work of the cross, the more you have access to true peace, confidence, and joy. So sing, however downcast or weary your soul may feel. Jesus is near and He is listening.

ROOTED IN SCRIPTURE

"Keep this Book of the Law always on your lips;
meditate on it day and night, so that you may
be careful to do everything written in it."
JOSHUA 1:8

HAVE YOU EVER considered all the verses that instruct you to place Scripture firmly in your mind? Reflect on these examples today:

Psalm 119:11 tells you to store up God's Word in your heart, that you might not sin.

Colossians 3:16 says to let God's Word dwell in you richly.

Hebrews 4:12 describes God's Word as living and active.

Deuteronomy 11:18–19 encourages you to put Scripture into your heart and mind, writing it on hands and foreheads, teaching it to your children, and talking about it at home.

Psalm 119:32 encourages you to run in the pathways of God's commands—for He sets your heart free.

When Jesus was tempted in the wilderness, how did He refute the Enemy? By quoting Scripture back to the Evil One. "It is written . . . it is written . . . it is written."

What steps can you take today to plant Scripture deeper in your heart?

PRAYER

God, I want a life anchored in Your Word so that I can live the life You've called me to. Grant me the discipline and fortitude to pursue this holiest of tasks.

THE JOY OF HIS GLORIOUS PRESENCE

To him who is able to keep you from stumbling and to present you before his glorious presence without fault and with great joy—to the only God our Savior be glory, majesty, power and authority, through Jesus Christ our Lord, before all ages, now and forevermore! Amen.

JUDE 1:24–25

JESUS HAS GIVEN you all you need for life and godliness. He has already won the war on sin, defeating death, hell, and the grave once and for all.

Ultimately, if we want to counter our sinful nature, we need to fix our eyes on Jesus. Start small, fight distractions, and begin by replacing impure thoughts with ones that line up with the character and nature of God.

Most importantly, remember that the peace of God—the one that Paul said surpasses all understanding—will protect your mind and heart. This peace is how God keeps you from stumbling and presents you to Himself blameless and pure. When you experience this peace, your spirit, like Jude, will be poised to cry out, "All glory, majesty, power and authority be Yours, God!"

PRAYER

Lord, Your strength is stronger than any of my shortcomings. I can't rescue myself; You are able to pull me out of the pit and keep me from stumbling. Thank You for the confidence that comes from Your great joy.

AIMING FOR A LIFE
OF OBEDIENCE

*Take captive every thought to make
it obedient to Christ.*
2 CORINTHIANS 10:5

OUR THOUGHTS CAN often get away from us. Sometimes, a lie we believe, like that we are unlovable, can start to spiral deeper into our souls. Other times, our thoughts lead to anxiety or anger. Thoughts can be hard to corral, much less make obedient to Christ. But it is possible for you today.

How? By taking your thoughts captive.

You take thoughts captive when you bind them in Jesus' name, aligning your Spirit with His in prayer and power. It might sound something like this: "God Almighty, I bind this thought in the name of Jesus. I take captive this thought because You commanded me to. I'm using the power that's available to me by the Holy Spirit, and I'm choosing to live in agreement with You. This thought is taken captive. The thought holds no power over me."

When a thought is obedient to Christ, it brings you freedom and brings God glory. Your obedience fulfills your soul and elevates His name. That is why you capture your thoughts and submit them to the authority of Jesus.

PRAYER

God, teach me to obediently pursue Your holiness through the transformative power of a renewed mind. For Your glory, I will fight to take my thoughts captive.

209

GRACE AND COMPASSION

Yet the LORD longs to be gracious to you; therefore he will rise up to show you compassion.
ISAIAH 30:18

MANY OF US are not the best at receiving gifts. *It's too much. I can't reciprocate. I don't deserve it.*

If we're not careful, this kind of thinking can inform how we approach God's grace. We certainly can't repay God for the gift of salvation, so our shame tells us that either we don't deserve to be in God's kingdom or that we have to work hard enough to repay God so the scales are balanced out.

But shame doesn't get to write your story—God does. And because of Jesus' work on the cross, He's declared that you can receive His goodness and forgiveness, no shame attached.

When you reject God's grace and feed your guilt, you're saying, "My opinion about what I should get trumps God's opinion about what He wants to give to me." Instead, choose to let God bless your heart. Trust that He longs to be gracious and compassionate toward you today.

A TOUGH LOVE

They disciplined us for a little while as they thought best; but God disciplines us for our good, in order that we may share in his holiness.

HEBREWS 12:10

IT DOESN'T FEEL good to be disciplined. But it's far easier to accept the accountability when it's coming from someone you respect.

When you ponder your heavenly Father, it is essential to understand and appreciate that God's love can be a tough love when it needs to be. He is exceedingly tender, but He's not a pushover. He loves you enough to speak sternly when appropriate, to always tell you the truth, and to discipline you when your decisions are leading you to a shipwreck. His motive will always be pure and rooted in love, but God will go to great lengths to ensure your best.

If God shows you tough love, it's not to hurt you. It's to move you toward holiness and to lead you into good. He's the One who was shattered on the cross so He could offer you a love that's indestructible, a love that will be yours from here to eternity. Don't push away; instead embrace His tough love.

PRAYER

God, I am grateful that You love me enough to correct me when I am going astray. Keep me on the straight path and guide my steps toward holiness.

FEAR IS NO MATCH FOR PERFECT LOVE

There is no fear in love. But perfect love drives out fear, because fear has to do with punishment. The one who fears is not made perfect in love.
1 JOHN 4:18

WHEN YOU INVITE God into your worry and doubts, you begin to dwell in an abiding relationship with Jesus, and your operating system shifts. Instead of fear being the motivator for your life, you start with love.

Did you catch that in today's verse? When you experience and internalize the perfect love of God, there is no room for fear because perfect love drives out fear. And once fear is gone, you no longer have the pressing need for control. Instead, you can be free to fully surrender and submit to the perfect love of God because you trust that His love is not only His best offering; it is what's best for you! And without that thread of control, there is nothing to worry about.

When you embrace God's perfect love, you find yourself with the freedom to confidently proclaim, as David did in Psalm 27:1, "The LORD is my light and my salvation—whom shall I fear?"

PUTTING YOUR STORY IN GOD'S HANDS

Put on the new self, which is being renewed in knowledge in the image of its Creator.
COLOSSIANS 3:10

IT DOESN'T MATTER where you're from, what you've been through, or what you've done—God is at work in your story, and He is bringing His plans to completion in your life.

You might feel like your whole book hasn't gotten off to a very good start, or maybe you feel like you have a couple of bad chapters. But there's not a decision you've made that Jesus cannot turn around for His glory and for your good.

It's easy to get stuck in regrets. But God is in the business of calling us up and out of our old ways. He tells us that when we put our faith in Him, He makes us a new creation. The old is gone. Done away with. True, there are still consequences. But the condemnation? Gone. It's taken away, as far as the east is from the west.

God is an expert Author, and His power allows Him to rewrite the narrative of your story for His redemptive purpose. So put it all in His hands today. Let Him write the perfect ending as only He can.

PRAYER

God, thank You for writing me into Your story. With a grateful heart I put on my new self and stand firm in Your love for me.

SUSTAINING GRACE FOR EVERY SEASON

Surely God is my salvation; I will trust and not be afraid. The LORD, the LORD himself, is my strength and my defense; he has become my salvation.
ISAIAH 12:2

EVERY DAY, WE have the opportunity to truly embrace this incredibly simple yet incredibly profound reality: Jesus is enough. This promise acknowledges there won't always be happy endings to our resurrection stories, at least not here on earth. Things break in this life and can't always be repaired. Not every story has a happy conclusion. We don't understand the reasons God allows grief to come into our lives, but it does.

Yet, within our journey, Jesus can become enough for us. This is called *sustaining grace*, a moment-by-moment grace. It's the type of grace that God offers for every moment of intense grief, frustration, sorrow, agony, or pain. This grace is a tailor-made grace specially designed for each person. It does not transfer over, and it's never repeated exactly the same way, and it's not experienced the same from person to person.

This grace is specific. Timely. Personal. And you can be sure that God will provide His sustaining grace for you if and when you need it.

GOD IS GOING PUBLIC
WITH HIS LOVE

And so we know and rely on the love God has for us.

1 JOHN 4:16

YOU MIGHT FEEL like there are days when you don't see or experience God's love. So how can you remind yourself of His deep, abiding care for you? Scripture gives you example after example to underscore how much and how intimately God loves you.

God shows His love for you in that while you were still a sinner, Christ died for you (Romans 5:8).

Nothing can separate you from God's love. Absolutely nothing (Romans 8:37–39).

God's love for you is so great, it surpasses human knowledge. The love of Christ is amazingly wide and long and high and deep (Ephesians 3:17–19).

God loves you so much He's engraved your name on the palms of His hands. He never forgets about you (Isaiah 49:15–16).

God's love delights over you with singing and rejoicing (Zephaniah 3:17).

Can you see it? Your heavenly Father is crazy about you and willing to go public with His love.

Yet all that love is for naught if you don't receive it and live in it.

PRAYER

God, I receive Your love fully and without fear today. Holy Spirit, transform this knowledge into belief, that I would be immovable in this great truth.

GOD FINISHES WHAT HE STARTS

Being confident of this, that he who began a good work in you will carry it on to completion until the day of Christ Jesus.
PHILIPPIANS 1:6

PRAYER

Jesus, You have never left me on my own because You are finishing what You started. May that truth shape the way I view myself today.

HAVE YOU EVER felt like you'll never *truly* change? Like you've stalled out and have no more strength left to take the next step forward?

The apostle Paul told us that what God starts in you and in me, He will bring to completion. He is faithful and steadfast. But we aren't told *how* God does that. We don't get a list of a dozen ways that God is actively changing you. He just points back to the *who*.

You may have been in your valley for a long time. You may have been listening to the lies of the Enemy for weeks, or months, or even years. You might have tried every method or tip along your journey. But before you give up, embrace this simple truth: Jesus is with you. In the valley. In the fight. In the struggle. He is *with* you.

Because He is with you, you can proclaim, as Paul wrote in Romans 8:31, "If God is for us, who can be against us?"

DEATH IS DEFEATED

He will swallow up death forever. The Sovereign Lord will wipe away the tears from all faces; he will remove his people's disgrace from all the earth.
ISAIAH 25:8

YOU CAN LIVE with the assurance there is a day on the horizon when death will be defeated once and for all. That's what the prophet Isaiah promised as he looked centuries ahead to the eternity-shaping work of Jesus when He died, was buried, and rose from the grave.

Paul also described this final victory in 1 Corinthians 15:57 when he wrote, "But thanks be to God! He gives us the victory through our Lord Jesus Christ."

Victory in the above verse is translated from the Greek word *nikos*. It specifically connotes victory that has come about due to a conquest. Jesus conquered all the powers of darkness and sin so that these powers will never again rule over any believer. The overall battle has been won.

In your spiritual life, Jesus gives you the same nikos. He gives you His accomplished work on the cross, the defeat of sin. Therefore, you can move forward in faith. From this foundation of victory, you now fight. That's your mindset to prayerfully embrace today.

PRAYER

Jesus, Your victory is my victory. You broke the power of hell and the grave so that I might stand and live in that line of eternal conquest today.

JUSTICE BELONGS TO THE LORD

Bless those who persecute you; bless and do not curse.
ROMANS 12:14

PRAYER

Lord, help me lay down my vengeance, trusting fully that You will make all things right.

WHEN YOU LOOK out at all the brokenness in the world, it can be tempting to get angry and try to take matters into your own hands. But human justice will never lead to righteous worship.

The way we righteously deal with our anger is by aligning ourselves with God's justice. He gives us the power to make peace with other people. He is the avenger of all injustice and all wrong in the world. One day God will right every wrong. And He's going to be fairer about it than you or I could ever be. He's going to be more comprehensive about it. The situation will find true justice, true peace, true reconciliation.

To relinquish avenging to the Lord is not to sweep our unresolved conflicts under the rug. There may be a needed step of confrontation, open communication, or restitution. But we must approach any such process from the position of forgiveness. Our freedom comes from anchoring our hope in the fact that our great God defends us and rights all wrongs.

Therefore, while you are waiting on God's justice, you can operate *from* forgiveness, not *for* it.

THE ANCHOR OF GLORIOUS GRACE

*Because your love is better than life, my lips will
glorify you. I will praise you as long as I live,
and in your name I will lift up my hands.*
PSALM 63:3–4

PRAYER

Jesus, thank
You for Your
love that
saved me even
when I wasn't
worshiping
You. Draw me
closer, that
I may praise
You as long
as I live.

WHAT DO YOU cling to when things get shaky? Often,
we reach toward—and end up worshiping—what we
think is the strongest, most stable thing in our lives.
If you think your job provides your security, you
might worship that. What about your family? Spouse?
Maybe your bank account? These are all too common
anchors people hold on to for steadiness and security.

But there is one anchor that is stronger than any
earthly alternative. When God's radical grace drops
down into your heart, you become connected to the
glory of God. And in light of His glory, you begin to
find true stability. Strength. Contentment. Joy.

The way you worship is often connected to the
worth of your anchor, and the radical grace of God
is the most worthy one of all. It always demands our
extravagant worship.

Are you pursuing this type of worship today? If
not, ask God to sink His anchor of glory deeper into
your soul.

GOD IS PURSUING YOU TODAY

Because this brother of yours was dead and is alive again; he was lost and is found.
LUKE 15:32

TRYING TO PLEASE God or earn His approval by your own strength is like running on a treadmill— you're putting out a lot of work and effort, but you're ultimately not getting anywhere.

In the parable of the prodigal son, the older brother thought he was loved because he showed up to work every day. He totally missed that he was loved simply because he was a son of the father. He was unfortunately toiling to get something he already had.

Through Jesus, God has already shown you how much He loves you. Yes, you are still going to make mistakes, and you will still need to work hard to live a holy life that aligns with God's grace. So you can step off the treadmill of working in your own strength.

God is pursuing you today. He doesn't want to lecture or condemn you. He wants to tell you that He loves you and that He is ready for you to come home. Take a step toward Him. Confess your sins and turn toward home. He'll be waiting for you the moment you turn toward Him.

THE BLUEPRINT OF HUMILITY

Have the same mindset as Christ Jesus: Who, being in very nature God, did not consider equality with God something to be used to his own advantage.

PHILIPPIANS 2:5–6

IF THERE IS anything that's making you anxious, humble yourself before God. Humility doesn't outright abolish anxiety. Only the power of the blood of Jesus in your life can help you put an end to anxious thoughts. But humility is a key that opens the door to the place where we can cast our anxieties on God. Humility puts us under God's mighty hand and allows us to exchange our anxiety for Jesus' peace.

We can make this exchange because Jesus Himself embraced humility. We see in Philippians 2 that though Jesus was God from the beginning of time, He humbled Himself to take on the form of humanity. He then went even further through His obedience to death, even to the cross.

Because Jesus humbled Himself so completely, God exalted Him to the highest place and gave Him the name that is above every name.

In doing this, Jesus' example has given us the blueprint of humility, and we are invited to live that out, both in our relationships with others and in our relationship with God.

PRAYER

Jesus, thank You for modeling humility so that I may follow in Your example. I surrender my pride in exchange for Your power.

SATISFIED IN CHRIST

You open your hand and satisfy the
desires of every living thing.
PSALM 145:16

HERE'S A CANDID truth many of us have learned the hard way: you will never find true fulfillment in the things of this world.

It's unfortunately all too common to look at a worldly source of provision—our jobs, our relationships, our social standing—and believe that these avenues will provide the contentment we seek. But as good as they may be, these things don't last. And when they begin to fade, if the stash is running low or just about finished, then we can find ourselves in a free fall of anxiety or sadness.

Every worldly thing is fleeting, but God is not, and He provides by His own supernatural means. Rest assured, He is continually working out His miraculous plan—even though we may forget it, and even when our faith is too small to trust God for miracles.

Only God can truly satisfy your desires and provide for you. Turn to Him and ask for what you need. Don't look to the left or right; instead, look up to God and let Him fulfill you today.

PRAYER

God, You have provided for me at every turn of the way. I have never gone needy while under Your care, so remind my heart again that You satisfy every good desire to its fullness.

AUGUST

BREAKING OUT OF THE NEGATIVE

We seemed like grasshoppers in our own eyes, and we looked the same to them.
NUMBERS 13:33

PRAYER

God, You will sustain me in every unknown. Help me uproot the things that are not giving me life and sow Your holiness there instead.

IT'S EASIER TO look for the negatives in a situation rather than focusing on the positives. Think of the last time you stepped into a situation you were uncertain about. You can probably still remember the things that didn't meet your expectations.

This was true for the people of God when they first entered the land God had promised to give them. It felt like a risky situation—the enemies were vast, the cities seemed strong, and the Israelite spies came back to the people with fear, complaining, and all-around negativity.

They forgot God had already promised them victory. They forgot that He was with them in every situation. God wanted them to trust that He would provide every blessing and answer their fears.

The same is true for you today. Victory can be yours. Right now. Victory is about trusting that God will fulfill what He has promised and provide beyond what you can imagine. Choose to toss out the negative thoughts that do not coincide with the heart of God, and commit to focusing on His power and goodness.

PRAYING WITH CHILDLIKE FAITH

"Therefore I tell you, whatever you ask for in prayer, believe that you have received it, and it will be yours."

MARK 11:24

ONE OF THE best aspects about seeing kids follow Jesus is listening to the way they pray. They ask God for everything they can think of! In the mind of a child, there is nothing the God of the universe can't do.

As we grow up, we seem to lose a bit of that pure and simple faith. So much of the time we let thoughts of *No way* or *That's impossible* inform our perspective and even our prayers. We forget we're walking in relationship with a God who was known by the Israelites in the Old Testament as "Yahweh." He is the great I AM. Nothing is too hard for Him.

So come to God in prayer and don't hold back! Believe again that He is the God of the impossible. What are you hesitant to ask for in your life? What's the most radical wish you have for Him? Petition to God for that today. He may not answer exactly how you'd expect, but you can be sure that He will hear and He will answer you because you are His child.

PRAYER

God, hear my heart today. I don't want to hold anything back. Answer me in Your good and perfect timing.

IN IT FOR THE LONG HAUL

Therefore, my dear brothers and sisters, stand firm. Let nothing move you. Always give yourselves fully to the work of the Lord, because you know that your labor in the Lord is not in vain.
1 CORINTHIANS 15:58

PRAYER

God, I don't want a quick fix; I want a heart that is content in You. Give me grace today for a long obedience in the same direction.

OUR WORLD OPERATES at a sprint pace. We want fast fixes. Instant gratification. Quick resolutions to our problems. But when it comes to matters of the soul, things cannot be rushed or fixed with a snap of a finger.

Things like jealousy, pride, or anger have never been overcome and defeated with a little spiritual duct tape. Becoming more like Jesus isn't an overnight process. It takes time. Intentionality. It requires that you abide in Him.

The counteragent for sin isn't quick bursts of holiness. It's the continual digging into the Word of God. It's receiving His good gifts and dwelling on what they tell us about God—that He is trustworthy, engaged, loving, and near to you.

The more you receive and the more you invest back into your relationship with God, the more you'll truly know Him. The more you'll look like Him. If you want to put your sins and struggles to death, commit to the long haul, and freedom will come along the way as you steadily pursue God.

BECOMING
SPIRITUALLY ALIVE

"I give them eternal life, and they shall never perish; no one will snatch them out of my hand."
JOHN 10:28

IF YOU WANT to live a fulfilling life, build your life on Jesus. It's as simple as that. John laid it out for us: "Whoever has the Son has life; whoever does not have the Son of God does not have life" (1 John 5:12). Do you know you have Jesus in your life? To ask it another way, are you alive in Christ?

In following Jesus, we realize we fall short of the glory of God. God is perfect, and He can't have anything to do with sin, so we are initially separated from God. Spiritual death overtakes us. But the good news is that Jesus Christ came to earth. He lived on earth for thirty-three years. He was crucified. He died. He was buried in a borrowed tomb. And then Jesus was miraculously raised to life again, all so we can have eternal life.

You are in that narrative. You were on His radar when He was accomplishing eternal salvation. Don't waste another minute looking anywhere else for fulfillment. Only in Jesus can you have the fullness of life.

PRAYER

Jesus, I choose today to follow You with all that I am. Thank You for calling me and for saving me, that I may have life to the fullest.

THE POWER OF A SONG

*About midnight Paul and Silas were praying
and singing hymns to God, and the other
prisoners were listening to them.*
ACTS 16:25

PRAYER

God, lift my
eyes to You
and off my
surroundings.
May others
around me
see that You
are my go-to
response in
every high
and low.

WHEN THINGS AREN'T going your way, what is your go-to response? Some people complain about the circumstances. Some shut down. Others avoid the situation altogether. But have you ever considered singing?

That's what Paul and Silas did in Acts 16. They were in the middle of a prison, at midnight, at the end of their ropes. They had no other options. What else was there to do but to cry out to God? As they sang their hymns of praise, all the prisoners listened, but the prisoners weren't the only ones. Heaven, too, was listening. Suddenly, the walls started to shake. Chains started to break. The prison door swung open, and the prisoners were eventually set free. Even the jailer and his family were saved and baptized. All because of the extravagant worship from these two men in the most unlikely of circumstances.

When the darkness closes in, when life doesn't add up, when you cannot make sense of your circumstances . . . sing. Choose to make worship your response to hard things, and let God do the rest.

ONE LITTLE WORD
CHANGES EVERYTHING

*For God so loved the world that he gave his
one and only Son, that whoever believes in
him shall not perish but have eternal life.*
JOHN 3:16

AUG 6

PACKED INSIDE THIS amazing love declaration is one little word, an incredibly potent little descriptor. Do you know the word?

So. God soooooooooo loved . . .

The text could just as aptly read, "God loved the world." Yet this tiny word *so* is added, a word so small it's almost completely overlooked in the text. But we cannot miss it—because its ramifications for us are huge. We need to camp out in "so land" and soak in the implications of why a great God would add such a tiny word to one of the most definitive proclamations of His love in the whole Bible.

He's trying to get through to us. He didn't merely love us. He *so* loved us. And that two-letter descriptor packs a terrific punch. He really, really valued and prized you to the point that He gave His ultimate treasure to hold you in His holy arms. God's love is not vague or general. His love for you is an intense, specifically applied love, and it leads to eternal life.

PRAYER

God, may Your abundance of love bring confidence and joy to my soul today. May I know more truly Your great love.

THE ONLY SUSTENANCE

"I am the bread of life. He who comes to Me shall never hunger, and he who believes in Me shall never thirst."
JOHN 6:35 NKJV

IF YOU'RE A thrifter visiting a yard sale or antique store, you're looking for value in things that other people may have overlooked—for more than what meets the eye.

Similarly, Jesus constantly sees value where others don't. He looks in unexpected places. At the poor and the downtrodden, the meek and those without power, and those for whom life hasn't worked out as hoped. Jesus sees great value in them, and He provides for them.

Jesus' answer in Scripture to people who are overlooked is not to take from them. He invites them to places of prominence and importance in His overall story. God looks at the people who are lowly and says, *Do you realize how incredibly important you are?*

You may feel low in your journey right now. You might feel worn down and heavy-laden. If that's you, know that Jesus is committed to taking care of your needs. In Him, you no longer need to hunger for peace or thirst for contentment. Allow Him to be your sustainer.

A NEW MINDSET

*For all of you who were baptized into Christ
have clothed yourselves with Christ.*

GALATIANS 3:27

TODAY, LET'S UNPACK what it means to be connected with Christ and His victory.

Second Corinthians 5:17 says we are "in Christ" and a "new creation," and in Galatians 3:26–28 we learn that we are "clothed" with Christ. This means that Jesus makes us brand new, and we're completely enfolded by the righteousness of Christ.

Further, Colossians 3:3 refers to our lives as "hidden with Christ." Imagine a hidden room in a house, or a hidden pocket inside a coat. When something is hidden, it's both concealed and secure. Our brand-new righteousness isn't fleeting. It's protected and safe. Train your mind and heart to believe that you are a new creation. Your righteousness is safe because of Christ.

There's more. Ephesians 2:6 says, "God raised us up with Christ and seated us with Him in the heavenly realms." That means we are united with Christ in victory. Since Christ was brought up from the grave, we are brought up together with Him also. That's how closely connected we are with Christ. Whatever Jesus has won, we have won also.

PRAYER

Lord, Your victory is my victory. May peace settle over my heart today because I am hidden in You.

PRAYERS THAT MOVE THE HEART OF GOD

"And when you pray, do not keep on babbling like pagans, for they think they will be heard because of their many words."
MATTHEW 6:7

PRAYER

God, thank You that You've made a new way to worship You—in a right and real relationship with Your Son.

HAVE YOU EVER felt like you're missing the fullness of drawing near to Jesus in prayer? Like you don't know the right words to say? Maybe you see other people worshiping Jesus through prayer and think, *Am I doing something wrong?*

If you are feeling discouraged, take heart. Learning to commune with God in prayer takes time and practice. We can easily get knocked off track when our prayerful pursuit of God starts to become a performance. Prayer isn't about how you lift your hands or say the kinds of words you think would impress your Christian friends. It's about what's going on in your heart.

More than the right *methods*, God wants you to embody the right *mentality*. He wants to break you out of the trap of *how* and lead you into a new direction of worship and prayer—the *why*—where your heart is alive and afire for Him. That's where you begin to pray prayers that move the heart of God.

THE SCARS ARE STILL
ON HIS WRISTS

*You, Lord, are forgiving and good, abounding
in love to all who call to you. Hear my
prayer, LORD; listen to my cry for mercy.*
PSALM 86:5–6

HOW DO YOU make the shift toward truly loving and blessing even those who hurt you, who persecute you, or who knock you down? You can begin by asking God to help you approach others with compassion and empathy.

When you near the end of your time on earth, you will never regret letting go of wrongs and forgiving others in the same way your Father has forgiven you. After all, the only reason you have eternal life is because He has forgiven you.

Rather, when you near the end of your life you will only regret the bitterness you harbored and the anger you held on to while on earth. When you get to heaven and see the risen Jesus, scars still marking His wrists and side, you will wish you'd trusted Him more to empower you to turn the tide of pain and loss and take your place as an agent of a better kingdom. When you see the mighty throne of God and understand fully that all justice rests in His hands, you'll wish you had extended more olive branches of peace to those around you.

PRAYER

God, break my heart for what breaks Yours. You show me that forgiveness is an abounding goodness, so empower me to be gracious today.

233

THE CROSS PROVES HOW MUCH GOD LOVES US

Don't be deceived, my dear brothers and sisters.
Every good and perfect gift is from above.
JAMES 1:16–17

PRAYER

Lord, You have given everything so that I may walk with You. I exalt You today and glorify Your name.

HAVE YOU EVER considered the tremendous benefits that exist for us on this side of Eden? Yes, we're living in a fallen, sin-stained, corrupted world. We're far from paradise. But we're also living with the knowledge of how far God Almighty will go for us.

If you're not careful, you can begin to look at the cross as ordinary and commonplace—as just another part of the story—when in reality, the cross *is* the story. It's everything.

For a long time, people who followed God had to look forward with faith that God would right every wrong and win the ultimate battle against sin. But for you, it's not theoretical or hopeful thinking. It has happened. Jesus died and rose again. The cross is proof of God's love for you.

The cross was the final sacrifice. It was the good and perfect gift, the ending hammer blow to sin and death. It is the invitation through which you find intimacy with God and the full requirement of your wage of sin. Think again about the cross today, and let its power fuel you to worship and glorify Jesus.

BEAUTY FROM PRESSURE

For you, God, tested us; you refined us like silver. . . .
You let people ride over our heads; we went through fire
and water, but you brought us to a place of abundance.
PSALM 66:10, 12

GOD IS AN artist. All of creation reveals His intentionality and beauty. Nature is His ongoing work of art—always in flux, developing and changing under His constant eye.

We can see in different areas of His creation that part of His design involves using pressure and tension to bring beauty to the surface. A diamond is a great example of this. One of the most beautiful stones forms only under the right combination of extreme temperatures and incomprehensible pressure. Or consider the Grand Canyon, carved by the strain of the Colorado River coursing through its channels.

When it comes to our lives, most of us would rather avoid periods of pressure and tension. We want beauty, but we don't always enjoy the process. But this is what His refinement often looks like.

As you experience the pressures of life, look for opportunities to shift your understanding of what God is doing. Pray that God would refine your heart and deepen your trust.

PRAYER

God, help me to embrace times of testing and pressure, knowing that through them You are creating something beautiful in me for Your glory.

MORE DELIGHT, LESS FEAR

The LORD your God is with you, the Mighty Warrior who saves. He will take great delight in you; in his love he will no longer rebuke you, but will rejoice over you with singing.
ZEPHANIAH 3:17

PRAYER

Father, Your voice comforts my soul. I rejoice in You because You first rejoiced in me.

THE PERFECT LOVE of God drives out fear and leads us to surrender our idea of control, which then leads to worry being replaced by worship. The more we discover about the love of God, the more worship we give to Him.

The amazing part of this reality is the more we delight in God, the more we discover that He also delights in us. That may be hard to embrace, but it's true. While He is fully content in and of Himself and doesn't need anything from us, He chooses to lavish us with His love and to rejoice over us.

God takes great delight in *you*. He quiets all forms of worry and anxiety with His perfect love. Whenever you are tempted to listen to the noise of the world, pulling you back into fear, remember that God says He rejoices over you with singing. His voice is all you need. His delight is your life. His love is your victory.

A FATHER TO THE FATHERLESS

Sing to God, sing in praise of his name,
extol him who rides on the clouds; rejoice
before him—his name is the LORD.

PSALM 68:4

IF YOU HAVE unprocessed anger in your life, it can often stem from feelings of betrayal or belittlement. It's possible the person who hurt you was an authority figure: a parent, a teacher, a boss. Their words may have marked you. Yet Jesus' voice speaks above it all. In His eyes, you are loved and safe, secure and significant because of Him. Thanks to Jesus, you have everything you need. Thanks to Jesus, you are loved and adored.

In the Psalms, we see David reveling in this love of God. David knew he didn't want anger to get the last word in his story, so he turned to God in song. This realignment to a posture of worship allowed David to find joy, no matter what had been said or done to him by others.

When you remember God's character, that He is a father to the fatherless and a defender of widows and orphans, your heart expands because this same God chose you. He loves you and He is singing over you today.

PRAYER

Lord, I sing a new song today. I choose Your ways, not mine! Your freedom and Your grace alone steer my heart today.

A ROAD MAP TO AWE

*Lift up your hands in the sanctuary
and praise the LORD.*
PSALM 134:2

PRAYER

God, show me
a step today
and I will
take it. I want
to worship
You with all
that I have.

KING DAVID OFFERS us a road map for how to import more awe and wonder into your life. It begins with kneeling in God's presence, gazing at His glory, and lifting up your voice. God's majesty demands a song! Awe is the only natural response to the grace and glory and love that He's poured out on us.

Has the promise of good news become dull to your ears? Has the gospel lost its luster? Has the wonder of your salvation turned to apathy? Quiet your mind and focus on the King of kings. He is the One who promised a Savior for the world and offered you His one and only Son. He is the God of David, Esther, and Paul. When you see the faithfulness of God throughout the stories of Scripture and across the generations of Jesus followers, your heart finds new joy to bring honor and praise to God.

You never outgrow your need for worship. Sing to Him, and then sing again! How wondrous it is to know you serve a God who pours out mercy and grace onto you. Lift your hands in praise!

ON GOD'S RADAR

Do nothing out of selfish ambition or vain conceit.
Rather, in humility value others above yourselves.
PHILIPPIANS 2:3

HAVE YOU EVER done something good but then found yourself frustrated that nobody noticed or seemed to care? Maybe you've felt like your contribution was overlooked, or your service was underappreciated? You might feel unseen by the world, but you can trust that you are never off God's radar.

God made you with uniqueness and specificity. He knows your talents and giftings. He wove them into you. He knows your strengths and weaknesses. He wrote down all the days of your life in His book before you were born. He knows how you're wired, what you enjoy, and what brings you to life because He made you in His image, and He invites you to be a daughter or son of His kingdom.

You don't need affirmation or acceptance from others around you—you have everything you'll ever need from your perfect and loving heavenly Father. You can willingly take up humility in every interaction around you. When you do, you'll mirror Paul's words in Philippians 2:3 and find that your life begins to look more like Jesus'.

PRAYER

Jesus, empower me today both to know my worth in You and to willingly lay it down, that I might serve those You have called me to care for.

HEALED AND FORGIVEN

Be kind and compassionate to one another, forgiving each other, just as in Christ God forgave you.
EPHESIANS 4:32

GOD DESIRES TO give you "revelation sight"—an understanding that you are a loved child of a perfect Father. This sight is not just to see God for who He truly is but also to see the cross of Christ and the resulting power as a source of forgiveness and grace to share.

God wants you to know that you have true power through Him. Power not to tightly grip the past or to withhold forgiveness. Instead, you can let go of anger and offer the person or people who have hurt you God's grace, even if you think they don't deserve it.

Forgiveness is not easy work, and often the seemingly easier route is to try to lock your disappointment and anger away in a closet. After all, the process of forgiving someone who has wronged us is sometimes as painful as the hurt we experienced in the first place. But the healing that comes from releasing your past pain to God is worth the hurt, not only for your soul, but for the person you are forgiving as well.

PRAYER

Jesus, soften my heart and plant empathy within me. By Your power, may I forgive those who hurt me, just as You've forgiven me.

240

MADE BY AND FOR GOD

*For in him all things were created . . . all things
have been created through him and for him.*
COLOSSIANS 1:16

IN HIS WELL-KNOWN book *The Knowledge of the
Holy*, theologian A. W. Tozer said, "What comes into
our minds when we think about God is the most
important thing about us."

Tozer didn't need to know the ins and outs of
your story or mine because he knew what God says
about us in Colossians 1:16, where we find the cornerstone of this truth.

First, you were made *by* God. He is your source
of origin. You didn't make yourself. You didn't happen randomly or by some cosmic accident. Since God
made you, you are incredibly important, valuable, and
prized. Second, you were made *for* God. That's your
central purpose on planet Earth now and into forever.
The reason He made you was so you could connect
with Him in a vital relationship.

Since we were made *by* God and *for* God, our
hearts search for the God whom we were made *by* and
for. Our souls want to respond to Him. If you are feeling that tug, lean into Him. He is closer than you can
imagine, and He wants to satisfy you today.

PRAYER

Father, You
have imbued
purpose and
design into
my life. May I
seek You with
all I have.

CONTENT IN THE STILLNESS

"Be still, and know that I am God; I will be exalted among the nations, I will be exalted in the earth."
PSALM 46:10

FOR MOST OF us, the difficult thing about abiding—the ongoing constant communion with God—is that it takes time. Just as it's hard to pour water into a shaky cup, it is difficult for the peace of God to flow into a heart that's in constant motion. When we quiet ourselves and sit before Him—really sit and create space to surrender our fears, our anxieties, and our burdens to Him—it becomes easier to truly abide.

When we spend undistracted time with God, when we read His Word and meditate on His truth and His goodness, we begin to unlock something sacred in our souls.

When it comes to our worries, we don't need a solution. We need a Savior. Thankfully, we have one. His name is Jesus. He's not just a nice guy floating through the pages of history. Jesus is an undisputed champion, death defeater, cosmos Creator, matchless light that sets darkness to flight. Because of who He is, you can be still and *know* that He is God.

GIVING WHAT YOU HAVE

*"Here is a boy with five small barley
loaves and two small fish."*
JOHN 6:9

WHAT MAKES YOU feel like you have "enough"? Some of us look to the balance in our savings account to make us feel secure. Others look to a beautiful home or a stable job. But if all the material things in your life disappeared, would Jesus be enough?

When you trust that God will care for you, the hope is you become more like the small boy in John 6, whose limited resources were multiplied by Christ so that everyone would have *enough*. This boy did not hoard his food but instead gave freely, trusting that God's provision would continue.

Maybe there's a need that has been placed right in front of you. You may not be able to fill the entire need, but you can still give what you have and trust that God will do whatever He wants to with your offering. When Jesus is enough, you can give open-handedly, knowing He owns it all and He can provide everything you need.

PRAYER

Jesus, I don't want to live a stingy life, missing out on Your abundant generosity. I put all that I have in Your hands, believing that You are enough.

WORSHIP IS A LIFESTYLE

*Let everything that has breath praise
the LORD. Praise the LORD.*
PSALM 150:6

WORSHIP IS NOT just a genre on the radio or the songs we sing in church. While that can certainly be an expression of worship, at its core, worship is a lifestyle, one of deep and revelatory gratitude.

Worship is a lifestyle.

When you get this view of worship in mind, it becomes a game-changing reality for your relationship with God. No longer do you have to worry about how well you sing or how musically talented you are. God isn't looking for your creative prowess. He simply wants you to direct your thoughts and emotions toward Him. He wants your affection. Your desires. Your voice. He wants your heart and all that really matters to you.

Embrace a lifestyle of worship today, and as you experience a little bit of heaven here on earth, watch how it changes you. Worship sharpens our sight, putting everything into perspective. It can transform mundane moments into extraordinary opportunities for joy. You were created with His wonder pulsing through you. Let your life be an expression of it.

REFLECTING GOD'S GLORY

*And we all, who with unveiled faces contemplate
the Lord's glory, are being transformed into
his image with ever-increasing glory.*
2 CORINTHIANS 3:18

IN EXODUS 34, after Moses encountered the presence of the Lord on the mountaintop, his face shone bright like a light. God's presence was so powerful that it altered Moses' very appearance, demonstrating to every Israelite that he had been with the Lord Almighty.

On this side of the cross, we have access to God that Moses could only dream of. Because of the death and resurrection of Jesus, you have the freedom to boldly come up the holy mountain of God. As you experience His glory and begin to comprehend His holiness, you, too, will be transformed to become more like Him—until your spirit shines bright, just like Moses' face.

With every trip up the mountain, something will change in your heart. Every time you're with God, your soul will be altered. He promises to mold you into His likeness, and that is what the world needs more than anything—for every one of us to look more like God. He will shape your heart and strengthen your hands so that you can carry His glory wherever you go today.

PRAYER

God, show me Your glory and transform me, that I may reflect Your glory to those around me.

A MOMENT-BY-MOMENT GRACE

God is the strength of [our] heart[s].
PSALM 73:26

PRAYER

Jesus, I need
Your grace
right now.
Strengthen me.
Uphold me.
Lead me
in Your
good and
gentle paths.
Shepherd me.
Make me more
like You.

THE TIMES WHEN life feels impossible are often the times when we make the most progress and see the most expansion in our personal relationship with God.

In those moments, we find a God who is sufficient, relatable, and dependable. He's the Satisfier. Our flesh and hearts may fail. The things we seek to fill our lives may fail. We might even let ourselves down. But God is our portion, and He will never fail or falter.

God often meets us most powerfully when we are willing to admit that we don't have the resources to move past the moment we're in. There is no plan B. We've run out of all human options. That's where the miracle happens.

Jesus supplies us with what we need for the moment, for the day, for the season. And then He provides another grace after that and another grace after that. Grace isn't a onetime deposit. It's a moment-by-moment relationship with God, where we trust Jesus to be in us and through us and for us. We trust He will come through in His own time and in His own way.

ACCESS GRANTED

In him and through faith in him we may
approach God with freedom and confidence.
EPHESIANS 3:12

AS CHRISTIANS IN today's world, we can become complacent with the access we have to God and His Spirit. It's easy to forget that this level of communion hasn't always been available throughout history. We often lose perspective of how truly wondrous prayer and worship can be.

In the Old Testament, God's people celebrated different feasts and special days, one of which was called the Day of Atonement. On this day each year, only one person—the high priest—was permitted to go into the presence of God. No one else had access, because before the life of Jesus, it was too dangerous for sinful people to worship so close to a righteous God.

But on the day that Jesus died, the veil separating us from God ripped in two. In that moment, total access to the Father became available. Jesus' death brought about a new way of worship. No longer was God separated from man; He was near! Fill your heart with that miracle truth today. You have unfettered access to the God of the universe, so don't waste it by not worshiping Him with your whole life.

PRAYER

God, I don't take for granted that You've made a way for me to approach You. Thank You for being a God who breaks down barriers so that I may come to You in freedom and confidence.

INTIMACY IS THE WAY TO TRUE FULFILLMENT

*For now we really live, since you are
standing firm in the Lord.*
1 THESSALONIANS 3:8

FINDING FULFILLMENT IN Jesus is not about following a set of rules. At its core, the gospel message is not "Don't sin." No, the message of the cross is more so an invitation to "Come, walk with God." The centrality of the gospel is that, through the finished work of Christ, our sins are forgiven. We are new creations, and we can step into a relationship with God Almighty.

As you live closely with Jesus, you discover that you can trust God. You can look back on your life and see times He carried you, times He held you close, times He steered you clear of danger, and times He pulled you through. Intimacy with God is the way to true fulfillment and a firm foundation that sustains you no matter what.

How can you prioritize walking closely with God today? Consider spending a few minutes in prayer or reading a portion of Scripture. Choose something and draw near to God, trusting that joy and satisfaction await you.

COME NOW

In your love you kept me from the pit of destruction;
you have put all my sins behind your back.

ISAIAH 38:17

DO YOU BELIEVE in the deepest parts of who you are
that God's grace is for you? Or are you still allowing
guilt and shame to obscure your view of your heavenly
Father?

God doesn't desire your perfection—He desires
your humility. Your invitation to know Him isn't
predicated on your work—it's predicated on His. You
don't have to wait to approach God until you clean
up your life, master obedience, or memorize enough
Scripture. Those aren't God's terms. God's terms say
that His Son was *enough*. You can come now through
the blood and the finished work of Jesus. Come
through His death, come through His burial, come
through His resurrection, and find the gift of eternal
life and a relationship with the almighty God.

It's easy to say you believe in the sufficiency of
God, but has that belief actually sunk deep down into
your identity? Navigating the shame of your past and
the guilt of your present can be a long road, but you
do not need to walk that road alone. Come to Him
and let Him show you mercy.

PRAYER

God, my guilt
is taken care
of in Your life
and death.
I choose to
embrace the
open arms of
Your Son.

BRINGING GOD INTO FOCUS

This is how God showed his love among us: He sent his one and only Son into the world that we might live through him.
1 JOHN 4:9

MAYBE YOU'RE WEARING glasses or contacts to help make the words you're reading right now legible. Most people can't see everything perfectly, and the same is true for our study of the cosmos. In order to see the vastness of the universe clearly, we invented telescopes to help us see what's all around us.

While man-made telescopes are spectacular, have you ever thought about the greatest telescope that God gave to His people—the Word of God? The whole Bible zooms in on one central scene—the cross. On this cross hung not just one of us but God Himself in human flesh. His name? Jesus. He chose to come to earth, embodying God's indelible proclamation: *I love you.* His incomprehensible death provided a covering for our fallenness, His resurrection life bridging the way back to the arms of our Maker.

When you look through this telescope, you can see the wonder of the cross clearly, and your heart can't help but feel awe and gratitude for His glorious grace that saved you.

LIVING ON THE HEIGHTS

The Sovereign LORD is my strength; he
makes my feet like the feet of a deer, he
enables me to tread on the heights.
HABAKKUK 3:19

IF YOU'VE WRESTLED with the problem of suffering in the world, if the calamities of life have been a hurdle for you in faith, you're not alone. God Himself is aware of and empathetic to your suffering.

He not only is aware but is also near. If we're not intentional about remembering God's nearness, the pain of our current circumstances can cloud His promises for the days ahead. We can become trapped in our view of the present and use that limited view to interpret our future—a future where living at the height of God's blessing and joy doesn't seem possible.

When you dive deeply into His Word, you regain certainty of your future—one that is good and merciful and joyful. The Scripture reassures you of the hope of God and the sure victory that's coming. There is life ahead in God, and it is wonderful.

In the power of a sovereign God, you can scale any mountain. Go to any heights. Withstand any storm. By His strength, you can reach the high places of God and find joy in your Savior.

PRAYER

God, I dwell on Your promises today to contextualize my pain. Strengthen my feet and make light my victory.

251

POWER OVER YOUR PAST

*One thing God has spoken, two things have
I heard: "Power belongs to you, God, and
with you, Lord, is unfailing love."*
PSALM 62:11–12

FOR THOSE WHO are followers of Jesus, your life is
not going to be likened to a run-on sentence of "what-
ifs" and "buts" and "if onlys." You are going to know
that you belong to the God of the universe and that
nothing can thwart His purpose and plans for your
life. You are going to discover new power inside, the
very power of the Spirit of God. And your eyes are
going to be opened to understand that God's power
can restore what was lost through the power of forgiveness and grace.

Think about it this way: if Jesus can overwhelm
the grave and rise from the dead, if He can can-
cel the debt of sin you owe, if He can make peace
between you and a holy God, if He has the power to
free you from death and raise you up to eternal life,
then He can certainly give you power over your past.
It all begins when you surrender your heart to Him,
embracing forgiveness and stepping forward in grace.

PRAYER

God Almighty,
if You can
overcome
my grave, I
can know for
certain that
You are
strong and
loving enough
to see me
through
the rest of
my days.

THE GREAT EXCHANGE

That is why, for Christ's sake, I delight in weaknesses,
in insults, in hardships, in persecutions, in difficulties.
For when I am weak, then I am strong.

2 CORINTHIANS 12:10

TODAY'S SCRIPTURE IS a commonly misquoted and misunderstood verse. So I'd like you to read it again, this time focusing on the great exchange of power.

Maybe you've always heard that last line this way: "For when I am weak, then He (God) is strong." That is very true. God is strong. But Paul wrote "I."

I am strong. I am strong because Christ's power lives in me.

Do you want to be a stronger student, a stronger husband, a stronger wife, a stronger parent, a stronger employee, a stronger leader? Then celebrate your weakness by admitting your vulnerability. Let Jesus embrace you as you are. Accept the invitation to step into His love. Let Jesus infuse His strength into your life. Allow Jesus to give you the power to exchange your weakness for His strength and walk on supernatural waters. Jesus will invite you, then, to do things you could not do on your own—in His power.

PRAYER

Lord, I acknowledge my own weakness and act in Your holy strength as You empower me to live for Your glory.

253

WHEN JESUS IS ENOUGH

*Whom have I in heaven but you? And
earth has nothing I desire besides you.*
PSALM 73:25

PRAYER

Jesus, I want
to want You
more. Remove
any obstacles
today that are
hindering my
full devotion
to You.

WHEN JESUS IS not only your all, but all you have left, then you begin to truly embrace what it means to say that Jesus is enough.

Look how the psalmist articulated it. His heart was full of grief, and he had experienced trouble after trouble, yet even at the very bottom of life, he proclaimed to God in Psalm 73:26, "My flesh and my heart may fail, but God is the strength of my heart and my portion forever."

That's the cry of someone who knows that Jesus is enough. When He is enough, we focus on what we have, not on what we don't have, nor on what we still might lose. When Jesus is enough, we gaze intently on God and run to Him, not away from Him. When Jesus is enough, we realize our hearts were made for Him and that the Son of God isn't just a theological idea—He's a person, and not just any person.

Jesus is the person our hearts and souls were made for. Draw confidence from that truth today: your heart and soul can rest fulfilled. Repeat this to yourself throughout today: "I have enough!"

SEPTEMBER

A SURPASSING GREATNESS

I consider everything a loss because of the surpassing worth of knowing Christ Jesus my Lord, for whose sake I have lost all things. I consider them garbage, that I may gain Christ.
PHILIPPIANS 3:8

PRAYER

Lord, help me to focus on the right things, that I would gain Christ in my pursuit of You.

WHAT IS SITTING on the throne of your heart right now? What do you consider most important? In other words, what do you spend the majority of your time and energy pursuing?

There are a lot of things in life that vie for our attention and affection. Work, relationships, even hobbies and goals. It's not wrong to work hard, love your friends and family, and enjoy some fun moments along the way. Rather, in this text, Paul was encouraging us to consider our heart's priorities and ponder the *why* behind the *what*.

It's easy to make an idol out of earthly "treasures"—but Paul knew that if these good things sat down and got comfortable on your heart's throne, then your worship would become distorted, and your heart would be led off track.

To shift your focus away from earthly idols to the heavenly and holy, consider the surpassing greatness of knowing Jesus. Only when you see His unrivaled value can you truly allow Him to claim the throne of your heart.

STAYING CONNECTED
TO THE TRUE VINE

"I am the vine; you are the branches. If you remain in me and I in you, you will bear much fruit; apart from me you can do nothing."
JOHN 15:5

YOU CAN COUNTER anxiety by abiding in Christ. But what does that mean? It means that you remain with Jesus. Dwell with Him. That you stay in a constant posture of surrender and dependency. Not in your own strength and your own power, but in His.

How beautiful are the words of Jesus in John 15:5? We see right off the bat what our role is in this whole story. We are the branches. Jesus is the Vine. He's the fount of life. Of nutrients—of richness and vitality. He is our Source. We are the receivers.

As branches, our job is to remain. We are to stay connected to the Vine; and when we do, we bear much fruit.

What kind of fruit do you bear when you are connected to Jesus? Paul talked about it in Galatians: "The fruit of the Spirit is love, joy, peace, forbearance, kindness, goodness, faithfulness, gentleness and self-control" (5:22–23). That is what is possible for you today when you abide.

PRAYER

God, as I remain in You, bear much fruit in me that glorifies Your name and brings good into my life.

A WATERFALL OF BLESSING

Deep calls to deep in the roar of your waterfalls;
all your waves and breakers have swept over me.
PSALM 42:7

THE WATERFALL OF God's fatherly blessing is not like one of those thin, ribbonlike waterfalls you see on the side of the road while driving through the foothills. It's more like Niagara Falls, or the great Victoria Falls on the border between Zambia and Zimbabwe. His love is like a torrent—relentless and unending, unconditional and pure, gently roaring His blessing over your life. And His love is pouring down on you right now.

If you close your eyes for a moment, can you picture it? Can you see yourself standing under a steady flow of love, smiling as the crashing water of a perfect Father's blessing washes over you? In Christ, that's exactly where you are.

Here are some incredible facts about this blessing you can take comfort in today: You will always have enough of His blessing (2 Corinthians 9:8). You will never exhaust His love (Jeremiah 31:3). You will never fully deplete His goodness (Psalm 23:6). Every single day His mercy will awaken you (Lamentations 3:22–23).

THE REFINING
NATURE OF GOD

*He is before all things, and in him
all things hold together.*
COLOSSIANS 1:17

YOU ARE UNIQUELY made by God, and your life has a specific purpose that He set in motion before you were even born. You have been created intentionally, and in Jesus, all of God's plans for you hold together.

But as the pace of life increases, and things pile up, it's easy to find yourself straying from God. While it's true that Jesus is never far from you, sometimes God allows your life to be stripped down to the bones so you can reach for Him and find Him anew. When things are going great—when your deals are succeeding, when your relationships are smooth, when your bank accounts are in the black—that's when it's hardest to be closest to God. But as soon as things are stripped away, that's when you remember that it's only Jesus who holds all things together.

God wants you to live out your unique purpose because He has given you assignments that only you can fill. So don't look elsewhere for validation or value. With Jesus at your center, go boldly into today, trusting that God will lead you in every moment.

PRAYER

Jesus, thank You that I don't have to hold it all together. I place my life in Your capable, refining, and holy hands.

259

ECHOING THE PRAISE OF HEAVEN

Praise the LORD. Praise the LORD from the heavens; praise him in the heights above. Praise him, all his angels; praise him, all his heavenly hosts.
PSALM 148:1–2

AT THIS VERY moment, heaven is roaring with worship for Jesus. As you read these words, the greatest choir in the history of the world is singing and shouting praise to the King. But it doesn't stop there. God is extending an invitation for you, too, to join in that chorus. As you stand in awe before His throne, He calls you to join the angels and echo back that same praise with every fiber of your being.

This is the song of eternity: Holy, holy, holy! Worthy is the Lamb of God; the sacrifice for our sins, Jesus Christ who was slain but has been resurrected to new and permanent life forevermore. Hallelujah!

When this melody takes root in your soul, you can't help but declare the praises of the One who is worthy of all worship. You can't help but share this good news with the world and reorient your entire life around this one goal—to echo the sound of heaven to the lost and hurting here on earth.

TAKING HEART IN GOD'S POWER AND MIGHT

David said to the Philistine, "You come against me with sword and spear and javelin, but I come against you in the name of the LORD Almighty, the God of the armies of Israel, whom you have defied. . . . The battle is the LORD's, and he will give all of you into our hands."
1 SAMUEL 17:45, 47

PRAYER

Father, I may feel surrounded by towering troubles, but You are my ever-present help and light. Guide me today.

LIKE THE SHEPHERD David, you may be facing a Goliath; a nine-foot-tall behemoth in your life that is intimidating and threatening you night and day. You might be up against past hurts, present disappointments, or future fears. If your giant is looming, the walls can feel like they're closing in. Darkness can seem to be overtaking the light.

In the face of the seemingly impossible, fight to remember that the power of God remains greater than your giants. No matter the size of the problems. No matter the hits that keep coming at you from every side. By His strength, He's able to take them all out. The battle is His.

If some form of bondage has tied you up, if some attitude can't be shaken, if some thought darkens your mind, turn to Jesus. Take heart because none of these are a match for our giant-killing Savior.

A NEW ERA

"I will give you a new heart and put a new spirit in you; I will remove from you your heart of stone and give you a heart of flesh."
EZEKIEL 36:26

PRAYER

Lord, help me today to embrace Your revealed righteousness and to chase after that which truly brings me life.

WHEN SOMETHING TEMPTING is before you, what are the thoughts that go through your mind? Do you believe you have the power to fight back, or do you remember the times you've fallen short or given in, thinking that sin is just an inevitable part of what it means to be human?

Apart from Jesus, sin reigned over all of us. But now because of the cross, if you have called on His name, you are saved by grace. You are a brand-new creation. In Jesus Christ you are not the same as who you were before you were saved. Jesus has ushered in a new era by removing your old heart and giving you a new spirit.

Even though you have a new heart, you are still not immune to sin. But now, the power of the Spirit within you gives you a new desire and new authority to overcome sin and its shame. The next time temptation knocks at your door, remember you have the power to fight back and to choose holiness over sin.

CO-HEIRS WITH CHRIST

Now if we are children, then we are heirs—heirs of God and co-heirs with Christ, if indeed we share in his sufferings in order that we may also share in his glory.

ROMANS 8:17

IF YOU'RE FEELING lonely or like you don't belong where you're at, rest assured that God sent His Son so that you can have life and belong to a new family, that you could become a child in His kingdom. Fully adopted. Fully new. Fully alive in Him.

How do you become part of the family of God? You must simply confess that you have fallen short of God's best and accept the forgiveness the Father offers through the cross. When you do, the Spirit of God enters you and everything begins to shift in accordance with His perfect love. This new birth firmly grafts you into God's family tree as a child and as a coheir with Jesus.

Let that new reality settle into your soul today. God offers you a place in a new spiritual family. He invites you to call on Him as your Father—a Father who overflows in His love for you. One who hangs on your every word. One who delights to meet your every need. So even as you faithfully wait and pray that God would restore relationships here on earth, trust that you already belong in the family of God.

PRAYER

God, through Your Spirit I have full inheritance as one of Your children. Therefore, I call on You, knowing You will always come through for me.

A MOSAIC OF GRACE

*Out of his fullness we have all received
grace in place of grace already given.*
JOHN 1:16

PRAYER

God, thank
You that You
take every part
of my story
and work it
into a beautiful
mosaic of Your
grace and love.

IF YOU'VE EVER found yourself in an old church, you've likely walked under some magnificent stained glass windows. But have you ever stopped to consider how many different and unique pieces of broken glass each window comprises?

When you reflect on your life, you might see a hodgepodge of experiences that seemingly have no rhyme or reason. Maybe some parts of your past are a little rough around the edges—some you wish you could forget forever. But every experience you've had—your pain, joys, successes, defeats—is part of the mosaic of God's grace in your life.

God is an expert craftsman, and He knows how to fashion beauty from our brokenness. That's the gospel at work. God takes our shards and, in His infinite goodness and wisdom, He makes something majestic and beautiful out of our lives.

It's also the message of the church. A multitude of unique pieces coming together to reflect a great and beautiful image—Jesus. His grace is available to all, so go out and tell the world about the God who takes broken things and makes them whole.

FORGIVEN TO FORGIVE

Forgive as the Lord forgave you.
COLOSSIANS 3:13

WHEN YOU'VE BEEN hurt, forgiveness can feel like the last thing you want to offer to someone else. But forgiveness is where your new story begins. When Jesus was hanging on the cross, He looked at the very ones who drove the nails into His hands and feet, and He forgave them.

The trajectory of your eternity began to shift the moment you opened the door to God's forgiveness. In the same way, when you've received God's forgiveness, your healing finds its fullness when you allow God to help you reflect His forgiveness to those around you.

Forgiveness is not turning a blind eye to wrong. God didn't do that with our wrongs. He leveled them squarely onto the innocent life of His Son and punished our sinfulness to the full extent of the law. When God offers forgiveness, He isn't ignoring our shortcomings and rebellious ways. Instead, He's made a higher way of peace.

Because Jesus has forgiven you of everything you've done and possibly will do against Him, you can offer that same forgiveness to others when they hurt you.

PRAYER

Jesus, how could I not forgive someone after how much You've forgiven me? Help me embrace this truth to become a display of Your grace to everyone around me.

SEATED AND REIGNING

Fixing our eyes on Jesus, the pioneer and perfecter of faith. For the joy set before him he endured the cross, scorning its shame, and sat down at the right hand of the throne of God.

HEBREWS 12:2

YOU HAVE VICTORY in Christ. This is not mere preacher talk or church rhetoric. Jesus has already won. He's seated in the place of victory at the right hand of God (Hebrews 12:2). When eternity unfolds, Jesus won't return to earth to fight sin again. He'll return as the ultimate victor.

Because Jesus has won the victory over sin, you have access to this victory too. You are freed from sin's quicksand by living in your new identity. The power to live freely comes from your close association with Christ and His victory.

Our battle isn't won because the pressure lifts from our lives or because circumstances change. We will still walk through dark valleys over the course of our lives. No, the battle is won because of who walks with us.

Since Jesus is seated at the right hand of the throne of God, Scripture says that you are seated with Him. Strive for holiness today, but only as one who is already seated with Christ.

WORTHY WORSHIP

*Let them praise the name of the LORD, for
at his command they were created.*
PSALM 148:5

THE GOD OF the heavens, who created the oceans
and the mountains and the rainforests and every living thing—the God above all—knows your name. He
has moved heaven and earth to reconnect with you
through the grace that is in Jesus Christ. And when
that truth plants deep in your mind, and you allow
His grace to fill your lungs, the only natural response
is worship.

Worship comes in many forms. It comes in a song.
It comes on our knees. It comes in our giving, and it
comes in our obedience. Over the years, I've defined
worship as our response, both personal and corporate,
to God for who He is and what He's done, expressed
in and by the things we say and the way we live. It is a
continuous posture of the Christian life.

When we truly see God for who He is—awesome
in power and holy in love and affection—we can't
help but offer Him everything we have. And when
the Spirit rises within us, we join the chorus of heaven.
Does this kind of worship define your day-to-day living? If not, ask God to inspire your heart toward His
magnificent grace.

PRAYER

God, my heart
exalts You,
for You have
made me holy
through the
blood of Jesus.

FREEDOM STARTS WHEN HUMILITY SINKS IN

He makes me lie down in green pastures,
he leads me beside quiet waters.
PSALM 23:2

PRAYER

Good Shepherd, I lie down today in Your green pastures. Restore and nourish my soul as I stay close to You.

ALLOWING GOD TO lead our lives feels counterintuitive to our "do-it-yourself" way of living. We all tend to think we're pretty good at calling the shots and setting the course for our lives—that we deserve to be in total control.

God is trying to get our attention with Psalm 23, which is why the imagery of Psalm 23 is not meant to be flattering. Being referred to as a sheep is not a compliment. Sheep are not the smartest creatures and struggle to survive without oversight and direction.

Knowing this, notice the first thing the Shepherd does in this psalm—He makes us lie down in green pastures. Most of us don't like to be made to do anything, yet surrendering to God means we obey as He prompts. He's not looking for control or power in our lives. He's seeking to lead us to what truly satisfies.

You can come to Him daily and admit you need His help. You can breathe out your inability and breathe in His all-sufficiency. You can trust that He will steer you through the valley to the other side.

ALIVE BY GRACE

Jesus answered, "Very truly I tell you, no one can enter the kingdom of God unless they are born of water and the Spirit."

JOHN 3:5

HAVE YOU EVER accidentally locked yourself out of your house? If you have, you know you'll need the right key to get back inside.

When the Jewish religious leader Nicodemus met with Jesus, he was trying to figure out: What is the key that allows someone to get into the kingdom of God? Maybe you've wondered that too. What do you need to do or believe to get into God's kingdom?

Jesus' answer is that you have to be "born again."

Jesus knew that sin makes us spiritually dead, and the only way to become alive again is through the gospel of God's grace. That's why He called salvation a "new birth."

You don't get into God's family by being good enough or trying your best. You need a Savior to pull you from out of your grave and stand you back on solid ground. Thankfully, God has provided you that opportunity through Jesus, and if you believe in Him, you'll have the right key to enter the kingdom of God.

PRAYER

God, You have allowed me to be born again, and because of that my only response is to worship You.

THE ROOT OF TRUE JOY

*I rejoiced greatly in the Lord that at last you
renewed your concern for me. . . . I am not saying
this because I am in need, for I have learned
to be content whatever the circumstances."*
PHILIPPIANS 4:10–11

GOD ISN'T SLOW to showcase His generosity, blessing us and meeting our needs. But if we're to find genuine contentment, we must be careful not to make our earthly blessings the source of our joy. Ask yourself honestly: Would you still be joyful without the tangible gifts that God has given you?

Near the end of Paul's letter to the Philippians, he demonstrated how his joy was rooted in Jesus, the only enduring source for true contentment in any situation. He knew that everything could be taken away from him—his work, his possessions, even his earthly freedom as he was repeatedly thrown in prison. And yet he rejoiced because he had the one thing that no one could ever take away: Jesus.

The same can be true for you. It's not bad to ask the Lord to bless you! Ask away! He wants to answer prayers and provide for you. But don't let your joy become anchored to the stuff or status you desire. There is only one unchanging anchor of joy in this world, and it's found in the person of Jesus.

RUNNING TO—NOT FROM—GOD

*Do not worry about anything, but pray and ask God
for everything you need, always giving thanks.*
PHILIPPIANS 4:6 NCV

THE WORD *WORRY* in this verse means "to rip into
pieces." It's the same for the word *anxiety* in Scripture.
Anxiety and worry tear our minds and hearts apart.
That's why we have the phrase, "I was worried to
pieces." Worry turns our *peace* into *pieces*. But here's
the good news: God wants us to bring every little
piece to Him through prayer. That's the first step in
how God brings us peace.

Back in Paradise when Adam and Eve sinned, they
immediately felt guilty, and hid from God. That's our
natural response when we know we have missed the
mark and fallen short of His glory. We run from God
when we need to be running to Him.

If you're stuck in the mire of worry and think
there's no way out, don't try to fix it on your own.
Instead, call out to Him. Invite Him into the web of
anxiety, and turn the negative energy of worry into the
positive action of prayer.

PRAYER

God, I
actively turn
toward You
in prayer
and invite
You into
what is
worrying me.
I don't want
to live in
pieces,
anxious and
afraid. I want
Your peace,
so lead
me today.

THE WAY OF RESTORATION AND REDEMPTION

*Because the Lord disciplines the one he loves,
and he chastens everyone he accepts as his
son. Endure hardship as discipline.*
HEBREWS 12:6–7

WHEN WE STRUGGLE in sin, God doesn't sit on the sidelines like an unengaged parent. He steps in. He convicts us of our shortcomings, but He only does so because He cares about us. He loves us so much He doesn't want us to continue down a harmful path.

If you feel the need to pivot in your thought life, to shift some action, or to apologize for something you said, it's likely that you're feeling the need for repentance; and that prompt is from God. He longs to restore you, and He gives you the strategy and the answer for how to go about realizing that restoration.

The solution is surrender.

Surrender comes when we raise our hands and say, *God, on my own, I can't change this situation. But Jesus, You can change me. I'm not going to hide from You anymore. I'm opening my heart to Your love and to the restorative work of the Holy Spirit.*

As God restores you, He reinvigorates you to live as a light for His gracious and holy kingdom.

GOD'S LEADING HIS PEOPLE

When Pharaoh let the people go, God did not lead them on the road through the Philistine country, though that was shorter. For God said, "If they face war, they might change their minds and return to Egypt." So God led the people around by the desert road toward the Red Sea.

EXODUS 13:17–18

EVEN THOUGH GOD'S plans rarely mirror ours, you can still be assured that He is in control.

When God led His people out of bondage in Egypt toward the promised land, He did not guide them to the shortest route; He led them straight into the desert. Sound familiar? We see a dilemma in our lives, quickly assess the situation, come up with a solution, and then inform God and wait for His intervention. But then God not only appears to ignore what we suggest; He does the opposite.

When He does this, God is still good and glorious. God knew the shortcut would be laden with challenges that the Israelites were not yet ready to face, so another plan was set in motion. For their best, God led His own into the wilderness. He might be doing the same with your life today.

PRAYER

God, lead me where You know it's best for me to go. No matter the terrain, help me to trust that You are in control and working things out for my good.

SET APART FROM THE BEGINNING

"Before I formed you in the womb I knew you, before you were born I set you apart; I appointed you as a prophet to the nations."
JEREMIAH 1:5

PRAYER

God, please uphold my hope. I trust that You are always faithful and that You are in control.

WHEN IT DOESN'T look like God is with you, when what's surrounding you seems to be defeat and darkness, you can be tempted to think, *Who cares? What difference does my life truly make?*

Look to the Word of God and see that, from the beginning, God set you apart. He appointed you as an ambassador of His love to the nations. He gave you a role in His redemption plan. He's set you on a course for good and not for evil. He gives you a hope, a secure future, and He has made Himself available to you. Call on Him, seek Him, and you will find Him!

When God created you, He wove a beautiful purpose into your story—to bring the good news of His gospel to others. So when the darkness closes in, when everything looks chaotic, you can fall back on His Word and His record of faithfulness. He won't let things end in darkness. Your story will continue. Reach out to Him and watch as He does the impossible once again.

SEEING THE CROSS AS BEAUTIFUL

Surely this man was the Son of God!
MARK 15:39

GOD DOESN'T JUST want you to know *about* the cross. He wants you to see it in such a way that it grips you in the deepest parts of your heart and awakens you to an eye-opening, jaw-dropping realization—the cross is *in* your story! That's the kind of clarity He wants to give you, and when you see it, nothing else can be the same again. Just look at the story of one of the soldiers who nailed Jesus to that beam of wood.

Just moments after Jesus breathed His last breath, the centurion declared a shocking truth. He had heard people say all kinds of things about Jesus, and about who He claimed to be. But in those moments while watching Jesus die, the centurion received spiritual sight, and he knew for himself exactly who Jesus was.

This verse reminds us of why it should be impossible to just breeze past the cross. Something powerful and gruesome and gutsy happened there. As awful as Jesus' death was for Him, it's the best thing that ever happened to you and me. Once you truly see it, you are free. It moves you to fall down in awe and wonder, and confess, "I am forgiven!"

PRAYER

God, give me a clearer picture of Your salvation work through Jesus on the cross.

BEING WITH JESUS

*When they saw the courage of Peter and John
and realized that they were unschooled, ordinary
men, they were astonished and they took note
that these men had been with Jesus.*
ACTS 4:13

WHEN WE READ what happened in Acts chapter 4, it's evident that James and John had been *with* Jesus. We see it in every fiber of their being. In their boldness. Their joy. And most certainly in their words. By communing with Jesus, the disciples naturally became more like Him.

Although we can't physically walk with Jesus today, we do have the Word of God, His breath on a page. We have His Spirit, which intercedes for us before the very throne of God. We have the power of the resurrection in our hearts. The worship of heaven in our lungs. The promise of His great and glorious return in our minds.

When you commit your life to being with Jesus, you begin to act, speak, and think like He did. And you begin to look like Him, modeling humility, which leads you toward a life of powerful peace and remarkable worship.

A CROWN OF LIFE

Blessed is the one who perseveres under trial because,
having stood the test, that person will receive the crown
of life that the Lord has promised to those who love him.
JAMES 1:12

MAKE NO MISTAKE: our God is a God of miracles
and wonders. Because He is wholly good and pure, He
cannot and will never bring evil into our lives. And yet
we still live in a broken and fallen world, so there *will*
be trials and temptations. That's why the Christian
life is one of perseverance.

In every challenge, you can trust that He is still
doing a good work in you. You might not see it, but He
is building something within you as He moves heaven
and earth toward His ultimate purposes. So when trials come, you can surrender your own expectations
and rely on Him. Only then will you see His resurrection power and live in the strength of your God.

We persevere in our faith by relying on Him
alone. Not our own cleverness, not our worldly
wisdom—just Him. And in every perseverance, you
will be blessed. Not just good or okay or barely making it. In every hardship, when you depend on Him,
your outcome is *blessed.* God is eager to offer you the
crown of life. Rely on Him and be transformed into
His likeness.

PRAYER

God, keep
my eyes
steadily on
You. Only
You can
transform my
heartache
through the
power of
Your
holiness.

A SIMPLE AND BATTLE-TESTED TRUTH

Then, after desire has conceived, it gives birth to sin; and sin, when it is full-grown, gives birth to death.
JAMES 1:15

PRAYER

God, I know the Enemy is lurking, but the more I linger in Your presence, the more confident I am that You will defend and supply my every need.

JAMES WROTE THAT we are "lured" and "enticed" by our own desires. That's why sin is so tempting. The Enemy knows what tempts you, and once those desires take hold, it leads to sin. Eventually, continual and unrepentant sin leads to death. Be aware! The Enemy wants to steal your sense of self-worth and kill your dreams. He wants to bury the purpose God has placed inside you. He's got all kinds of time and no mercy.

Despite the Enemy's malicious intent, you don't have to live fearful or paranoid. God is greater than the Enemy, greater than your sin. Because of God's Spirit in you, you are an overcomer. God has given you weapons of righteousness—His Spirit, His Word, His Church—to help you fight back against the darkness. You are not the victim in this story, but in Christ, you are the victor! Sin no longer reigns over you, but you have been born again to new life in Christ!

That's how you can find peace and learn to say no to the wrong desires. Don't let the Enemy steal what is rightfully yours—your victory.

HIS CRUCIFIXION KILLED EVERY CURSE OF SIN

It is written, "Cursed is everyone who hangs on a tree."
GALATIANS 3:13 NKJV

JESUS TOOK EVERY curse that is over your life onto Himself. And because of Christ's work, you can claim this over your life today:

You are healed because Jesus was cursed. You are accepted because Jesus was rejected. You are released from the weight of sin and shame because Jesus experienced the wrath of God's righteous judgment. Your shattered destiny can be put back together again because Jesus was broken on the cross. You can become the righteousness of God in Jesus because He became sin for you. You can find healing because He was wounded for your transgressions and rebellion.

Once your eyes are opened to the transforming power of Jesus' death, you understand that the cross is not just an important moment in history. The cross is the place where your hope becomes reality and you find grace to cover everything you need today.

PRAYER

Jesus, no amount of gratitude can convey my debt of joy at Your selfless sacrifice. You became a curse so I could be cured before You. I will live as that new creation today.

THE GREAT AND GLORIOUS LIGHT

The people walking in darkness have seen a great light.
ISAIAH 9:2

GOD IS THE source of all joy, abundance, and goodness on this earth. His light can shine through any darkness and can fuel your faith. But if you've found yourself day after day walking under gray skies, it can be hard to believe that God's powerful light can still break through.

What keeps your heart and mind in step with heaven is remembering that you are not off God's radar. You may not see Him, but He is still at work. There is evidence of His light in your life. You have received mercy even when you were far from God. He has chosen you. Your God is not a "bad news" God, and you do not have a "bad news" story. In fact, if you are in Christ, your story is guaranteed to end in redemption.

If the darkness is masking your vision today and the clouds feel thick and immovable, you can rest assured that God's light is still shining through to offer you grace and peace. He is near, so your life can be forever marked by His great light.

PRAYER

God, shine through my shadows today and direct my gaze back toward Your throne of steadfast love.

A PERSONAL AND INDIVIDUAL LOVE

"For I know the plans I have for you," declares the LORD.
JEREMIAH 29:11

GOD LOVES YOU personally. You are His creation, handcrafted by Him before the earth began. He knows you specifically—the number of hairs on your head and every hue and shade of color in your irises. He knew your name long before you entered this world, and He has a specific plan and purpose for you. He didn't set out to make you like someone else, because He wants the unique worship that only you can offer.

If we're honest, it's easy to look at other people and say, "Wow, I wish I were more like them." But God is saying to you today, *I took care to make you exactly the way you are.*

Though we are all made differently, we have something massive in common. God loves each of us individually and intimately, in remarkable and specific ways. Take a moment today to slow down and dwell on this powerful truth. God knows your name. He knows your story. Look up and say yes to His love and plans for you.

PRAYER

God, You created me on purpose and for a purpose. Therefore, I can stop trying to be like everyone else. Instead, I can rest confidently in the plans You have for my life.

THE MISSION OF
THE GOSPEL

For we are to God the pleasing aroma of Christ among those who are being saved and those who are perishing.
2 CORINTHIANS 2:15

PRAYER

God, You
have given
me a purpose
greater than
myself. May I
elevate Your
mission as
I step out
in faith to
proclaim Your
name to those
around me.

IF YOU FOLLOW Jesus, every day of your life is saturated with purpose. There are other people waiting on you—whether a close family member, a coworker, or even a stranger you may run into—to take a step of faith and to talk about the person who has changed everything for you. Jesus isn't inviting you to look like Him and think like Him so that you can go love others like the world loves them. He wants to invite you to purposefully join Him on His mission.

When we are close to Jesus, we can bring hope and life and freedom and strength to people trapped in despair and darkness. We can help to draw people one step closer to Jesus by showing them how much He has changed our lives. Trusting in the gospel means you extend the aroma of Christ to those around you. Because life is short and you serve a big God, the gospel prompts you to proclaim the truth that "Jesus saves" to those who He puts in your path.

THE GREATEST SYMPHONY

Shout for joy to the LORD, all the earth. Worship the LORD with gladness; come before him with joyful songs.
PSALM 100:1–2

DO YOU REALIZE that worship has been hardwired into your being? No one has to be taught to be a worshipper. You already are. It is in the DNA of your soul. You don't get to choose if you're a worshiper, but you do get to decide if you'll add your worship to the greatest symphony of praise ever assembled.

At all times, the entire cosmos sings a song of praise to the almighty God. At this very moment, the waves worship in wonder. Mountain peaks shout His glory. Trees of the field and the forest clap their hands. The stars burst forth, declaring His glory. The leaves on the branches rustle an anthem of His might. The thunder and lightning reverberate with the greatness and the power of God.

So lift your voice and join in! Tell everyone and everything of His goodness and His everlasting love. With every cry of praise, you are becoming a truer version of who you were called to be. Sing with all you have, and let your heart swell before the throne of heaven. Rejoice that the God of the universe pours out His love on you.

PRAYER

God, I join with all creation today to proclaim that You are worthy of all honor, praise, and glory!

THE KING COMES BACK FOR THE KING'S THINGS

"To one he gave five talents, to another two, and to another one, to each according to his own ability."
MATTHEW 25:15 NKJV

PRAYER

Jesus, thank You for the talents You've given me. Since You know my ability, I can trust You will empower me to do all the work You have assigned to me.

WHEN WE FRET and fixate on the future, we tend to miss that the most significant things are what God has placed in our hands right now. Yes, the future is important, and wise preparation will almost certainly be beneficial, but most things we worry about coming to pass never end up happening. So we need to get out of the stream of worry and what-ifs and get back on the path of making the most of what God has assigned to us today.

God puts things into your hands according to your ability and His power to work in and through you. If He's entrusted it to you, you can carry it. If He's calling you to it, He will be faithful and help you through it. If He's placed it in your hands, you don't need to worry about where it will end up. You just need to prepare, plan, and stay ready—because the King will come back for the King's things.

BY HIS WOUNDS WE ARE HEALED

He was pierced for our transgressions,
he was crushed for our iniquities.
ISAIAH 53:5

HAVE YOU EVER wondered why, exactly, Jesus had to come to earth? Jesus didn't just come to do some good works and heal diseases. He wasn't on earth just to walk on water and raise His buddy Lazarus from the dead. Jesus came to die for our sins, to do what no other person ever born could do. Born of a virgin and without sin, Jesus lived obedient to the Father, ultimately exchanging His innocent life for yours, so that you could have eternal life.

This is the glorious gospel story that fuels everything about the Christian message, and this heavenly exchange offers you a new reality that is almost beyond comprehension.

Jesus willingly took on all the wrongs of every one of us on the cross and bore the guilt of our sinful ways, and He was crushed by the weight of God's wrath that we deserved. By coming to earth and bearing your transgressions, He made you free from every sin—past, present, and future. He made it possible that you can live in relationship with God forevermore.

PRAYER

Jesus, Your wounds have made me free. I praise You with everything I have today. You took my guilt and gave me grace. Hallelujah!

OCTOBER

LAYING DOWN YOUR SELF

"Whoever wants to be my disciple must deny themselves and take up their cross and follow me."
MARK 8:34

WE ARE LIVING in a selfie culture. You don't have to look far to find examples of "build your own" or "you do you" or "what's in it for me?" ways of thinking.

But if you want to worship God intimately and authentically, you're going to have to embrace the sacrifice of self. You're going to have to buy into the invitation to take up your cross and follow Jesus. This isn't God trying to punish or restrict you. The Spirit of the Lord isn't one of condemnation and fear but of freedom. He loves us and wants what is best for us, which He knows is more of Himself and less of us.

If you are afraid to surrender your whole life to God, let the gospel sink down into the very depths of your heart. Let the nail-pierced hands open the doorway to eternal freedom. The truth is, when you lay down your ways to embrace His holiness and love, you actually win in the end. In laying down your life and taking up His cross, He gets glory, and you get everlasting life.

THE PATH YOU DON'T KNOW IS THERE

Your path led through the sea, your way through the mighty waters, though your footprints were not seen.
PSALM 77:19

THE GOOD SHEPHERD will not tell you that you're not going to make it. You will never find Him telling you that life is hopeless. That there's no way out. That you may as well abandon it all. That is not the voice of the Good Shepherd. The Good Shepherd says, *We're going through this valley, and I'm going to be with you all the way through. And guess what? We're going to have a story to tell on the other side.*

This is how God delivered His people from bondage in Egypt. He didn't build a bridge over the Red Sea; He parted the sea so they could walk through it. You might feel like your back is against the wall, and you may not see the path out, but if God is with you, you always have a way forward.

You are going through whatever circumstance you're currently in. And your Shepherd is going through it with you.

PRAYER

God, open my eyes today to see the ways You are sovereignly providing pathways of peace that I can walk down, despite what may be raging and rising all around me.

SURRENDERED TO THE KING

Do not merely listen to the word, and so deceive yourselves. Do what it says.
JAMES 1:22

PRAYER

God, I want my faith to be genuine. Would Your Spirit help me to live in a way that reflects what I believe?

IF YOU FOLLOW Jesus, it means you're going to have to change. The things that used to fill you and used to satisfy you no longer will. You're under new leadership. You aren't the boss of you anymore, and that's actually the best news you could ever hope for.

James said we can't just let our faith sit on the shelf. It has to infuse itself into our everyday living. We must let the gospel change us as we surrender our desires, our plans, our time and energy and resources to the Lord of lords. You can't follow Jesus and continue as king of your own life. You must submit yourself to His teaching and follow His ways. To be in His kingdom is to live like there is a King who is seated on the throne ruling over your life.

The great news about God's kingdom is that your surrender is ultimately for your good! His kingdom is a place of mercy, goodness, and peace. As you cede your seat on the throne, as you die to yourself and surrender to the God of the universe, rest assured that you'll find freedom under His rule that will always result in your delight.

MORE THAN ANY BLUEPRINT

"Now this is eternal life: that they know you, the only true God, and Jesus Christ, whom you have sent."

JOHN 17:3

LOOK AT YOUR friendships, especially with those you're closest to. Isn't it stunning that what's often most important about community is spending time together and not necessarily having the whole blueprint of friendship planned out? That's because who you are with is almost always more important than what you are doing.

The same is true with God and your relationship with Him. He is far more interested in developing a deep and meaningful relationship with you than He is in giving you all the details and plans in a concrete blueprint for your life.

God wants us to constantly lean into a relationship with Him. The moment we feel like we have a blueprint, we're prone to think, *Okay, this is all I need. I'm off and running. If I run into any big obstacles or need Your help, I'll let You know. Thank You very much.*

No, God is looking for intimacy. He wants to know you. He's less interested in handing you long-range, detailed plans and more interested in cultivating a personal, day-to-day relationship with you. He wants your heart.

PRAYER

Jesus, You have made it possible to draw near in personal relationship to the Father, and I rejoice in the eternal life that comes through knowing You.

OCT 5

TWO TESTAMENTS LINKED BY PROMISE

"Behold, I will send you Elijah the prophet before the coming of the great and dreadful day of the LORD. And he will turn the hearts of the fathers to the children, and the hearts of the children to their fathers, lest I come and strike the earth with a curse."
MALACHI 4:5–6 NKJV

PRAYER

God, Your Scripture shows me Your faithfulness in leading Your children back to You. Lead me closer to You today, that I may delight in You.

HAVE YOU EVER noticed what the last words of the Old Testament recorded in Scripture are? Do you know what message God left His people before He went silent for four centuries?

The Old Testament ends in Malachi 4:5–6 with a promise underscoring God's desire to restore fatherhood. He wanted to reconnect the hearts of fathers to their children and reposition children under the waterfall of their fathers' blessing. When we flip the page to the New Testament and read the Gospels, we see that this is exactly what Jesus did.

God is still seeking to reestablish His future children to their spiritual Father, leading to a right understanding of Himself and His ways. Even today, the God of the universe wants you to realize that He is working, even when we can't see it, to draw you closer and to help you to know Him as Abba Father.

GIVING BACK TO GOD

"All these people gave their gifts out of their wealth; but she out of her poverty put in all she had to live on."

LUKE 21:4

IT CAN BE challenging to want to be generous when you feel like you're lacking. Our culture is constantly telling us to make sure we have *enough*. Make sure you feel secure—and *then* you can be generous.

But that's not how God's economy works. One of the greatest examples of generosity in the Bible is the story of the woman with two copper coins. She didn't have much; in fact, she had far less than nearly everyone else around her who gave gifts. But her willingness to surrender what she had to God wrote her into scriptures that we're still reading today. She gave not because she had enough but because she knew that the God who owns everything was able to meet her every need.

Even though this woman only gave a "mite," Jesus still noticed her heartfelt generosity. It moved His heart, and He admired her worship. The same can be true of you today. Even if you feel like you're lacking, trust God and put all that you have in His hands.

God, everything in my possession is already Yours. Today, I give back what You first gave me.

JESUS KEEPS OUR CUPS OVERFLOWING

You anoint my head with oil; my cup overflows.
PSALM 23:5

KING DAVID, WHO wrote Psalm 23, understood what God meant when He promised to be with us in the valley of the shadow of death. David battled a giant, survived many attacks on his life, and even battled a lion and a bear. Even in these trials, David didn't write that his cup was half full or completely full—his cup *overflowed*. How did David confidently do this? Because of his access to God.

You have access to that same God. Jesus is in the middle of the pressure with you, and He's not just standing around with His hands in His pockets. He's there to rescue you when necessary, to protect you at all costs, and to fill your cup to overflowing.

When you focus on your Good Shepherd, as David did, you can find rest in the face of death. You can walk confidently through difficult seasons by keeping your eyes fixed on Him. You can be sure that when you draw near to God, the Enemy will try to pull you away, but stay close. By God's side you can be fulfilled.

Jesus, thank You for overflowing Your grace and mercy in my heart. I rejoice, for You are an abundant and generous giver of joy.

MOVING TOWARD JESUS

*Be diligent in these matters; give yourself wholly
to them, so that everyone may see your progress.*
1 TIMOTHY 4:15

HERE'S AN ENCOURAGEMENT for you today: you
don't have to get it all right. Not this week, or this
month, or this year. Which is good news because the
truth is, no matter how hard you try, you won't get it
all right. That's why the aim of the believer isn't perfection. The goal is making progress.

How do you make progress today? You point
your feet toward Jesus, and you begin to move, step-
by-step, in the direction of the King. Yes, you might
encounter some detours along the journey. But if your
destination is set, you can move confidently toward
God, knowing that every step closer is making you
more Christlike.

Instead of trying to get it all right today, just try to
take one step at a time. Acknowledge your desires and
your fears to God. Confess what is consistently knock-
ing you off the road, and begin to surround yourself
with like-minded people who are just as eagerly moving toward the King.

Don't let a sense of needing to be perfect keep
you from pursuing Jesus today. Embrace the path of
making slow and sure progress.

PRAYER

God, cover
me in grace
and draw
me slowly
and patiently
into Your
arms today.

TRUST IN A GOD WHO SUFFERED TOO

You will keep in perfect peace those whose minds are steadfast, because they trust in you.
ISAIAH 26:3

PRAYER

Jesus, I choose to keep Your cross in view today. Because of Your sacrifice, I know You will give me encouragement and endurance for every hardship I may face.

JESUS NEVER PROMISES us a problem-free life. Even when you walk closely with Christ, chaos still comes. Painful circumstances can appear in a flash. But thank God, Jesus will lead you through every valley.

The way you stay satisfied in the midst of chaos is to keep your gaze fixed on the cross. You don't come to believe in God's love for you because of the circumstances around you. If that were the metric, there wouldn't be much cause for faith. No, you draw assurance of His love for you because of the circumstance of Christ on the cross. If you're walking through hardship, remind yourself that Jesus knows all about suffering. Whatever you're going through, you are not alone in your pain. He knows exactly how you feel.

Even though He suffered, He rose again. That truth can anchor your hope. In Christ, you can trust that no matter what, good will come again. Keep your eyes fixed on Jesus. Deliberately and consistently set Him before you, and watch as your heart expands in confidence and joy.

ALL YOU'VE EVER WANTED

Keep me as the apple of your eye; hide
me in the shadow of your wings.
PSALM 17:8

IF YOU EVER feel like something is missing or lacking, try shifting your focus to the truth that God not only knows what you want, but He is perfectly able to fulfill your every desire. He's not just satisfactory; He's incomparably wonderful. And you can trust in His provision because He's already stepped toward you in love and grace.

From the pages of Scripture, you can know that you are the apple of His eye. He saw you long before you saw Him. And He has been leaving you breadcrumbs, little invitations here and there throughout your life, from the beauty of the stars to those moments of coincidence that don't totally seem to add up. You've been loved by Him since before there was time. He sought you, paid a ransom for you before you did one thing to deserve it.

Before God ever asked anything from you, He gave everything *to* you in the gift of His Son. He can provide everything you could ever want and need, and it brings Him joy to care for you as His child.

PRAYER

God, in You is life, and life abundant. Keep me in Your shadow as a child of Your affection, that I may worship You all day long.

THE JOY OF EVANGELISM

*Because we loved you so much, we were
delighted to share with you not only the
gospel of God but our lives as well.*
1 THESSALONIANS 2:8

PRAYER

God, expand
my awe of
You, that I
may joyously
serve and
share the
gospel
with those
You put
around me.

GOD IS AN almighty God who, in the very beginning,
brought the universe into being with just a simple word.
Imagine the power and authority of that moment! He
is not only a creator but a restorer. When humanity
walked away from Him, He bridged heaven and earth
with the life of His Son, who took on human flesh and
absorbed our penalty, our spiritual death.

As this gospel truth takes root in your heart and
you accept the love God has poured out for you, the
only appropriate response is deep gratitude and love
that overflows into your everyday life. You don't have
to be convinced that when you love something, you
talk about it. That's what we do in all areas of our
lives, so if we've been saved and redeemed, how much
more should we share about this love of Jesus? Sharing
the gospel isn't an obligation—it's an opportunity and
a delight!

Make the sharing of God's Word your delight
today. God has given so richly to you, and therefore it is your joy to look outward and love on those
around you.

ALL GLORY TO GOD

*So whether you eat or drink or whatever you
do, do it all for the glory of God. . . . For I
am not seeking my own good but the good
of many, so that they may be saved.*

1 CORINTHIANS 10:31, 33

TRUSTING IN GOD'S sovereignty isn't the same thing
as living a life of passivity. Even when we don't know
the answers to our questions or when we can't see the
way forward, God invites us to keep doing the very
best at whatever He has put in front of us. He is in
control, and we are faithful to follow where He leads.

When our view of God expands so we can see Him
as He truly is—as a big and extraordinary God—we
have less need for specifics. We've seen God act before.
We trust Him for how He's going to act in the future.
We know we're loved by Him and called by Him and
chosen by Him and created by Him. And if all those
things are true, then we are free to wait well and still
give our best, doing everything to the glory of God,
that salvation might come to those around us.

PRAYER

God, I work
unto Your
glory, but I
wait for Your
power and
provision. No
matter what
You call me
to, I will trust
Your goodness
and want to
glorify You in
all I do today.

THE THUNDER OF HIS POWER

How faint the whisper we hear of him! Who then can understand the thunder of his power?
JOB 26:14

PRAYER

My God, I am amazed at Your power and proximity. You reign over all, and yet You know me personally.

WHAT'S THE MOST powerful thing you've experienced? Maybe you've been in a terrible storm, felt an earthquake, flown in a fast jet, or joined the roar of tens of thousands of people at a massive sports game?

While they can all feel formidable, none of these displays of strength come close to rivaling the overwhelming power of God. Linger over this for a minute: the God who created the cosmos—every black hole, meteor, solar flare, and solar system; every sun, every moon, every mile of outer space making up every light-year of galaxies—that same God knows your name and listens when you pray.

When you lose sight of the immeasurable power of God, you're prone to see your present trials as being undefeatable. You start to say things like, "I'll never be free" or "This is just the way it's going to be."

But you can speak to your soul. You know the One who thunders in power and who shakes the earth with His glory. He is bigger than whatever is threatening your peace, and He is guarding, providing, and loving you today.

WISE STEWARDSHIP

Be very careful, then, how you live—not as unwise but as wise, making the most of every opportunity, because the days are evil.
EPHESIANS 5:15–16

WHAT DOES THE Bible say about planning for your future? In Matthew 25 Jesus told a parable about a master who went away for an extended period. Before he left, he gave a considerable amount of money to three of his servants.

Each servant did something slightly different with the money, but when the master returned, he praised the servants who had invested well. The master said that they were "good and faithful" (25:21). They planned well and were concerned for the welfare of the work assigned to them. The master rewarded them by giving them even more than they were originally entrusted with.

Planning isn't a bad thing. In fact, being a good steward with our time and resources is one of the ways we can glorify God in this world. On the other hand, when your planning tips over the edge and spills into the grip of having to control everything, then you're in trouble. Don't let the Enemy confuse planning with posturing your life before God.

PRAYER

God, I put my plans into Your hands and ask that You do what You will with what You have given me.

YOU'RE IN A NEW STORY

For you did not receive the spirit of bondage
again to fear, but you received the Spirit of
adoption by whom we cry out, "Abba, Father."
ROMANS 8:15 NKJV

PRAYER

Lord, would
You remind me
consistently
throughout
the day that
I belong to a
new family?
That You have
given me a
new spirit,
and my former
ways have
no authority
any longer?

IF ANXIETY HAD a stronghold in your life before you met Jesus, it may be time, in the power of the Spirit, to turn the page. If fear had a strong grip on your heart, if defeat was your lead story and dejection was where you set up your camp, it's time to look forward and realize that through Jesus, you have a new narrative of life and victory.

To say it another way: You're living in a new story. You are no longer a slave to fear and anxiety because you have received the Spirit of sonship or daughtership. You are a part of the family of the King of kings, loved and cherished by Him, adopted into all strength, beauty, hope, and peace. You are His, and in His presence, your former way of life must fall and flee.

As you speak that new narrative, you'll begin to see changes in your walk with God, starting with how you daily interact with and depend on Him.

GOD FULLY PROVIDES

"So do not worry, saying, 'What shall we eat?' or 'What shall we drink?' or 'What shall we wear?... *Your heavenly Father knows that you need them."*

MATTHEW 6:31–32

JESUS TOLD HIS disciples in Matthew 6 that He knew they had things they needed and plans they were hoping to accomplish. Like the disciples, Jesus isn't unaware of what is going on in your life. He knows what is keeping you up at night—what is weighing heavy on your heart.

He also knows that God has a perfect record of coming through for His people. He's never failed. Not once. Ever. In the history of humanity and beyond, because God is the Alpha and the Omega, the beginning and the end. He's provided for every need—big or small, basic or complex.

And as He provides, He invites you to seek His kingdom. To put His righteousness first. To know He will meet your needs means you can surrender your anxieties and fears to Him. And when you do, you'll find a new sense of freedom to meet the needs of others and to love those He puts in your path.

PRAYER

God, keep my priorities straight and my pursuit of You at the forefront of my heart. I put You first today.

KNOWING GOD IS YOUR FATHER

Therefore we do not lose heart. Though outwardly we are wasting away, yet inwardly we are being renewed day by day.
2 CORINTHIANS 4:16

PRAYER

Father, You have given me a spirit of power, through Your Son, which means I don't have to lose heart. May I feel Your renewing sense of goodness in every area of life today.

THINGS CHANGE THE more you understand what it means to be a child of God. As that wonderful and paradigm-shifting truth continues to sink deeper into your soul, you begin to realize that you have at your disposal an unfathomable power. A power that unlocks prison doors, heals wounds, and propels you into a greater sense of purpose in your life.

Knowing God as your Father can revolutionize your life. Old things pass away—disappointments, guilt, sorrows, and struggles. Habits change for the better. Your relationship with God is transformed. Your worship is revived. You see changes in the things you longed for and hoped for.

This life-altering relationship becomes yours when you trust in God through Jesus Christ. God brings your heart to life, and you are born anew. This spiritual birth not only brings you to life on the inside; it immediately places you in a new family with a new and perfect Father.

DINING AT THE KING'S TABLE

"Put the bread of the Presence on this table to be before me at all times."

EXODUS 25:30

WHATEVER YOU ARE battling, internally or externally, God has set a table in the middle of the trouble, at the epicenter of conflict, and He's saved you a seat. He knows that your heart is most fulfilled when you're dining with the King.

Sometimes the Bible uses the term *table* as a shorthand expression for God's salvation, peace, and presence. In the days of the Bible, every Jewish listener would immediately know the significance of being invited to sit at someone's table, especially the table of the Lord. It would have been the pinnacle of intimacy and honor.

Today, we have to fight to not let it be lost on us that our God invites us to dine with Him. He isn't threatened by what's threatening us. He's set a feast before you and He wants to help you tune out every distraction as you focus on Him.

When you're at His table, you can experience the fullness of intimacy and joy. The battle might still rage and swirl around you, but in His presence, nothing can befall you.

PRAYER

Lord, I claim my seat at Your table today. I understand that I am not sitting here because of anything I did, but I relish Your grace that made a way for me to be with You.

NO CHECKING OUT

"I will make you into a great nation, and I will bless you; I will make your name great, and you will be a blessing."
GENESIS 12:2

PRAYER

God, keep me ready and poised to follow Your call. I place all that I have in Your hands and say, "Use me as You know best."

HAVE YOU EVER started a new dream later in life than you thought you would? Maybe you went back to school or took up a hobby. For Shelley and me, we planted Passion City Church when I was in my early fifties!

The Bible specifically notes that Abram (later Abraham) was seventy-five years old when God made an unconditional covenant of blessing with him. Seventy-five! This blows up two common myths. First, that a person needs to have life figured out when he or she is in their twenties, and second, that God doesn't give great callings to people when they're older and more established in life.

God never wants anybody to check out, no matter how old or young. God is looking for people to take steps based not on age but on how we're gazing at His greatness. God wants us to keep an open hand, to continually say to Him, "I trust You to lead me." If you've slowed down in trusting God, lean back in and put your yes back on the table.

A PROMISE OF FAITHFULNESS

Let us hold unswervingly to the hope we profess, for he who promised is faithful.
HEBREWS 10:23

IF YOU'VE BEEN following Jesus for any length of time, you know that the Christian walk isn't always easy. Some days, our joy in the Lord comes quickly; other days, it's a struggle to take a single step. But God predicted our unpredictability, and it's already accounted for.

The beauty of a relationship with God is that He's in it for the long haul. He's already gone before you, and nothing you can do will change or alter that. Even when you don't feel like pursuing Him, He's actively pursuing you. When you're faithless, He is faithful. When you experience a hard stretch or you grow distracted by the things of this world, God is still there, kindly and gently beckoning you back into His arms.

We can be secure in His faithfulness. He doesn't write us off or scratch us out of His book when we fall short of His glory. He's patient and kind. You might feel far from God, but you can still profess this promise—that He is faithfully close. He hasn't left you, and He never will.

PRAYER

God, anchor my hope in this: You love me unceasingly. Help me to set my eyes on You.

HE CALLS YOU HIS OWN

*"Don't you know . . . ? Anyone who has
seen me has seen the Father."*
JOHN 14:9

JESUS WENT ABOVE and beyond to emphasize one
name of God in Scripture. In fact, 189 times in the
four gospels alone, Jesus referred to God as a Father,
far more than any other term, distinction, or charac-
teristic. It begs the question for us today: What is the
name of God that you most often relate to?

Some of us view God as our Lord. The total
authority. Some view Him as Judge. A warden oversee-
ing sinners. Others might see Him as King, demanding
obedience. But what if we followed in Jesus' example
and chose to see God first and foremost as *Father*?

When Jesus was baptized, God the Father showed
that His relationship with His Son wasn't a contract.
It was a connection. A family connection. A real,
heart-to-heart life connection where the Creator of the
universe acknowledged His Son. And God extends a
similar kind of relationship to you. God loves you,
and God is proud to call you His very own.

SATISFIED BY CHRIST

The woman said, "I know that Messiah (called Christ) is coming. When he comes, he will explain everything to us."

JOHN 4:25

THE GOD-FEARING PEOPLE of Jesus' day carried a desire deep within their hearts. It was based on a promise God had made, one that had been passed down from generation to generation and family to family. God had said that His Messiah would come to make the world right once more, and there was an eagerness to see that promise fulfilled.

When Jesus came, He changed everything. He showed that God was able to meet and exceed our deepest desires. Through His death and resurrection, He not only satisfied God's necessary requirements of redemption, but He also satisfied every human heart longing for freedom and new hope.

Like those who waited on Jesus to arrive, if you feel like there is an unfulfilled desire in your soul, know that through Jesus you can find the contentment you long for. The purpose you crave. The comfort you need. The family you desire. The heaven you hope for. You can experience that joy of having your deepest desires met by a God who cares immensely and intimately for you.

PRAYER

Jesus, You fulfilled every hope, and Your death brought me back to life. I stand secure in You today, knowing I am loved eternally.

309

HE'S WITH YOU NO MATTER THE STORM

"When you pass through the waters, I will be with you; and when you pass through the rivers, they will not sweep over you."
ISAIAH 43:2

PRAYER

God, I know You are with me, no matter what today may hold. So I draw from You—Your strength is my strength, Your hope is my hope, Your joy is my joy.

WHEN YOU FEEL overwhelmed, hold fast to the truth that God is with you. He's with you in the sickness. He's with you at the graveside. He's with you when the job opportunity doesn't come through. He is with you when you receive hard news. God Almighty—your Good Shepherd—is right there in the midst of the difficulty with you.

This understanding shifts a lot of things about your faith and personal relationship with Jesus, but none more so than your prayer life. If God is right next to you in your hardship, you no longer have to invite Him into your story, but you can praise Him for already being with you. You don't have to shout or put in a long-distance call; you can just lean over and tell Him what's on your mind. When you know that Jesus is close, you have a present source of peace, victory, and freedom in the midst of problems, pain, and loss. Praise God that no matter the storm, He's with you.

FORGIVEN AND MADE RIGHTEOUS

For us, to whom God will credit righteousness—
for us who believe in him who raised
Jesus our Lord from the dead.
ROMANS 4:24

IF YOU HAVE ever paid off a debt—a car, college tuition, or even just a personal IOU to a friend—you know how good it feels when your ledger hits zero and the accounts are balanced.

If that's the peace that comes with balancing your earthly debts, how much more joyous and stunning is the fact that God paid off our spiritual debt! Though we didn't deserve it, He provided redemption through the blood of Jesus. While we were still sinners, He forgave us by putting our sins on Him who knew no sin. The debt has been canceled. Wiped out. Sent packing.

He hasn't simply paid our debt. He has credited us His righteousness. Jesus has put His perfect life and the fullness of His holiness and intimacy with God in our account forevermore.

God doesn't just forgive you. He restores you. You've got a good God. A perfect Father. The almighty God who runs the universe knows and cares about you. Worship Him today for what He's done for you.

PRAYER

God, Your grace is more than I can ever truly appreciate or grasp. All I can say is thank You.

THE WOVEN THREAD
OF GLORY

*For the earth will be filled with the knowledge of
the glory of the LORD as the waters cover the sea.*
HABAKKUK 2:14

ONE OF THE greatest pitfalls of the modern Christian
is the tendency to make everything about us. We
reduce Jesus to a self-improvement technique, saying,
"He helps me feel better about my life." If we're not
careful, in the end, the person of Christ, the promise
of the Word, the gathering of the people, the work of
the cross, the hope of heaven can all become about
"me."

God wants you to experience the fullness of who
He is. He wants you to know that you're a vital part of
the story. But it's not all about you. God does not exist
for us; we exist for God. We are not His maker; He is
our Maker. The central aim of our lives is to glorify
God and enjoy Him forever.

We are designed to be dependent on our Creator
and reflect His greatness and glory. You get the fullness of life and breath and gifts and opportunities,
and God gets credit and glory and praise from your
life. This is what you are made for and why glory is
woven through every fiber of your being.

THE BEST IS YET TO COME

Trust in the LORD and do good; dwell in the land and enjoy safe pasture.
PSALM 37:3

WHAT DOES IT look like for you to cultivate faithfulness, being content where you are while you're waiting and trusting in the Lord for His next step? How do you counter fear with faith and anxious thoughts with assurance of God's steadfast love?

You recenter in the truth that you haven't seen all the purposes of God fully unfolded yet. In this journey of faith, your confidence comes from God's character, what's been revealed about Him in the Bible. And your confidence also comes in trusting that God is working even when you don't understand or see what's happening around you.

God is at work even amid whatever problem you're going through. He's working in both seen and unseen ways. He's working to put you on a path that you'll never regret, a path of extraordinary goodness that's a reflection of His character. That means that today you have one major assignment: trust God for your future and cultivate faithfulness for whatever is in your hands now while believing that the best is yet to come.

PRAYER

God, I don't have to worry about tomorrow, so I choose today to enjoy where You have me right now and to do good with what You have gifted me.

A NEW APPROACH TO YOUR RELATIONSHIP WITH GOD

"Our Father in heaven, hallowed be your name."
MATTHEW 6:9

IT CAN FEEL frustrating when it seems like your prayers aren't being heard, let alone answered. God may seem far off, which may dampen your desire to live for His glory. But don't let the quiet lead you to stop praying or stop listening. God is tuned into your heart—as a good father is with his children.

When Jesus showed us how to pray, He didn't begin His prayer with "Dear sir," or "Your Majesty," or even "Most Holy Lord." No. Jesus said in Matthew 6 that when you talk to God, you start by saying, "Our Father . . ."

Earlier in that same message, Jesus talked about how best to live. He said faith in action is like a light that you set on a hill, so you can give glory to who? To your Father. When you embrace the truth that God is a father, your heart shifts and your hands open as you go to Him for your needs.

Talk to your Father in prayer today. He wants to hear from you. The closer you get to walking with and knowing your Father, the more you shine for His glory.

PRAYER

My Father, You are before me and beside me always. Thank You that I never have to question where I stand with You again; I am Yours and You love me.

CHOOSING JESUS' WAY

And now, dear children, continue in him, so
that when he appears we may be confident
and unashamed before him at his coming.
1 JOHN 2:28

PEOPLE WHO WANT to become the fullest versions of themselves embrace all sorts of sacrifices. They sacrifice money, reputation, relationships, time, sleep, or a dozen other things to pursue what they desire.

But when it comes to faith, we're sometimes less willing to embrace the sacrifices associated with pursuing Jesus. He calls us to die to ourselves. To seek His kingdom first. To rely on His sufficiency and trust in His promises and obey His commands.

That kind of pursuit is costly. It requires you to give up making yourself the center of your own story. You can't put your agenda first, rely on your strength, or live by your created standards of holiness. You have to make the decision to forgo your worldly desires to take up Jesus' heavenly promises.

The more you embrace these spiritual sacrifices, the more you will abide in Him. And the more you dwell in Him, the more assured and fulfilled you will become as you pursue your greatest desire—intimacy with Jesus.

PRAYER

God, I choose to continue in You today. I choose to align my life with Your plans and Your agenda.

OCT 29

SALVATION IS HERE TO STAY

Surely He has borne our griefs and carried our sorrows.
ISAIAH 53:4 NKJV

YOU CAN FIND hope today because Jesus has already won the final battle. We are not waiting for the good news of salvation. Salvation is here! Jesus accomplished our redemption by taking our place and dying the death we deserved.

Scripture says in Isaiah 53 that Jesus "took up our pain and bore our suffering" (v. 4). He was "pierced for our transgressions" (v. 5). If you've ever thought that one day you'd make things right with God, there's news for you—God's already made things right for you.

Jesus can carry what is weighing you down. He has already carried what was meant to kill you. He took on your sorrows, your shame, your doubts, and disappointments, and He buried them in His grave.

When you're tempted to worry, fear, or look for other solutions apart from God, how can you grow your confidence and dependency on Him? How do you win the fight to lay down yourself and find peace, especially when the world around you seems out of control? By surrendering your need for self-sufficiency to the One who is in control.

PRAYER

God, You have carried me long before I knew who You were. You hung on the cross for me, and You will keep carrying me until the end of my days. I trust You to come through again today.

316

THE CROSS HAS THE FINAL WORD

You see, at just the right time, when we were still powerless, Christ died for the ungodly. . . . But God demonstrates his own love for us in this: While we were still sinners, Christ died for us.

ROMANS 5:6, 8

THE WORK JESUS accomplished on the cross defines your life. It gives you victory over death. You are identified with Christ. You are a brand-new creation. You are not unwanted, unlovely, or worthless. You are wanted by God, made in the image of God, and worthy of Christ's love because He has chosen to place worth on you. Your identity was born in the death, burial, and resurrection of Christ.

Don't let anyone try to convince you of anything that wasn't demonstrated to you when Christ gave His life for you. You are forgiven. Made right. You are holy in Christ. You are born into a new family. Woven into divine plans and purposes. Your guilt is gone. You are free.

Today, rejoice in your newfound position and freedom in Christ. Shout out as the apostle Paul did, "Therefore, if anyone is in Christ, the new creation has come: The old has gone, the new is here!" (2 Corinthians 5:17).

PRAYER

Lord, I will not listen to lies that don't align with Your love proven by Your death on the cross. I am a new creation in You, and I'm claiming that truth today!

THE HABIT OF GRATITUDE

*Give thanks in all circumstances; for this
is God's will for you in Christ Jesus.*
1 THESSALONIANS 5:18

PRAYER

God, break
through my
barriers that
keep me from
gratitude, and
elevate my
eyes, that I
would give
thanks to
You always.

IT'S EASY TO practice gratitude when things are going our way. When we get the job or cross the milestone or win the competition. But unfortunately, life doesn't always consist of those mountaintop moments. There are far more times when your gratitude will be tested by the barrage of trivialities and inconveniences of everyday life.

If that's you and you're struggling with gratitude, the encouragement is simple but effective: pray. Pray continually. When you spend time directing your thoughts toward God, you realize that gratitude is a response first and foremost to God's continual love. It's about gaining the right perspective on your life, a humble human before a loving Lord. With this lowly posture, you'll more quickly move past annoyances and find your way back to rejoicing.

Pray today for a mind that has been captured by God's brilliant love. Ask Him to replace callousness and cynicism with awe and wonder in your heart, and watch how gratitude permeates your every breath.

NOVEMBER

DAILY MERCIES AND DAILY BREAD

Because of the LORD's great love we are not consumed, for his compassions never fail. They are new every morning; great is your faithfulness.
LAMENTATIONS 3:22–23

PRAYER

Jesus, I won't look ahead to tomorrow or backward to yesterday. I know that You are with me today, in this moment, and You have supplied me for all that I could need.

RIGHT NOW, YOU can live a life that is characterized by a rich and daily sense of joy and freedom. How? By living in view of God's mercies and His provision, both of which He specifically sets out for you, each and every day.

Imagine how you would feel if you woke up each morning and your first thought was, *I have new mercies for today.* And not just new mercies, but the specifically tailored-for-today mercies. Well, that's your reality! You have daily mercies—strength when you feel weak, hope when you feel downcast, love when you feel unworthy—handcrafted for every hurdle and hardship you will face today. But there's more.

You don't only have daily mercies; you have daily provision as well. That's why Jesus instructed His disciples that when they pray, they should include the line, "Give us today our daily bread" (Matthew 6:11).

Daily mercies and daily bread. Compassion and contentment. You have all you need today.

A NEW WAY

*At that moment the curtain of the temple
was torn in two from top to bottom.*
MATTHEW 27:51

IF YOU'VE EVER believed the lie that you are not good enough for God, felt too much shame to open your Bible, or feared the doors of church—you need to know this: you are welcome and wanted by the Creator of the universe.

Your heavenly Father longs to have a relationship with you. God is not saying to you today, *Hey, you've messed your life up, and now you have to clean your act up and make your way to Me.* No, instead God has already made the way for you. When Jesus died, He made the way by ripping that veil that signified separation between you and God. He tore it in two so you can walk into His holy place with joy and confidence—no matter who you are or what you've done.

God loves you and sent His Son to die for you. There is nothing you can do to make God love you more, and there is nothing you can do to make Him love you less. So be at peace, and come have a relationship with a holy God. You have access to mercy and grace and holiness, so don't delay in running back to His arms.

PRAYER

God, I choose to cease my striving and rely on Your strength. Guide me to You today.

ALIGNING WITH HIS DESIRES

*Take delight in the LORD, and he will
give you the desires of your heart.*
PSALM 37:4

MOST OFTEN, OUR best next move you can make in life is to choose to simply delight in God. When you do, God gives you something in return—the desires of your heart.

It's an extraordinary promise, but before we start jumping to asking God for all those things we want, like a big wish list, we've got to notice the sequence of how this verse is laid out. The delighting comes first. The fulfillment of our desires happens second. We don't need to worry about what our desires may be, because it's our delighting in God that drives our desires. When we make Jesus our first priority, our desires morph and change over time as God shapes them.

Jesus' desires for our lives are far greater than anything we could dream of. If we commit to pursuing His desires first and foremost, then we'll begin to see the windows of heaven opened as we align with His abundant blessing.

PRAYER

God, I delight in You right now. Stir up my affections and deepen my awe at Your holiness, that I may know You more.

THE GOOD NEWS OF THE GOSPEL

For the wages of sin is death, but the gift of God is eternal life in Christ Jesus our Lord.
ROMANS 6:23

WE LOVE IT when we get good news. The right news at the right time can make our whole day, or in some cases, even our whole year, How amazing is it, then, to stop and consider that we've already been given the best news we could ever hope for—the gospel of Jesus!

The gospel says that sin doesn't make you a bad person. It makes you a spiritually dead person. And being dead is a major problem because dead people can't do a thing to help themselves.

That's why what God has done for us is called good news! Jesus didn't leave heaven and die on a cross to make bad people better people. He gave His life as a sacrifice for our sin and rose again so He could bring us from death to life.

God's love set a rescue plan in place for you not because you deserved or earned it but because of His great love for you. Rejoice in that good news! Shout with joy. Dance with celebration. You were dead, but now you are alive in Jesus.

PRAYER

God, Your gospel is miraculous and magnificent. I am so thankful today for the eternal life You have set within my soul.

A HEAVENLY HOME

*Open my eyes that I may see wonderful
things in your law. I am a stranger on earth;
do not hide your commands from me.*
PSALM 119:18–19

PRAYER

God, You
are eternally
secure, so I
find confidence
today that
through Your
strength, I will
always be able
to stand firm.

WHEN YOU REALIZE that you are a stranger on this earth, that you have the promise of a better home ahead of you, then you can take hold of the invincible faith that God offers His children. Circumstances no longer have to define you. Your hope is in a future glory that nothing can shake or change.

Even though the psalmist was feeling under threat, boxed in, and on the run, he wasn't focused on the things happening around him. Rather, he shifted his soul to better understand more from God's law and to see God move in his life. His confidence in God's future promise transformed his present living.

Knowing you've got a better home ahead doesn't mean you only ever live in the future. Being freed from this world means you can now spend your days on earth worshiping, evangelizing, and shepherding more fully. You can live in alignment with God, knowing that every day you are drawing closer and closer to the perfection of all joy, hope, and peace.

THE RADIANCE OF BEING FORGIVEN

Those who look to [the Lord] are radiant;
their faces are never covered with shame.

PSALM 34:5

DO YOU EVER find yourself fixated on something shameful in your past? It's easy to wallow in these emotions for a long time, even for a lifetime. Whenever we wallow in guilt and shame over our sins, it's as if we are stamping ourselves as "damaged goods."

But Psalm 34:5 points you in a different direction. Have you ever thought of yourself as "radiant"? That's a powerful image, one that's strong enough to counter shame. When you look at God, you're focusing on someone glorious rather than on the griminess of a broken world. Your face is reflecting the light and love of Christ. Sin no longer gets to be your lead story.

It can be hard to forgive yourself. Yet your new identity doesn't spring from you letting yourself off the hook. Your new identity springs from the realization that Jesus forgives you. Jesus took on your debt and paid your wage. Your new identity truly comes into focus when you agree with Jesus. He says you're a son or daughter of God. Jesus says you're forgiven. Do you agree with Him? If Jesus says you can go forward, you can go forward.

PRAYER

Jesus, Your resurrection changes my reality. Guilt and shame are no more because You have set Your radiance, Your righteousness, on me.

GRATITUDE DRIVES A VICTORIOUS HEART

Therefore, since we are receiving a kingdom that cannot be shaken, let us be thankful, and so worship God acceptably with reverence and awe, for our "God is a consuming fire."
HEBREWS 12:28–29

PRAYER

Let my heart say a hundred times today, *Thanks be to God!* Over and over again, let gratitude move my spirit toward victory.

IF I WERE to ask you what you are grateful for, what quickly comes to mind? Maybe you would name some people in your life. Or your job, your home, your health. But how often do you practice *gratitude* for God's faithfulness and His mercy?

It's no secret that you'll face trials and difficult circumstances. You might be facing some today. But no matter *what* you're facing, you can shift *how* you approach your days. If you take on the attitude of Jesus, you quickly begin to see opportunities for gratitude instead of grumbling. You can say, "I am in Christ, and Christ is in me. I am a brand-new creation. Christ is the victor, and I am walking in all the victory Jesus has won for me."

Your new mindset reminds you that God is faithful. You begin to practice gratitude for God's goodness toward you. Your circumstances don't get the final word. True to His promise, God already gave you the victory. So rejoice! Thank Him for His faithfulness and commit to practicing gratitude today.

AN ETERNAL WEIGHT
OF GLORY

For our light and momentary troubles are achieving for us an eternal glory that far outweighs them all.
2 CORINTHIANS 4:17

NONE OF US are immune to days that feel distracted, meaningless, or challenging. In unexpected hardship or long seasons of waiting, we ask ourselves, *What good will come from this?*

This is the battleground of the soul. This is where we must take heart! We know that God will use every moment of our lives for His glory and our good. The Bible is full of histories of hardship, stories of lost and confused people waiting on God to move and come through. And time and time again, He does.

God hasn't left you in your hardship. He's not doing nothing while you waste away. He's going to redeem all your pain in a powerful way for His name. Your suffering will not win the day. In the end, you're going to be standing by the power of a sovereign God who makes all things new.

Have confidence in the long arc of the story that God is writing. Nothing is meaningless. Even if your reward on earth seems small, your troubles are producing an eternal weight of glory that far outweighs everything else.

PRAYER

God, nothing is meaningless in my story. Give me endurance today to keep living for You and Your glory.

FREEDOM AND VICTORY

*If we confess our sins, he is faithful and
just and will forgive us our sins and
purify us from all unrighteousness.*
1 JOHN 1:9

PRAYER

God, Your
humility and
sacrifice have
changed
my life
forevermore.
Praise the
Lamb that
was slain!

HAVE YOU EVER felt too embarrassed to talk to God?
Like you weren't worthy enough to be in His presence?
If so, I have good news. That's natural. On our own,
full of sin, we aren't worthy to be in God's presence.
But that's not our final reality. We can be made worthy through the blood of Jesus' sacrifice. Through His
death, burial, and resurrection, Jesus rang the bell of
our freedom. God took our guilt and placed it on His
innocent and righteous and willing Son.

Then God took the innocence and righteousness of His Son and made it available to us. Through
Christ, you are innocent. You are set free by a holy
and righteous God. All your guilt was taken by Jesus.

For those who are moved by the Spirit of God, the
result of such joyous news is to confess your sins and
to depend fully on Christ. Through that confession,
you realize the fullness of His faithfulness to transfer
His righteousness to you. Guilty no more, let go of
embarrassment and embrace your clean slate before
God today.

STUNNING GRACE THAT UPENDS DEATH

"Greater love has no one than this: to lay down one's life for one's friends."

JOHN 15:13

IF YOU HAVE ever been tempted to question God's character and motives, Scripture helps us remember that in a real moment in history, Jesus gave His life by enduring death on a cross. Jesus Christ laid down His life for us so we could be forgiven and have eternal life. There is no greater proof of God's character and motives than this.

Think of it this way: You, and everyone on this planet, are on a trajectory that inevitably ends in death. Yet God has stepped into the story with stunning grace and upended the power of death (1 Corinthians 15:26–28). It was His plan from the beginning of time (Acts 4:24–28). You can fully trust that the One who overcame death, hell, and the grave loves you and gives His victorious life to you through Jesus Christ. He promises to care for you. Guide you. Protect you. And you can trust Him because He's already endured the worst on your behalf.

PRAYER

God, whenever I begin to question or doubt Your goodness, point me back to the cross. Show me again the scars that prove how far You went to bring me back to You.

CALLED INTO MORE

*But the Lord said to Ananias, "Go! This man is
my chosen instrument to proclaim my name to the
Gentiles and their kings and to the people of Israel."*
ACTS 9:15

BEFORE HE WAS saved, Paul actively worked against
Christians and the new church. But when he met the
risen Jesus, his life changed practically overnight. He
left his entire past identity behind, and he stepped into
a radically new calling on his life. He encountered the
majesty of God, and he could never go back to who he
was before God's grace captivated his heart.

Similarly, when you put your faith in Jesus, God
is inviting you into a new calling. He invites you into
His plan and gives you an assignment to leave behind
your former ways and to follow Him, sharing the good
news of Jesus with those He puts in your path.

The weight of this new calling to go and share
His name is immense, but be encouraged. The same
God who called you will equip you. Protect you.
Provide for you. He is not to be underestimated. Go
in confidence today, knowing He is faithful and He
will surely do it.

PRAYER

God, I want
to be used to
share Your
gospel with
those around
me. Empower
me and
give me the
opportunities
to share Your
good news.

NOTHING CAN LIMIT
THE SPIRIT

Grace and peace to you from God our Father and the Lord Jesus Christ.
EPHESIANS 1:2

WHEN PAUL WAS moved by the Holy Spirit to write to the Ephesians, he was in a crazy, dangerous situation. When you realize and remember Paul's surroundings, it becomes noteworthy how Paul *didn't* begin Ephesians. He could have started out by talking about being in prison and how he was miserable there.

Instead, Paul launched straight into the letter with a huge encouragement sending grace and peace from God. It's as if he was saying, "Even when you're under house arrest, the Holy Spirit can still flood your life in powerful ways. I might be in chains, but my circumstances can't limit God from doing what God wants to do through my life. You may be stuck in your circumstances, but you are still free to be used by the Spirit of God to do whatever it is that God wants to do in and through your life."

That's a big takeaway for us, because some of us are in lousy circumstances. But whatever conditions you find yourself in today—high moments or low—your surroundings don't have to hinder God from doing what He wants to do in your life.

PRAYER

God, no matter what is surrounding me, You have given me grace and peace through Your mighty arms that always lead me exactly where I need to be.

FINDING CLARITY THROUGH GOD'S FATHERHOOD

The Word became flesh and made his dwelling among us. We have seen his glory . . . who came from the Father.
JOHN 1:14

PRAYER

God, I'm stunned today by the fact that I can know You. You are a good Father, and I'm thankful You're inviting me, Your child, to cling to You today.

HAVE YOU EVER thought you knew every angle of a topic or situation only to learn something new that changes what you think? Sometimes this new information can help you love something more, or it can steer you away.

Jesus showed us in Scripture, both through His relationship with His Father and His teaching, that we can see God in a new way. He showed us that God is powerful and glorious, but even more than that, He showed us that all of God's characteristics are wrapped in the person of a Father.

Seeing God through this lens can help you immensely, because so many of God's attributes are difficult to grasp. The fact that God is a Father means He can become relatable to us through the work and person of Jesus. He's knowable, not just in some bookish, academic way. He's family.

When you begin to understand this new revelation of God as a perfect Father, you begin to want to walk with Him through the ins and outs of life.

AN INFINITELY POWERFUL CREATOR

Day after day [the heavens] pour forth speech; night after night they reveal knowledge. They have no speech, they use no words; no sound is heard from them.

PSALM 19:2–3

EACH OF US has a different approach to science and all the staggering details about space and the cosmos. But everyone, everywhere, at some point in life, has gazed into the night sky and felt a sense of wonder.

When you look at the stars and consider how big the universe is, there is a stirring that happens inside the soul, beckoning you to something greater, something more. This is where worship often begins—in wonder and awe at who God is and what He has created.

The longer you look up, the freer you become—lost in the wonder and mystery of God's vastness, lost in praise of the One who set each star in place. When you see God's infinite power, your heart can't help but feel overwhelmed in awe. So let that feeling come and wash over you. Let the wonder of God's mightiness lift you up, and commit once again to relying on His majesty today.

PRAYER

God, stun my heart anew, that I may be in awe of Your mighty power and how You hold every star in its place.

JESUS' WORK IS YOUR WEAPON

Take the helmet of salvation and the sword of the Spirit, which is the word of God.
EPHESIANS 6:17

WHEN YOU'RE FACE-TO-FACE with temptation, loss, or hardship, you've likely felt that you need something more powerful than some routine prayers or half-memorized Bible verses. What can you turn to that will help you stand firm and secure?

Thankfully, the Spirit of God equips you with weapons that have divine power. Those weapons are outlined in Ephesians 6:10–18. These weapons have the power to demolish anything that sets itself up against God. So how do you wield them? You take the initiative to depend on the work of Jesus.

In Christ, you have been given the opportunity because of His death and resurrection to move forward, fighting in power. The power comes from Christ. The victory comes from Christ. Yet you must agree with Christ; it's time for you to step up and take responsibility to partner with Christ in your destiny and your future and your victory.

JOYFUL ADORATION

"I have told you this so that my joy may be in you and that your joy may be complete."
JOHN 15:11

WE DON'T REALLY need a lot of extra convincing to get excited about something that we love. You don't have to go up to a person going to the championship game of their favorite sports team and say, "Can you just get a little more excited?" Odds are, that person is already talking your ear off, giddy about what's to come.

The same is true for us when we go all in on Jesus. Something unlocks in our hearts when we embrace a childlike spirit in our communion with God. When we begin to grasp the depth of God's sacrificial love, following Him becomes a delight. We become excited about His Word. His grace. His holiness. The things that might have seemed difficult or even boring before now seem attractive and enticing.

When you trust that you serve a heavenly Father who wants to bless you, His sanctifying work in your life becomes your joy. And not only that, but you buy into the mission of making His name known. You are eager to share this good news with whoever will listen because you love this God who loved you more than you could ever ask or imagine.

PRAYER

God, let my worship be saturated with the joy of Your salvation. Let my song rise to You, not out of obligation, but out of authentic awe.

THE KING OF GLORY

Who is he, this King of glory? The LORD Almighty—he is the King of glory.
PSALM 24:10

IF YOU WERE asked to paint a portrait of Jesus, where would you start? How would you go about trying to capture His essence in a meaningful way?

When the apostle John was caught up in a vision writing the book of Revelation, the very first thing John saw was Jesus. Not Jesus the carpenter, not the softer side of the Savior, but Jesus the King of glory.

John saw Him in Revelation 1. Jesus unveiled. Jesus as holy and majestic. Awesome and terrifying in His glory and goodness. No human being able to stand in His presence.

When the Enemy tries to tell you that God can't fix your problem, remember this picture of Jesus. When the Enemy tries to convince you how strong and scary he is, remember your mighty and powerful King. You do not belong to a weak and feeble god. He is holy and awesome in wonder. Keep this picture in your mind as you go about your day. It will change the way you worship.

PRAYER

God, reinspire my awe at Your holiness and greatness. May that awe fuel an overwhelming and all-consuming worship today.

FINDING ULTIMATE SATISFACTION

LORD, our Lord, how majestic is your name in all the earth! You have set your glory in the heavens.

PSALM 8:1

AS YOU FOLLOW Jesus, cling to these two life-altering truths that bring an eternity-shifting understanding of God.

First, God wants you to know who He is. He is not obscure, mysteriously engaging in a cosmic game of hide-and-seek. No, God is announcing His presence with every sunrise and declaring His beauty with every sunset. He has gone the extra mile to pursue you and reveal Himself to you. God wants you to see Him in all His glory and splendor.

The second truth is similar: you, like all humanity, are on a desperate search to know who God is.

You may know what it is like to seek the things of this world and not be satisfied. Yet under every human longing is a desire to find the One who made us, the God who stamped His very image onto your soul. When you know Him, you've found the source of endless satisfaction, the One whom you can look to today for fullness and fulfillment.

PRAYER

God, Your glory is set in the heavens, and You are actively revealing Yourself to me. Thank You for making Yourself known.

SAINTS AND NOT SINNERS

Greet all [the saints] in Christ Jesus. The brothers and sisters who are with me send greetings.
PHILIPPIANS 4:21

PRAYER

God, I start today with who You declare I am—a saint in Christ Jesus who has been brought back to new and everlasting life.

WE DON'T USE the word *saint* to describe ourselves often, but it's a word Paul consistently used to refer to those who believed in God. These were ordinary people, but because they were connected to Jesus, everything had changed. *Saints* is powerful because it's a strong identity word, especially for people who have called themselves "sinners" all their lives.

This is an important distinction, because starting from the place of being a saint is the opposite of religion. Religion starts with what you do (sin) and works its way toward what you might become (saint). Maybe you've been caught up in that, the thought that if you do enough good things and change how you behave, then maybe you can become the person God wants you to be.

God doesn't work like that. God starts with an act of faith in which we join our lives to Jesus. Something happens inside us. We become brand-new creatures in Jesus Christ. God starts with who we've become in Him, and then from that identity, He empowers us to live out a holy and obedient life to Him.

HOPE THAT EXCEEDS ALL EXPECTATIONS

And hope does not put us to shame, because God's love has been poured out into our hearts through the Holy Spirit.
ROMANS 5:5

THE GOD WHOSE hand carved out the oceans and their boundaries is the same God who created you in His likeness. He knew your name before you were born, and He goes with you moment to moment, day after day. Not a single thought in your head or step you take goes unnoticed by Him.

This God of constant care speaks grace over every second of your life today, offering you mercy and affection in every breath you take. This God has a purpose and a plan for you. He's masterfully weaving every moment together—even the seemingly mundane ones—in His great and glorious story. Nothing is wasted. Nothing is off His radar.

When you come to Him in prayer, He's not going to just meet your expectations. He'll exceed them in every way. And every day, you can live with the hope that one day you will be face-to-face with this wondrous, holy God, worshiping Him for all eternity. So fight for joy and hope today. You are held by love, and you have all you need.

PRAYER

God, I focus on Your hope today, so by Your Spirit, stir my heart toward Your heavenly throne.

NOTHING IS BIGGER THAN JESUS

"The thief comes only to steal and kill and destroy; I have come that they may have life, and have it to the full."
JOHN 10:10

PRAYER

Jesus, I rejoice today that Your desire for me is an abundant life. May my heart come to know and believe that true abundance is found only in You.

WE HAVE A destructive inclination to label sin in our lives as "minor." Even though we know it goes against God's will, we tolerate it. We justify its existence, convincing ourselves it's not so bad. We might be annoyed that it's there, but wrestling with it feels harder than just giving in to the temptation.

Don't let the thief steal the fullness of life from you. He comes only to take and tear down. Jesus offers an abundant life to everyone who follows Him. He didn't come to earth to die on the cross and be resurrected from the grave so you could settle for a reduced amount of God's best. Jesus intended for you to "really live" (1 Thessalonians 3:8). You can live freely in the power of what He has accomplished for you.

It starts with seeing and believing that whatever sin you come up against may be big—but it's not bigger than Jesus. He intends to set you free.

GOD'S VICTORY DEFINES YOU NOW

The law was brought in so that the trespass
might increase. But where sin increased,
grace increased all the more.
ROMANS 5:20

IF YOU'VE EVER thought, *I'm too broken for God to want me,* rest assured that the whole church was founded by people with a past. If there was anyone who should have been counted out of doing great things for God, it was Paul. He spent years ruthlessly persecuting the church and followers of Jesus, and he later called himself the "chief of sinners."

And yet, this chief of sinners would go on to write most of the New Testament! Paul's past didn't define his story; Jesus did. When Jesus bore the weight of sin on the cross, His righteousness transferred to all His followers. And so, Jesus made a way for this enemy of the gospel to become one of the greatest missionaries of all time.

If you're still defining yourself by your sin, the Lord can set you free. You may have a broken past, but all have sinned and fallen short of the glory of God (Romans 3:23). Like Paul, embrace the love of Jesus, and the finished work of the cross.

PRAYER

God, thank You that You chose me, even when I didn't deserve it. Use me to share Your story of grace.

OUR PATHWAY TO
THE FATHER

Jesus answered, "I am the way and the truth and the life. No one comes to the Father except through me."
JOHN 14:6

PRAYER

God, I cannot capture the fullness of my amazement at Your character and power. But I can praise Jesus even more because He has made the way back to You possible.

IF YOU WANT to know more about who God is and how He cares for you, look to the life and death of Jesus. When you look at the cross, you witness that God is powerful, holy, omnipotent, ruler of all things, greater than all things, loving, saving, good, generous, compassionate, and much more.

Yet there is something even more amazing that Jesus teaches us about God, and it's a revolutionary truth that sets us free to become everything God created us to be. The number one image of God that Jesus paints for us again and again is that God is a Father. He is our perfect Abba Father.

This might have been the most counterintuitive truth that changed everything for those in His day. The same can be true for you. Jesus wants you to know that this Father-child relationship is available to you today, and like any good father, God would love to talk to you, provide for you, defend you, and lead you where He knows you need to go.

THE ENEMY LIED

"You will not certainly die," the serpent said to the woman. "For God knows that when you eat from it your eyes will be opened, and you will be like God, knowing good and evil."

GENESIS 3:4–5

AT THE BEGINNING of humanity, God's beautiful plan of Paradise was sabotaged by two people who made a fatal choice. Their action, while not outside of God's sovereign control, brought consequences into an otherwise glorious circumstance.

The first humans reached for the forbidden fruit from the Tree of Knowledge of Good and Evil and took a brazen bite. Believing the Enemy's accusations (Is God good? Can He be trusted?), Adam and Eve did the one thing the Creator warned them not to do. They wanted to be in charge—or at least wanted as much authority and knowledge as the God who had formed them. But, as they quickly discovered, God wasn't trying to keep anything from them. In fact, He was seeking to protect their peace.

Where are you trying to control what God has promised you? Ask Him to help you unclench your hand from what was never meant to be your responsibility. He has this. You can trust Him.

PRAYER

God, I obey You because I can trust in You. Protect me from the illusion of control through Your promised provision.

JOINING WHOLEHEARTEDLY WITH JESUS

"I tell you the truth, whoever believes in me will do the same things that I do. Those who believe will do even greater things than these."
JOHN 14:12 NCV

PRAYER

God, because I am in You, You empower me to live and love like Jesus. Give me more faith to see You move in mighty ways in my life.

EVERYBODY WANTS GRACE and peace, but few know where to truly find it.

For those who are surrendered to Jesus, we know that grace and peace are reflective of our new position in Christ. When we put our faith in Jesus, we don't join an organization. We join *with* Jesus. And when we join *with* Him, our lives and stories and pasts and presents and futures are inseparably joined together with Jesus' life and story. Our abilities are joined to His abilities. Our dreams are joined to His dreams. Our destiny is joined to His destiny.

That means that becoming a Christ follower involves more than simply saying we believe in something. We are joined to Someone! We join our lives to His, which is why we can declare that Christ is in us, the hope of glory.

This isn't based on how we feel on any given day. It is a reality from the instant we come to life by faith in Christ. Praise God today that you are in Christ and He is in you.

HOPE OVER THE HORIZON

Instead, they were longing for a better country—a heavenly one. Therefore God is not ashamed to be called their God, for he has prepared a city for them.
HEBREWS 11:16

THE DARKEST MOMENTS of your life often bring out the richest qualities of your faith in God. To live by faith and not by sight requires assurance in the One who is ultimately in charge of your life.

How can we find that confidence? We learn the story of God's steadfast love. The Bible offers us historical accounts of God's faithfulness and security. It gives us a glimpse into His unshakable provision. It reveals the evidence that helps us believe He is who He says He is.

But faith is also future-oriented. Our confidence is bolstered not only by what God has done but also on what He promises to do. We have great hope just over the horizon. Take heart that you are headed for a better country, where death and sorrow will be no more. If you feel yourself wobble in your confidence, fix your eyes on the heavenly city, on spending eternity with Jesus. Let that future joy work backward into your heart today. Rejoice because your salvation is secure and is coming sooner than you think.

PRAYER

God, give me a glimpse of heaven, that my hope would be brimming over today.

345

THE PICTURE OF GOD ON EARTH

The Son is the radiance of God's glory and the exact representation of his being, sustaining all things by his powerful word.
HEBREWS 1:3

HAVE YOU EVER seen a kid who looks exactly like their parents? We know scientifically that who you come from shapes you. This is what the author of Hebrews was communicating by saying that Jesus is the exact representation of God. Jesus left heaven and came to planet Earth, becoming human, in part to show people what the Father was like.

He looked like His Father, so by studying the life, words, and work of Jesus, you can start to see the Father more clearly. You can better grasp attributes of His character like His love, mercy, and power.

If you've been born again into the family of God, you are a son or daughter of this perfect heavenly Father. So ask yourself today, When people look at you, are they seeing Him? Are they able to better know God because you reflect His character through your life? Pray that He would help you radiate His goodness and glory today.

LIVING UNDER GOD'S MIGHTY HAND

Humble yourselves, therefore, under God's mighty hand, that he may lift you up in due time.

1 PETER 5:6

IF YOU EVER feel the crushing weight of anxiety pressing in on your heart and mind, you can turn to 1 Peter 5, particularly verses 6–11. Jesus invites you to cast all your anxiety on Him, not just because He's the best one to carry it, but because He cares about you. How stunning! The God of the universe cares for you so much so that that He invites you to give Him everything that's weighing you down.

In the original Greek language, the word used for *anxiety* in this verse means "to divide" or "to pull apart." That's what happens to our hearts when we are anxious about something. That's why Jesus offers to carry this weight for us if only we surrender it to Him.

Once you can name what is weighing down your soul, you are on the road to freedom. When you can identify it, you can specifically cast it on Jesus in a meaningful way. You can transfer the burden and concern to His care, knowing He cares about you. In humility, pray today for God's peace and put your problems once more in His hands.

PRAYER

Lord, I know You care for me. I come today with my concerns—not because You command or coerce but because You care, and I lay them under Your mighty hand.

OUR ARMOR IS GOD-MADE

*Put on the full armor of God, so that you can
take your stand against the devil's schemes.*
EPHESIANS 6:11

PRAYER

Father, I
commit to
putting on
Your spiritual
armor today,
that I would be
equipped to
fight against
the darkness
and dwell in
the light.

THE ENEMY IS cunning and strategic. He attacks where he knows his hits will hurt you the most, doing anything he can to throw you off course. The rude comment at work. The unexpected car trouble when your finances are on the rocks. The friend who disappears right when you need them the most.

But you can be encouraged today, because as a follower of Christ, you are not left defenseless against these schemes and attacks.

You have been given God-designed armor that is strong, forged with truth and righteousness. When you put on this armor, you have the gospel of peace and the shield of faith. You have the helmet of salvation and the sword of the Spirit—the Word of God—to help you push back the darkness.

Your armor isn't the old clunky suit you'd see in a museum. Your armor was crafted in the fires of God's holiness. All that's required of you is to submit yourself before God and put it on. Go forward with the peace that you're prepared to face all things.

YOU'RE IN THE FAMILY

To them God has chosen to make known among the Gentiles the glorious riches of this mystery, which is Christ in you, the hope of glory.
COLOSSIANS 1:27

IF YOU HAVE younger children, you don't spend time trying to convince them to believe they are a part of your family. They are *in* your family, and from that truth, they can experience all the benefits of being in your family.

The same is true with Christianity. Your new identity is that you have Christ living in you. You are supernaturally joined with Jesus. You have moved from death to life. From sinner to saint. You are *in* God's family. And not only that, but Jesus is *in* you.

That means that if Jesus died, you died. It means that if Jesus rose, you rose. If Jesus lives, you live. If Jesus wins, you win. If Jesus says that this is the way, you walk in it.

It's Jesus in you, not you in Jesus. You're inseparably linked by grace through faith. It's not Christ and you, it's Christ in you! Draw from His immeasurably great power and grace today.

PRAYER

Jesus, because I am tethered to You and Your vine, grant me wisdom to depend fully on You and nothing else. You are my hope of glory, my worthwhile inheritance, and I look only to You.

DECEMBER

LET GOD BECOME YOUR VIEW

Before the mountains were born or you brought forth the whole world, from everlasting to everlasting you are God.
PSALM 90:2

THERE ARE SO many things vying for your attention and affection. In the cacophony of voices, how do you find a right and truthful way of living?

You start with a right view of God. Scripture tells us that He has been a solid and firm foundation throughout all generations. That He is unshakable. That before the mountains were born or the seas were filled, He was there, holy, sturdy, and secure. He is everlasting.

What could be better than building your life on someone who has never failed? Who never diminished one single ounce of goodness or glory? Who never surrendered an inch of ground to an opponent?

When you start with a right view of God, every other viewpoint, every other voice that's competing for your attention becomes small and quiet in comparison. God doesn't just ruin every other viewpoint; He becomes *the* view. So make sure you have His grace and His glory in your sights today, and let the rest fade into the background.

THE DIVINE FORCE
BEHIND IT ALL

For since the creation of the world God's invisible qualities—his eternal power and divine nature—have been clearly seen.
ROMANS 1:20

PRAYER

God, when I look around at the world You have created, my heart can't help but cry that You are holy! In awe, inspire me to seek You deeper.

HOW DO YOU develop an accurate view of God? He's not hard to notice. He is constantly revealing Himself, and what you see of Him in the cosmos is just the beginning of His might. But that doesn't mean it's easy to really see Him, to view Him in all of His glory.

In Romans 1, God wants to make sure we know who He is and that we see Him correctly.

Anybody, anywhere on planet Earth, can look around and consider the universe—the mountains and sunsets, the stars and volcanoes, the marvelous flight-producing design of a feathered bird, the half a billion neurons in the motor cortex of your brain that are present just so you can talk—and conclude that there must be some divine force behind it all.

That's good news. Nature shows us that indeed there is a God—a creative, beautiful, intelligent God. But even more than that, through Jesus, we know that this God is not far off, but can be known. You can walk with Him today, step-by-step.

STEPPING INTO RESURRECTION POWER

And if the Spirit of him who raised Jesus from the dead is living in you, he who raised Christ from the dead will also give life to your mortal bodies.
ROMANS 8:11

PRAYER

Hallelujah,
You have
redeemed
me! You
have made
straight my
paths and
changed my
eternal
destiny. I
praise You
in splendor
and holiness.

EVEN AFTER YOU put your faith in Jesus, you'll still be tempted to live in your old ways—giving doubt, insecurity, anger, or pride power over your life. Becoming like Jesus isn't a one-day event.

The difference between who you were before putting your faith in Jesus and who you are after is this: You no longer need to accept the lies or thoughts the Enemy tries to plant in your mind. He formerly led you to sins that choked the life out of your heart, but they no longer get to rule over you.

Jesus has broken the power of sin, and God now invites you, by the power of the Spirit living in you, to embrace a new mindset. A new way of living. In Jesus' name, you are dead to the power of sin. In Jesus' name, you can win the battle for your mind. You are no longer bound to fear. You are set free. You are alive. Praise Him today that you are a child of God, and step into your resurrection power as you fight against temptation.

MOVING TOWARD GOD

"This is what the Lord says . . . , 'Call to me and I will answer you and tell you great and unsearchable things you do not know.'"
JEREMIAH 33:2–3

GIVE GOD A chance. Call out to Him today. He wants to open your eyes to see Him as the kind of Father He truly is. He wants to tear down any misconceptions that have formed in your mind about Him. He knows what you've been through. He knows your story, and He wants to walk with you through the hard stuff, the pain you have endured as a result of living on a broken planet.

God wants to bring you to the place where you believe and receive that what He says is true. Only He can do that. Only God can declare that you are a child of the King of the universe. And He wants you to live fearless and free. He always stands poised and ready to take a step toward you. You just need to give Him the nod, then simply be willing to take a baby step toward Him. This drawing near is the beginning of strength and courage and will invite confidence into your heart through Christ.

PRAYER

God, I will not be terrified, because You are with me. I will not be discouraged today because in You, I cannot be shaken.

COMFORT THROUGH SORROW

"Ah, Sovereign Lord, you have made the heavens and the earth by your great power and outstretched arm. Nothing is too hard for you."
JEREMIAH 32:17

PRAYER

God, comfort me today with the fact that nothing is too hard for You and that You are able to bring good from hardship.

NO MATTER WHO you are or where you come from, you've likely suffered some form of loss. If you are in that tension right now, you may feel like you're on the brink of collapse, or like the loss you've experienced is too heavy to keep going. Know today that you're not alone in these feelings. If you are in relationship with God, He is able to heal and restore every wound and worry.

When we say God is able, that's not a little Christian slogan to throw around. It is reality, and we have proof of His power all around us. We just have to look up and see His creation—the entire cosmos—to know that God is all-powerful. The God who made the galaxies knows exactly what you are walking through, and He is actively and compassionately working in your life.

Our God is a God of order, and He still has a plan for you. Nothing is too hard for Him. Loss doesn't get the final word—the God of all creation does. This is who journeys with you today.

ASSURANCE VS. AVOIDANCE

*Since we live by the Spirit, let us
keep in step with the Spirit.*
GALATIANS 5:25

IF YOU'RE TIRED of feeling like you need to figure out your life on your own, it's never too late to start depending on the Spirit. Through Jesus, you have all the power you need to shift from self-reliance to Spirit-reliance.

This might feel overwhelming or awkward at first. It's like the first workout when you're trying to get back in shape. But stick with it and keep showing up. If you commit and start down this path, the Spirit will continue to empower you to fight the good fight.

Sin ultimately tries to get you to avoid any hardships that *might* come against you. The closer you stay to God, the more you'll come to realize that *avoidance* isn't the desired outcome of the Christian life. The goal is *assurance*. Assurance is what turns a *what if* into an *even if* through the truth of *what is*. God *is* good. Loving. Kind. Mighty in power. He *is*, and because of that truth, you can have assurance no matter what comes against you.

PRAYER

God, help me stay in step with You today. I want to live with holy assurance of Your power; show me how to make that shift here and now.

THE CLEAR CORNERSTONE

"If you remain in me and my words remain in you, ask whatever you wish, and it will be done for you."
JOHN 15:7

PRAYER

Jesus, I want
to depend
more on You
today and less
on myself.
Steer me
sweetly back
into Your arms
that I would be
secure on Your
cornerstone.

When you think your life depends solely on you, each stress and strain can feel overwhelming, if not frustrating. Yet when God calls you to hard things, it's never all on your shoulders.

Peter was destined to be the cornerstone of the early church, but Jesus knew that Peter wasn't going to be ready for that responsibility until Peter understood that Jesus was the real cornerstone. Peter needed to be completely clear on that. As long as Peter believed it all depended on him, Jesus couldn't use him. Peter needed to depend on Jesus first.

But like so many of us, Peter had forgotten that. He tried to do things his way. He'd denied Jesus, but Jesus knew Peter's heart and He knows yours. He knows the plans He has for your life, and instead of you figuring them all out on your own, He invites you to stay close. To trust Him. To remain in Him.

That is where the fruit is. The joy. The peace. The cornerstone to stand on. That's how Jesus leads you, allowing you to rely on Him for His strength and sufficiency.

HE LOVES YOU TODAY

"Everyone who is called by my name, whom I created for my glory, whom I formed and made."
ISAIAH 43:7

IT'S ONLY NATURAL to question how someone can have faith in the midst of this pain-filled and broken planet. In light of so much devastation, how can we still worship God in spite of what we see around us?

You can find assurance because God isn't unaware or unconcerned with what is happening. He cares so much that He is right in the midst of the devastation with you. In real time, He is empowering you. Comforting you. Leading you. Yes, God did amazing miracles in the past. And victory is coming in the future. But what's so remarkable about the Christian faith is that it's not just a "back then" or a "someday" relationship. It's a "right now" relationship, where moment-by-moment you are walking with Jesus in every circumstance.

He knows your pain. Empathizes with you. He understands your heartache. And He gently and lovingly leads you right where you are. He made you, and He won't let you go a single day without being by your side. So call on Him. Lean on Him. Let His love wash over you today.

PRAYER

God, You have called me by name, so in faith, I will move toward You in worship today. I will give You the honor due Your name.

359

THERE IS ONLY ONE CROSS

For we know that since Christ was raised from the dead, he cannot die again; death no longer has mastery over him.
ROMANS 6:9

EVEN AFTER YOU'VE put your faith in Jesus, it can be difficult to bring your whole self to Him. It's tempting to keep the things we're most embarrassed or ashamed of hidden off to the side and away from Jesus. But He wants you to know that He's already paid for every sin and shortcoming.

Jesus died one time—for all time. He never needs to go to another cross. Period. The work of defeating death and all hell's power is finished. Completed. Done. Accomplished. Jesus has defeated all of sin, all of death, all of hell, all of darkness.

He is the ultimate Enemy defeater, demolishing the devil with a defining and deafening blow. Death doesn't carry a sting anymore. There is nothing in your story that can separate you from Jesus—no shame, no secret, no sin. Bring it all to Him. Open up every part of your heart and trust that His good love will wash over you today.

PRAYER

Lord, thank You for allowing me to bring You my sin, without shame or condemnation. I celebrate and shout with joy at Your ultimate and eternal victory!

AN UNENDING AND UNASSAILABLE LOVE

The LORD bless you and keep you; the LORD make his face shine on you and be gracious to you.

NUMBERS 6:24–25

HISTORY RECORDS THAT the God of heaven is for you. He made you. He sees you. He Himself wants to be your Father, and He wants to shower you with His blessing. He wants to raise you up, show you the ropes, help you grow strong, and cheer you on as you pursue your God-given passion. He wants to put a safety net of His love under you so you can spread your wings and take flight without the crippling fear of failure holding you down.

The blessing God wants to give you is not to be discounted. In fact, the blessing of your heavenly Father is actually way beyond any human relationship. The best possible earthly father giving the most excellent blessing can't compare to the smile of your heavenly Father. His love is supernatural and powerful, unending and unassailable.

And His love means this for us: If you know Him as Father, you will never be left behind. You will never go unwanted. You will always have a place of hope and a home with Him.

PRAYER

God, open my eyes to more intimately understand Your great blessing, how You have gone before and behind me in victory, singing over me with steadfast love.

361

LET HIS WORK SPEAK THROUGH YOU

"But you will receive power when the Holy Spirit comes on you; and you will be my witnesses . . . to the ends of the earth."
ACTS 1:8

PRAYER

God, help me proclaim Your name, that the people around me would know the same hope that You've given me.

IN THE STORY of the gospel, God shows up in your story and offers you the chance to exchange your "bad news" with His good news. He offers hope when you have none and promises you an eternal life in His presence. It doesn't end there. When you say yes to that exchange and receive the Spirit, you receive a new calling on your life—to awaken people around you to the grace and mercy of Jesus Christ.

God could have chosen a multitude of ways to make Jesus known to the world, but He chose you to be a part of His church. As you begin to share the gospel of Jesus with others, you'll find your testimony is one of your greatest tools. Every word, answered prayer, and blessing that He provides demonstrates His victory over death. The God who rose from the dead is resurrecting you! Don't take His work and hide it. Let the ends of the earth witness His power in your life, so that they, too, may know the redemptive work of Christ. This is your greatest calling.

GOOD HEART, STRONG ARMS

Though my father and mother forsake me, the LORD will receive me.

PSALM 27:10

NO MATTER YOUR relationship with your earthly dad, you have a perfect Father in heaven who loves you and wants to pour out His blessing on you. That's what David spoke of when he wrote the words in Psalm 27:10 that have comforted countless people who are living in real tension with their earthly families.

Even if the blessing of our dad escapes us, the love of our heavenly Father can still find us. Even if our dad is no longer with us, our Father God can still hold us close and lift us up. If we have experienced a breakdown in our relationship with our dads, it doesn't mean we can't experience a miracle recovery in our relationship with God. Even though we may bear wounds inflicted by our earthly fathers, God can restore us and raise us up healed and whole.

God is a Father, but He's not the same as your earthly dad. His heart is good, and His arms are strong. You can run to Him and He won't ever let you down.

PRAYER

God, You are not just the best person I can think of. You are the exact fulfillment and perfection of all things holy. You are good, and I am Your child.

BUILDING AN "EVEN IF" FAITH

*Though the fig tree does not bud and there are
no grapes on the vines . . . yet I will rejoice in
the LORD, I will be joyful in God my Savior.*
HABAKKUK 3:17–18

PRAYER

Lord, I want
to live with
an "even if"
faith. Help me
to be so sure
and confident
of Your great
love that no
matter the
circumstance,
I stay rooted
with You.

IT'S HARD NOT to marvel when you read throughout Scripture about people who encountered intense
trouble yet went all in with their faith. One less-quoted
but faithful leader is the prophet Habakkuk. Even in
the midst of utter despair, notice the two phrases that
Habakkuk repeats three times in his closing prayer:

"Even though . . ."

"I will . . ."

Habakkuk basically said, "Even though life is
desolate and difficult, I will still be joyful and glad
because the Lord God is my Savior. I have not lost my
faith. In fact, my faith is even greater. I'm still going
to rejoice in the Lord. I'm still going to worship God."

That kind of faith doesn't just have to remain in
the pages of Scripture. It can be true of your life, and
it can rise in your heart when you see Jesus as the ultimate treasure of your soul.

THE GREAT PIVOT
OF CHRISTIANITY

And if Christ has not been raised, our preaching is useless and so is your faith.
1 CORINTHIANS 15:14

IF YOU FEEL powerless, defeated, or even half-victorious, know that the same power that raised Jesus from the dead is available to you. It's at work, right now, revitalizing the parts of your story that need a new touch of power.

The resurrection is the great pivot on which the Christian faith hinges, and it's the source of abundant life and grace for a believer. Don't overlook this. It's not something to be shrugged off—the resurrection power of almighty God that brought Jesus up from the grip of death and hell is living in you!

We need to be sure that we understand how important the resurrection of Jesus Christ is to us personally. When we live from that power, it truly changes everything. First, it guarantees that we can be freed from the need to pay for our own sins. And second, it makes overwhelming grace and power readily available to us so that we can leverage our whole lives toward making much of Jesus. Embrace that truth today and get ready to see how God will use you.

PRAYER

God, give me a deeper and richer appreciation for Your resurrection and salvation today. Help me to stand firmly on Your good and life-giving truth!

365

GOD REVEALS AS WE SEEK

One thing I ask from the LORD, this only do I seek: that I may dwell in the house of the LORD all the days of my life, to gaze on the beauty of the LORD and to seek him in his temple.

PSALM 27:4

PRAYER

God, I want to seek You more. Help me to dwell with You today, that I would gaze on Your beauty with joy.

CHRISTIANS AROUND THE world worship in different forms. Different volumes, different music, and different traditions. While our worship may differ, one thing remains the same: God is eager to reveal Himself to those who are eager to find Him.

He isn't playing some cosmic game of hide-and-seek where you just need to look hard enough or long enough and then He'll pop up and yell, "Surprise!" No, He wants to be found. He wants to show you more of Himself because He knows that when you gaze upon His beauty and dwell with Him in His courts, you fall more in love with Him. And you get all the benefits of being in His presence.

So don't get so caught up today in *how* to draw near. You can sing. Journal prayers. Dance. Kneel in the dark. There are a thousand *hows*, but there is only one true *why*—to see and savor the beauty and majesty of King Jesus.

CONCEALING DOESN'T CURE ANYTHING

Therefore confess your sins to each other and pray for each other so that you may be healed.
JAMES 5:16

TODAY, BY THE power of God, you can examine your shortcomings and bring them to Jesus, allowing the light of Scripture to wash over them and through them. You can immerse yourself in the goodness and greatness of God and let Jesus write the story of your redemption.

But be mindful, the Enemy won't want you to surrender your sins without a fight. He'll try to get you to cover up your sin, minimize it. After all, if your sin is concealed, it will eventually just go away, right?

Unfortunately, that's not how sin works. Even if you can hide your shortcomings from everyone else, God knows. He sees. He is aware of every broken act and misplaced thought. But for those who believe in Jesus, He offers grace from the guilt. Freedom from the failure. Because God is steadfast and loving, we don't need to conceal our sin. We can confess it, both to Him and to our community of believers. That's how we'll ultimately find healing.

PRAYER

Father, would You give me the strength today to confess my shortcomings and surrender my pride?

OUR SHINING LIGHT OF HOPE

The light shines in the darkness, and the darkness has not overcome it.
JOHN 1:5

PRAYER

Jesus, I turn
to You first,
before any
other source
of strength.
Because You
are my Savior,
I can walk with
full confidence,
knowing You
will never let
me down.

WHEN YOU ARE in the middle of a dark day or a dark season, it can be hard to imagine finding your way back to the light. But in faith, you can have confidence because God promises to lead you *through* the valley of the shadow of death. He won't leave you behind; He'll always provide a way out.

This may sound simplistic and elementary, but it's amazing how often we first look to a website, a friend, a diagnosis, or a book for our support and answers— when the God of heaven is standing right in front of you, offering to be your Shepherd in whatever valley you are in.

What proof can you have of His provision and guidance? He came to planet Earth, God in human flesh. He lived among men. He was crucified, though He had done nothing wrong. He died, was buried, and then resurrected. His ultimate victory over all darkness proves that He can be all that you need today, a source of light that can lead you out of any darkness.

THE INCREDIBLE INVITATION

"I am the good shepherd; I know my sheep and my sheep know me."

JOHN 10:14

PSALM 23 DEPICTS God as a personal and attentive Shepherd, One who intimately cares for the sheep yet is tough enough to defend them against attacks. In time, we see this Shepherd most clearly in the person of Jesus Christ.

In John 10:1–21, Jesus outlined how He Himself is our Good Shepherd. He protects us from attacks that will try to knock us off course. He provides for us and meets our daily needs. He guides us, and we are able to listen for and know His voice. And in the end, He lays down His life for us.

Jesus is a personal, involved God who is saying, *I want to be your Good Shepherd.* Can we just stop and breathe in this reality? The Good Shepherd, who also happens to be God, is offering to lead you through every moment of your life! He wants to walk with you personally and be involved in your day-to-day living. Let your heart be encouraged today by God's intentionality and His desire to live in a right relationship with you.

PRAYER

God, You are mindful of me! You want to shepherd and steer my soul, so I release the reins of my life, trusting that You will guide me perfectly.

CREATED WITH GIFTING TO GLORIFY

Whatever you do, work at it with all your heart, as working for the Lord, not for human masters, since you know that you will receive an inheritance from the Lord as a reward. It is the Lord Christ you are serving.
COLOSSIANS 3:23–24

PRAYER

God, You have set before me good works to walk in. Knowing this, I aim to excel in what You have given me, doing this work with all my heart as for Your glory.

GOD HAS WIRED each of us with unique abilities, aptitudes, and desires. He has put His stamp on our souls and He's pressed a gifting onto our hearts that we would follow Him all the days of our lives.

That's why the core of our reason for being is to know and love our Maker and enjoy Him forever. Nothing is more important than that; nothing—no earthly title, relationship, status, or success—surpasses that central purpose. Yet within our relationship with God, He tailors us to make our unique contributions to the greater good for His glory, giving our individual lives very specific meaning and direction.

His plan for you is not mere existence. It's way beyond monotonous drudgery. He has woven into your heart a gift and a dream so that you can invest your days in meaningful pursuits that make your heart come alive and give Him much glory.

REJOICING IN THE HOUSE OF THE LORD

I rejoiced with those who said to me, "Let us go to the house of the LORD."

PSALM 122:1

IF WE'RE NOT careful, church can quickly become about attendance and not about engaging with the living God. But church was never meant to be about simply checking a box. God has far more in store for those who actively lean into their local church than just another rule to manage.

From the very beginning, the church has been a deep-rooted source of life, worship, friendship, and accountability. It has been the people of God walking together as they all become more like Jesus. It is the place where worship is exponentially elevated as people from all backgrounds join under the banner of Christ's glory.

Worshiping together with our church family helps readjust our hearts. It provides fuel for our faith that can't be found anywhere else. It shows us a glimpse of heaven and inspires our trust in the power of a holy and loving God. Don't neglect the opportunity to be in church. Embrace it and watch how your awe of God blossoms.

PRAYER

God, I want to be with Your people, singing Your praises. Inspire me, ignite me, that I may worship You with all that I have.

WORTHY OF IT ALL

In a loud voice they were saying: "Worthy is the Lamb, who was slain, to receive power and wealth and wisdom and strength and honor and glory and praise!"
REVELATION 5:12

HOW DO YOU determine the order of authority in your life? Who gets the final word? Work? Your family? God? When it comes to your priorities, what gets the top line?

When the apostle John wrote the book of Revelation, he got a glimpse into the throne room of God. Everything in the throne room was oriented around the person standing in the center: the Lamb of God, Jesus, who was slain for the sin of the world. All heavenly beings bowed to worship around Him. Everything in creation recognized His ultimate power and authority.

Will you join the chorus of the angels and order your life around the one true King? God is the only One who deserves to be on the top line of our lives. He is worthy of all honor. All glory. All praise.

So praise Him! Right now, right this second. The Lamb of God isn't just somewhere in the cosmos far away. He's close. He's with you. So bow, right where you are. Worship. Acknowledge what Jesus offered for you, give Him the top line, and respond with praise.

THE FIERY FURNACE

If we are thrown into the blazing furnace, the God we serve is able to deliver us from it, and he will deliver us from Your Majesty's hand.

DANIEL 3:17

WHEN LIFE GETS tough, where do you turn? It feels easy to follow Jesus when everything is going according to plan. But what do you stand on when hardship comes or when the bottom starts to fall out?

If you are fighting for your faith right now, think of three Hebrew young men—Shadrach, Meshach, and Abednego—who worshiped God in an era when King Nebuchadnezzar had commanded everybody to only worship a huge gold statue of himself.

It might have seemed logical for them to abandon their faith. But the faith of Shadrach, Meshach, and Abednego didn't deflate in the heat of the trial. Instead, their faith inflated. Even on the edge of a fiery furnace. They chose to believe that whether they were rescued out of their circumstances or left to go through the fire—God would show up.

Likewise, when you realize that Jesus invites you to follow Him even though life is hard, you exercise faith that will last through any situation.

PRAYER

Jesus, I'm not sure how this situation will end, but I am confident that You will be with me in the fire.

JESUS HAS ALL AUTHORITY

Then Jesus came to them and said, "All authority in heaven and on earth has been given to me."
MATTHEW 28:18

PRAYER

God, You are victorious over every sin. Give me confidence and hope to stand firm and fight the good fight.

HAVE YOU EVER felt like your sin is stronger than the Spirit of Jesus living inside you? It might feel strange to admit, but sometimes, sin seems to have the upper hand, and we start to listen to the voice of our Enemy more than the voice of our Savior.

But Jesus is not some puny god. And He's certainly not flimsy or frail or helpless or toothless. The reason Jesus came to earth was to crush the power of sin and death. That's what Jesus did. The work is finished.

Yet even though Jesus completed the work on the cross, sin still plagues us today. We are new creations living in a fallen, broken world.

When you feel this tension, remember that you are not left alone to sort this all out. You have the Spirit of God to guide and lead you each and every day. He does this by reminding you of who you are and where your true power comes from—Jesus, the One who has all authority over sin and death.

THE FULLNESS OF JOY IS WITH GOD

For He Himself has said, "I will never leave you nor forsake you."
HEBREWS 13:5 NKJV

NO MATTER WHAT you are walking through, your Father remains present with you. In fact, this has been a trait of God from the beginning. In the garden, God walked with the first humans in the cool of the day. When His people were navigating the desert after being freed from bondage, God had Moses build a Tent of Meeting where His presence descended in a cloud that covered the tent as God talked with Moses face-to-face. In time, the tent was replaced by a tabernacle, and then a temple, and in each place, there was the promise of God's presence.

However, things dramatically changed when one night in Bethlehem, Jesus was born. God was no longer in a tent or a temple, not in the cloud or some other manifestation of His nearness. God was now among men in the person of Jesus, whose name is called Emmanuel—God with us.

The psalmist wrote, speaking about the perfect Father, "In Your presence is fullness of joy; at Your right hand are pleasures forevermore" (Psalm 16:11 NKJV).

PRAYER

God, Your consistent presence with me brings great joy and great strength. Because You are close, I can know true contentment.

375

GOOD NEWS, GREAT JOY

But the angel said to them, "Do not be afraid. I bring you good news that will cause great joy for all the people."
LUKE 2:10

PRAYER

God, thank
You for
providing
lasting peace
and joy. You
rescued me,
and I rejoice
in Your
wisdom and
salvation.

WHEN THE ANGELS appeared to the shepherds at the time of Jesus' birth, their first reaction was to cower in terror. But as the story goes, we know there is no reason to fear for those of us on whom God's favor rests. Following Jesus guarantees heavenly good news. It guarantees joy. It guarantees peace.

The peace the angels proclaimed at Jesus' birth is a blood-bought promise that redeems God's people back to Him. Jesus chose to be the solution—humbling Himself unto death—so that anyone who would seek Him could spend eternity with God. This is our one true joy!

Glory to God, peace among men. Glory to God, He favors you. Glory to God, He didn't want to leave you out of His story. We serve and worship a great and glorious God beyond our wildest imagination, who chose to love and value us, come for us, and rescue us so that we could be included in the great story of His glory. Don't let fear stand in your way of joining in the worship of Jesus.

HIS BREATH
CONQUERED DEATH

"This is what the Sovereign LORD says to these bones: I will make breath enter you, and you will come to life."
EZEKIEL 37:5

WHEN JESUS WAS born, He was still God, but He was also a human being. He took His first breath on planet Earth, and that breath signaled a cosmic shift in the war against sin and death. What all of humanity had failed to do since being expelled from the garden of Eden—make our way back to God—was made possible by God in that first breath of Jesus.

The God of the universe came to dwell with us. He came so that you would know that you can take a brand-new breath of life in God. When you accept Jesus as your Lord and Savior, you are filled with His Spirit and new life enters your lungs. You can breathe anew, just like the army of dry bones that God brought back to life before the prophet Ezekiel. And with that new breath, you worship! It's His power, His breath, that brings you to life. Instead of hoarding or hiding it, sing back to Him in praise! Shout your worship and thank Him for saving you through the sacrifice of Christ.

DEC 26

PRAYER

Jesus, Your first breath signaled the end of the reign of death. Your breath is in my lungs, so I give my praise to You today.

377

HIS VERY GREAT PROMISES

What, then, shall we say in response to these things? If God is for us, who can be against us?
ROMANS 8:31

IF YOU WANT to live a revolutionary life of blessing and experience the supernatural mercy of God, then renew your mind with this truth: No matter what you see in the natural world, God is working out His plan. No matter what you perceive about your circumstances, God is doing something remarkable. He is always at work.

Maybe you know the longing of praying for years, only to have your requests seemingly go unanswered. It's so common for us to question if God has forgotten us, feel rejected, and then opt to take matters into our own hands—trying to win God's favor through a spiritual formula of more good deeds than bad ones. But that's simply not how faith works.

Your blessing won't come from a ten-step formula of living well. It comes from living a life of surrender and faith-driven confidence. So be blessed with the fact that *God is for you.* Remember that all things work together for good to those who love God and are called according to His purpose (Romans 8:28).

God, I don't come to You looking for the secret way to derive favor from You. You've already blessed me with Your Spirit, so I rejoice today at simply being with You.

YOU'RE NOT IN CHARGE

*"Since you cannot do this very little thing,
why do you worry about the rest?"*

LUKE 12:26

WORRY WANTS TO entice you to believe that if you just think long enough about a struggle or situation, you can control the outcome. But in the end, control is an illusion that distracts you from your best plan of action: depending on God by His grace.

You are not God. While worry wants you to think you're in the driver's seat, worry really locks you in the trunk of the car. Jesus asked, "Who of you by worrying can add a single hour to your life?" (Luke 12:25). If we can't add even an hour to our lives, how "in control" can we actually be? The answer is not at all. But thankfully, we are known and are loved by the One who is in total control.

Worry will try to keep you up at night by convincing you that you don't need anyone else to step in and intervene. That you can muscle through. But in the end, peace comes by admitting that you are not God. Therefore, you are not in charge. You don't run the show. But you can trust and obey Him as He leads because you know He loves you.

PRAYER

Lord, You invite me into great freedom when I release my attempts at control and shift my hopes into Your hands.

HIS PERSONAL AND PROFOUND LOVE

*From heaven the L<small>ORD</small> looks down and
sees all mankind; from his dwelling place
he watches all who live on earth.*

PSALM 33:13–14

PRAYER

God, Your
holiness
invades the
innermost
parts of my
heart as I
realize that
You know me
personally and
profoundly. I
pray I sense
Your nearness
as I draw
near to You.

FOR ALL OUR straining to see what God has made in
the cosmos, He will never have to so much as squint to
see you. Though high above the heavens, and capable
of measuring the entirety of space with the breadth
of His fingers, God has no trouble seeing you—His
prized creation and most loved possession.

When you might be tempted to believe that God
is too big to be concerned with the things that are
weighing you down, you can fall back on His Word
to remind you of His intentional love.

He's so passionate about you that He sent His Son
for you—the same Son who made and named each of
the billions of stars in the night sky. Just as He named
those stars, He also named you, and even more, He
died for you to redeem you and restore you back to
new life.

God is big, but He's not too big to be personal to
you if you'll draw near to Him with awe and wonder
in your heart.

YOU'RE GOING TO MAKE IT

"Do not be afraid or terrified because of them, for the LORD your God goes with you; he will never leave you nor forsake you."

DEUTERONOMY 31:6

YOU'RE GOING TO make it. This is the gospel ending we're promised. At the end of the day, you are going to stand holy and blameless before the Lord. God will finish the work to make you strong, mature, and complete. In the end, you are on the winning side.

How does knowing the ending change how you live today? You no longer have to live afraid. Instead, you can live confidently in His grace. You can stand firm in His commandments. If you need more proof, wait and watch what a glorious God will do for the ones He loves. He does not forsake; He does not abandon. He is majestic and mighty, and no force on this earth will ever diminish His power or change His heart toward you.

Give your fear to Him. Let Him take it for you, and in exchange He will give you incredible courage and a sense of confidence rooted in His immeasurable power. If God says you are going to make it, take heart that no trial or hardship can take you out today.

PRAYER

God, I will not fear, because You go with me. I declare today that I will make it through this season with Your support and strength!

381

THE ULTIMATE PRIZE

Now there is in store for me the crown of righteousness, which the Lord, the righteous Judge, will award to me on that day.
2 TIMOTHY 4:8

IN THE END, it doesn't matter where you live, what you do for work, or who you know. Yes, God can and does use all those details. But none of those things are the end goal. Instead, as followers of Jesus, we all have the same aim, the same greatest treasure. We are running after the same prize.

Paul knew that at the end of the race of his life, there was going to be a great reward of a "crown of righteousness" stored up for him in heaven. But even more than that crown, Paul was looking forward to seeing the One who would present the crown, the holy and righteous judge, Jesus Christ the Lord.

You have a similar promise waiting for you, so keep running, keep believing, and keep trusting. At the end of the race is a person, and He makes the whole pursuit worthwhile. When you finish well, you don't just get a crown. You get Jesus, the ultimate source of life and celebration.

ABOUT THE AUTHOR

LOUIE GIGLIO IS PASTOR of Passion City Church and the original visionary of the Passion movement, which exists to call a generation to leverage their lives for the fame of Jesus.

Since 1997, Passion Conferences has gathered over one million college-aged young people in events across the United States and around the world, all under the banner of leveraging their lives for what matters most—the name and renown of Jesus.

Louie is the national bestselling author of over a dozen books, including *Don't Give the Enemy a Seat at Your Table*, *At the Table with Jesus*, *Goliath Must Fall*, *Indescribable: 100 Devotions About God and Science*, *The Comeback*, *The Air I Breathe*, *I Am Not but I Know I Am*, and others. As a communicator, Louie is widely known for messages such as "Indescribable" and "How Great Is Our God."

An Atlanta native and graduate of Georgia State University, Louie has done postgraduate work at Baylor University and holds a master's degree from Southwestern Baptist Theological Seminary. Louie and his wife, Shelley, make their home in Atlanta.

Bestselling author and pastor Louie Giglio shares practical ways to overcome the enemy's lies in *Don't Give the Enemy a Seat at Your Table*. Discover how to break free from the chains of negative thinking and experience true freedom from unhealthy thoughts and emotions.

Available wherever books are sold.